BEYOND

TERROR AND MARTYRDOM

THE FUTURE OF THE MIDDLE EAST

BEYOND

TERROR AND MARTYRDOM

THE FUTURE OF THE MIDDLE EAST

GILLES KEPEL

TRANSLATED BY

PASCALE GHAZALEH

THE BELKNAP PRESS OF HARVARD UNIVERSITY PRESS

Cambridge, Massachusetts, and London, England • 2008

Library of Congress Cataloging-in-Publication Data

Kepel, Gilles.
   [Terreur et martyre. English]
   Beyond terror and martyrdom : the future of the Middle East / Gilles
Kepel ; translated by Pascale Ghazaleh.
     p. cm.
   Includes bibliographical references and index.
   ISBN 978-0-674-03138-8 (alk. paper)
   1. Terrorism—Middle East.   2. Martyrdom.   3. East and West.
4. Jihad.   I. Ghazaleh, Pascale   II. Title.
   HV6433.M513K46 2008
   363.3250956--dc22   2008027923

CONTENTS

BEYOND

TERROR AND MARTYRDOM

THE FUTURE OF THE MIDDLE EAST

INTRODUCTION

In launching a "war on terror" after the attacks of September 11, 2001, President George W. Bush and his advisers sought to reshape the political world by delivering it from evil. Their strategy was breathtaking in its simplicity. Destroying Al Qaeda in Afghanistan and eliminating the regime of Saddam Hussein in Iraq would induce the birth of democracy throughout the Middle East. Simply by appearing on the scene, democracy would cause the collapse of the anti-American theocracy in Iran and would undermine authoritarian Middle East regimes, where Islamist militants preaching jihad—holy war—had distracted the masses from the corruption of their leaders and had produced the nineteen 9/11 hijackers. Under the benevolent hegemony of a victorious United States, Arabs and Muslims would see their best interest in a regional recognition of Israel's right to exist, and the land considered holy by three ancient religions would find its place in a harmonious scheme of globalization. With cheap oil flowing from the Persian Gulf to irrigate the world's economy, the entire planet would bloom with the promise of a "new American century"—prophetic words invented by neoconservatives in a Washington think tank long before the terrorist attacks of 2001 gave the Bush administration grounds for military action.

President Bush won reelection in the fall of 2004 to pursue this ambitious program. But his second term in office was marked by a stunning set of reversals, as the realities on the ground proved resistant to his simple prescription. Iraq—the testing ground for the war on terror—sank into chaos. Political strife between Arabs and Kurds, Sunnis and Shiites led to sectarian massacres, ethnic cleansing, kidnappings, torture, and suicide attacks. Having failed in their bid to capture or kill Osama Bin Laden in Afghanistan, U.S. military forces found themselves reacting to spiraling violence in Iraq, where jihadists linked to Al Qaeda had joined the battle with—and against—local insurgents.

As Iraq teetered on the brink of anarchy, Iran—contrary to the White House's optimistic projections—elected Mahmud Ahmadinejad as its president in 2005. Like Bush, he was also determined to reshape the world, in his case by practicing nuclear blackmail. Ahmadinejad's call for Israel to be wiped off the map frightened his wealthy, fragile neighbors on the Arabian peninsula and placed the global petroleum market at the mercy of Gulf security, which now found itself under potential nuclear threat. The United States' deepening disorientation in Iraq increased Iran's opportunity to influence Shiites in that country as well as in Lebanon, making a resolution of the crises in both of these states impossible without Iran's consent.

In March 2008 Ahmadinejad made an official visit to Baghdad, where he toured the Green Zone under the protection of the 160,000 U.S. troops present, in a stunning display of Iran's new clout. Then in May, after Iran's protégé in Lebanon, Hezbollah, swept the streets of Sunni Beirut and the Druze mountain in fighting that left scores dead, a conference in Qatar made arrangements for the opposition, led by Hezbollah, to have the right to veto decisions of the Lebanese government. This precondition was set by Tehran's local allies in order to elect the long-awaited new Lebanese president. Throughout the Middle East, President Bush's war on terror had strikingly and inadvertently reinforced the power of Washington's old nemesis, the Islamic Republic.

As for Israel, that embattled nation was not made more secure by the war on terror—far from it. Israel's pointless Thirty-Three-Day War against Hezbollah during the summer of 2006 served only to cast the militant Lebanese Party of God and its Iranian mentor as champions of resistance to Zionism, American imperialism, and the decadence of the West. Grievances and frustrations grew sharper every day, aggravating a theme with inexhaustible media value: the problem of Palestine. Israel had scored an irrefutable military victory with its response to the second intifada, launched in late September 2000. That Palestinian uprising was broken after the Israeli government mercilessly repressed the militants and proceeded to erect a barrier wall on the West Bank. But Ariel Sharon and his successor, Ehud Olmert, were no more able than George W. Bush to convert military victory into political success. When Israeli troops pulled out of Gaza in 2005, the Islamist nationalist party Hamas portrayed the withdrawal as a victory for the armed jihad it had waged since the second intifada. And on the strength of that claim, Hamas won a majority in the Palestinian legislative council six months later.

Bush's war against the "axis of evil"—which he identified as Iraq, Iran, and North Korea in his State of the Union address of January 2002—deliberately echoed the struggle against the Soviet "evil empire," a phrase that President Ronald Reagan had coined in 1983. The defeat of terrorism and jihadism would be an extension of the victory over communism, guaranteeing the triumph of Western democracy in the Muslim world just as the fall of the Berlin wall had done for the countries of the Warsaw Pact. On April 9, 2003, after the conquest of Baghdad, a cable attached to a U.S. tank toppled the colossal statue of Saddam Hussein that had stood in the capital. For television audiences worldwide, the scene was intended to evoke the moment when statues of Stalin and Lenin were pulled down in the former Soviet Union, symbolizing the collapse of the communist system and the flourishing, on its rubble, of democratic nation-states. Just such an efflorescence of democracy was what Washington foresaw for Iraq once it was freed from the dictatorship of Saddam Hussein.

But in formulating this analogy between the war on terror and the cold war, the Bush administration ignored several fundamental differences between the former Eastern bloc and the Middle East. By the time the Soviet empire collapsed in 1991, almost no one believed in communist ideology anymore. It had become merely the mask of a bureaucratic regime, a discourse cut off from any social base. In the Muslim world, on the other hand, references to Islam, then and now, permeate the culture, fertilizing a deep-rooted concept of civilization and dictating the routines of daily life. Islam is subject to many diverse, often contradictory, appropriations, which clash in a bid for control over meaning and values. Yet over a billion believers spread throughout the world adhere to Islam with equal conviction, even as their interpretations of their common faith differ.

By initially identifying terror as the enemy to be targeted by war, President Bush and his advisers sought to avoid any possible amalgamation of hundreds or thousands of "bad" Muslims with the many millions of "good" ones. The very notion of "terrorist" was supposed to identify those comparative few who were to be eliminated. But the borders of the group tagged as terrorists quickly became politically subjective. From Washington's perspective, "terrorism" was represented first and foremost by Al Qaeda and its Taliban host in Afghanistan, but the definition quickly expanded to include not just Saddam Hussein and his Iranian enemy to the east but also Hezbollah in Lebanon and Hamas in Palestine—two organizations with a significant popular base, vast support and sympathy beyond the borders of their countries, and victories in democratic elections—the kind of elections in whose name the war on terror was being fought.

In opposition to Bush's war on terror, Bin Laden and his followers sought to perpetuate the strategy of "martyrdom operations" that had shocked the world on 9/11. Their plan was to duplicate suicide missions indefinitely, until the final apotheosis of Islam and the destruction of the West were achieved. Here too, the ultimate goal was nothing less than to cleanse the world of evil. But the jihadists would accomplish their aims through voluntary death in combat, in a sublime, phantasmagorical act of self-sacrifice on the part of believers.

From their sanctuary in Pakistan, Bin Laden and Ayman al-Zawahiri sent out a flood of jihadist proclamations after 9/11. According to these narratives, the hijackers were not murderers but martyrs who laid down their lives for Islam. They, and their thousands of imitators in Afghanistan and Iraq, were the vanguard of a larger community of believers that Al Qaeda sought to recruit to its cause. Bush's war on terror, in the view of Al Qaeda, was nothing less than a last, doomed crusade intended to humiliate Islam, and in the fight against this ignominious assault Al Qaeda was the best defender of the faith—an umbrella organization well suited to coordinate the multiple martyrdom operations of local jihads.

Spurred on by rhetoric from Al Qaeda, waves of would-be martyrs flowed into Iraq following the American invasion. But unlike Israeli victims of suicide bombers during the second intifada, most of the victims of martyrdom operations in Iraq were not "infidels" such as coalition troops but were fellow Muslims—Iraqi Shiites killed by Sunnis who took advantage of the chaos to settle scores with their age-old foe. The cult of martyrdom promoted by Al Qaeda, far from leading to triumph over the enemies of Islam, became a devastating war of Muslim against Muslim.

In Europe, the dubious quest for martyrdom was epitomized by the suicide attacks of July 7, 2005, which targeted London's transportation system. They were followed by other operations, almost all of which were foiled at the eleventh hour. This unprecedented, stupefying violence dealt a blow to preconceived notions of British multiculturalism and induced a soul-searching review of what was supposedly at stake in the Muslim presence in Europe. The 7/7 bombings mingled with other crises, like the assassination of Theo Van Gogh in the Netherlands by an Islamist of Moroccan origin; the outcry over the Danish cartoons; the riots in the French banlieues; and even the pope's declarations about the Prophet Muhammad. But contrary to the expectations of Al Qaeda's leadership, the strategy of martyrdom did not galvanize or mobilize the Muslim masses, especially in Europe.

The struggle between the Bush administration and Bin Laden's Al Qaeda for the minds and hearts of more than a billion peaceful Muslims coincided with the dawn of the digital age, where the possibilities for uncontrolled communication were practically infinite. Satellite television networks were the first media to broadcast the competing narratives of terror and martyrdom, and some stations, like Al Jazeera, made this their specialty. But the Internet, with its proliferation of sites in all languages, offered limitless opportunities to tout the self-sacrifice of the jihadists or stoke the outrage of America's warriors. Unlike the propaganda of the cold war, which was carefully policed by both sides, Zawahiri's declarations were joined on the air and online by the interrogation and beheading of blindfolded hostages, raids and bombings, the suffering of detainees at Guantánamo, and pornographic piles of naked prisoners in Abu Ghraib. All these images played simultaneously on ideological edification and morbid voyeurism, in a register where traditional vocabulary and postmodern grammar intertwined, the better to erase critical thinking, historical perspective, and social context.

When Saddam himself was hanged for crimes against humanity on December 30, 2006, the fallen dictator's execution should have provided an object lesson in the triumph of law and universal justice over barbarity. But instead, Saddam's death turned into a lynching—a shameful settling of accounts between Sunnis and

Shiites, captured in stolen images taken on cell phones by witnesses and replayed on the same Internet sites that had displayed beheadings of Western hostages and torture at Abu Ghraib.

By that time, Iraq was awash in blood, with over 34,000 people having met violent deaths in 2006 alone. Most were victims of suicide bombings; many others had been kidnapped and tortured before being killed. The number of U.S. soldiers dead exceeded the number of victims of the 9/11 attacks. The war became so unpopular in the United States itself that the Republicans were routed in the November 2006 midterm elections, losing their majority in the Senate and the House. The Baker-Hamilton report, compiled by the Iraq Study Group at the urging of several members of Congress and with the agreement of President Bush, drew up a catastrophic tally of the costs of the Iraq occupation and advocated a radical change of strategy, but in vain. The president's response was to initiate a military "surge" which temporarily halted deterioration on the ground by dividing Iraq along territorial and sectarian lines. High concrete T-walls separated Sunni from Shiite neighborhoods—similar to the barriers separating Palestinians from Israelis on the West Bank.

Despite its narrative of good versus evil, democracy versus totalitarianism, the war on terror embodied the same policy objectives that the United States had pursued in the Middle East since 1945. For Bush and his advisers, the presumed weapons of mass destruction in Iraq merely offered a new opportunity to square the circle—to guarantee both Israel's security and the unimpeded flow of oil from the Persian Gulf. In the bid to eliminate Saddam Hussein, the aim was to control Iraqi oil fields, take Iraq out of OPEC, break the anti-Israeli Arab front, weaken the Saudi oil monarchy, punish that kingdom for failing to suppress radical Islamists, and provoke a grassroots demand for regime change in Iran, following the model of a newly democratic Iraq.

Along the same lines, the grand narrative of martyrdom was supposed to lead the Muslim masses to identify with Al Qaeda, to hasten a general uprising against "apostate" pro-Western governments such as Saudi Arabia, precipitate the establishment of a universal Islamic state, and crush the nation of Israel. And like the war on terror, this ideology, in its turn, crashed against a wall of reality within the Muslim world. The Al Qaeda jihadists were hijacked by other political and religious actors with their own agendas. The Sunni Muslim Brothers and figures linked to them, such as Youssef al-Qaradawi, a superstar Islamic preacher on Al Jazeera, condemned the 9/11 attacks even as they applauded martyrdom operations in Israel and, for a time, in Iraq. They took advantage of Washington's democratic model for the Middle East to put forward their own anti-American candidates, who, to Zawahiri's chagrin, swept the polls in Egypt, Palestine, Bahrain, Saudi Arabia, and Turkey. Zawahiri could not find language strong enough to denounce the Muslim traitors who swapped the blood of jihadist martyrs for electoral victories.

More galling still, Ahmadinejad recycled the grand narrative of martyrdom to the benefit of Iran's own political interests and nuclear ambitions in the region. In so doing, Iran returned to its roots, for the Islamic Republic had invented the modern suicide attack in the 1980s, when it sent waves of young Shiites to blow themselves up in Iraqi minefields during the eight-year-long Iran-Iraq war. Iran then went on to inspire Hezbollah, whose "martyrs" in Lebanon willingly drove to their deaths in booby-trapped vehi-

cles that killed hundreds of American, French, and Israeli soldiers.
Hamas in Palestine and finally Al Qaeda in the 9/11 attacks had
merely adapted this revolutionary Shiite tactic to the Sunni world.

Terror or martyrdom—these were the two grand narratives created to transform the international landscape, particularly the
Middle East, at the beginning of the second millennium. This book
aims to analyze them in detail, and for the most part it will tally
their failures. Bush, Cheney, and the neoconservatives on one
hand, Bin Laden, Zawahiri, and Al Qaeda on the other—both sides
staked their claim to power on a vision of global rectification
through violent means. But the utopian ends that supposedly justified those means—universal democracy or a universal Islamist
state—proved impossible to achieve, and in a few short years the
opposing dreams of Bush and Bin Laden had devolved into an
endless shared nightmare.

What caused the failure of these two ambitious, transformative
fictions, and what lessons can help the world emerge from the hor-
rible reality they created in the Middle East? This book will explore
these questions, in an effort to discover the disastrous assumptions of the antagonists and to disentangle the tragic, unforeseen
consequences of their decisions. It will then go on to examine the
case of Europe, home to diverse populations of second- or third-
generation Muslims, where the challenges and richness of lived
experience suggest some alternatives to the fantasies of violence
perpetrated by ideologues on both sides of this dangerous divide.
Europe has been a hostage of the war on terror and a target of martyrdom operations, but it sits at the heart of one of the world's

most dynamic regions—a vast area centered around the Mediterranean and reaching to the North Sea and the Gulf—whose economic power is on a par with the American and Asian poles. This region hosts a civilization with a shared cultural legacy over fifteen centuries long. How can Europe, in collaboration with countries surrounding the Mediterranean and the Gulf, turn the crisis that has deepened since September 2001 into a factor for peace and prosperity, when the war on terror failed in this task? How can it make the saga of martyrdom obsolete?

In its final pages, this book will sketch a way to move forward—a third "narrative" that draws together the multicultural experience, economic strength, security, and diplomacy of Europe, the investment capacity and energy resources of the Gulf states, the entrepreneurial ambitions of their educated youth, and the vast labor pool and rich cultural traditions of Mediterranean countries from the Levant and North Africa. Running counter to the narratives of both Bush and Bin Laden, which considered force or violence to be a prerequisite for change in the Middle East, a new framework for sustainable prosperity would take up the challenge of building an integrated civilization stretching from the North Sea to the Gulf. Grounded in the kind of economic dynamism that remains at the core of the European Union, this alternative vision would meet the stability requirements of the United States and address the security needs of its ally, Israel, and the viability of a Palestinian state.

Intelligence services regularly express their greatest fear, a culmination of the dialectic of terror and martyrdom—that some terrorist/martyr from Birmingham or Karachi will carry out a nuclear suicide attack in a Western metropolis, by blowing up a plutonium charge stolen from the arsenal of the former Soviet empire. It is impossible to rule out this apocalyptic scenario, but we can minimize the risk by nurturing a web of social and economic relations that transcends the conflictual logic of terror and martyrdom.

CHAPTER ONE

FROM THE WAR ON TERROR
TO THE FIASCO IN IRAQ

Freedom from terror, justice under the law, and democracy were
the fundamental themes of the grand narrative the administration
in Washington created after 9/11 to drive U.S. foreign policy for
the duration of Bush's presidency. This narrative was dubbed the
Global War on Terror (GWOT), but it was quickly shortened to the
"war on terror."

The antagonist was the "terrorist," recognized as a "bad guy" not
just by Americans but also by Europeans, all honest Muslims, and
indeed the rest of the civilized world. The Bush administration
highlighted the figure of the "terrorist" as a way to reveal the reality
behind the mask of the "martyr": he was a despicable individual
whose fanatical ideology, based on hatred, death, and devastation,
culminated in the massacre of innocent civilians through his own
self-destruction. By targeting the terrorist as the symbol of evil *par
excellence*, Washington expected to rally a vast alliance of nations
behind the United States in its quest to rid the world, particularly
the Middle East, of this villain. The administration also hoped to

gain the support of Muslim populations by showing that so-called martyrdom operations were nothing but suicide bombings carried out in the name of a wildly distorted misinterpretation of religious commandments.

This American grand narrative encountered a number of problems from its inception, however. First, the very word "terrorist" implied that the United States government was waging war in defense of an opposite set of civilized values that terrorism presumably threatened. Yet the detainee camp set up at Guantánamo, where the civil liberties of hundreds of suspects were suspended without recourse to judicial hearings or even statements of the charges against them, gave an early indication that America's role in upholding the values of freedom, justice, and democracy would not be played to the satisfaction of its world audience or its own citizens. Later, the abuses at Abu Ghraib prison, where inmates were humiliated, terrified, and tortured, would further undermine the central themes of the United States' grand narrative.

Second, identifying who was a terrorist and who was not turned out to be extremely difficult. Apart from the hijackers on 9/11 and those who masterminded that operation, the category of "terrorist" had very porous boundaries indeed. Should Palestinians who blew up explosive devices on the streets of Israel be targeted in the war on terror? In both the United States and Israel, many people said yes, tracing out an equivalence between suicide attacks in Tel Aviv and in New York. But others disagreed, insisting that the two cases were very different. While condemning the 9/11 attacks, they justified or even applauded Palestinian operations in Israel. Viewing the violence in Palestine on the Al Jazeera news network, Arabs and Muslims around the world, along with Third Worldists and anti-imperialists, classified Palestinians who blew themselves up in order to resist Israeli occupation as nationalist heroes or jihadist martyrs following God's path. From that perspective, the Israeli occupation of Palestine was an act of terrorism, not the Palestinian resistance to it. Setting and resetting the boundaries of terrorism turned into a battle over the meaning and direction of the war on terror. This issue triggered deep disagreements among the United States' supporters—a very large coalition at first, but one that diminished precipitously with the invasion of Iraq in the spring of 2003.

Having identified the figure of the terrorist as evil incarnate, the U.S. administration required an exorcism to cast it out. The immediate focus was on authoritarian governments in the Arab and Muslim world that harbored terrorists. According to the hypothesis of the neoconservatives surrounding President Bush, by limiting pluralism of thought and freedom of expression these regimes left opponents and dissidents with only one alternative: violence. By overthrowing these authoritarian governments or leading them to repent their ways, Western allies could clear a space for pluralist political systems to flourish. The Middle East, which had remained isolated from the wave of democratization that swept the world in the 1980s and 1990s, would be integrated into the global community, under the benevolent peacekeeping umbrella of the United States.

Pushing forward such a large-scale operation required the rhetoric of a "just war." And indeed, the first armed intervention of the war on terror—targeting Al Qaeda and the Taliban regime in Afghanistan—gained much of the world's approval under this banner. But the second intervention, aimed at Saddam Hussein and his presumed stockpile of weapons of mass destruction, struck the global community as a more dubious proposition, and far less justifiable on ethical grounds.

The mirror image of the war on terror was jihad, or holy war, which Islamist radicals had declared against Western infidels and their Muslim collaborators. Founded on divine injunctions and reaching its apotheosis in martyrdom, jihad was a just war by definition, from the perspective of those who believed in it. It sought to eradicate evildoers from Muslim lands (the American "crusader," its Zionist ally Israel, and pro-Western heads of state in Saudi Arabia, Egypt, and other nations) and to change the Middle Eastern scene by establishing states governed by Islamic law (*sharia*). In this narrative, the "blessed double raid of September 11th" was a harbinger of Islam's ultimate victory over the declining West.

A Bad Omen in Afghanistan

The first phase of the war on terror—military operations against the Taliban in Afghanistan and the hunt for the leadership of Al Qaeda—extended from the fall of 2001 to the spring of 2003, when a "coalition of the willing" invaded Iraq. Contrary to the expectations of Bin Laden, who had hoped to trap the international allies in Afghanistan just as the Red Army had been trapped there in the 1980s, the Taliban regime fell easily and without arousing much regret, since its sectarian character had alienated a large segment of Muslims worldwide.

The Northern Alliance pulled together a group of Afghans who were just as Muslim as the Taliban to spearhead the land offensive against Al Qaeda and bring about regime change in Kabul. The very existence of these indigenous Muslim forces, which received training and financing from the West along with air support from the United States, prevented Mullah Omar's supporters from swaying Arab and Muslim public opinion with the idea that the Afghanistan operation was tantamount to an infidel invasion of Muslim lands. Only a handful of preachers advanced this interpretation, and these individuals were at the extremist fringe, without much of an audience—people like the Saudi imam Hammud al-Shuaybi, who was also one of the few to give legal sanction to the 9/11 attacks but was known only in jihadist circles.[1] No international "defensive jihad"—a war that Islam requires Muslims to wage when their land has been invaded and occupied by unbelievers—materialized in Afghanistan in the fall of 2001 comparable to the resistance movement against the Soviet invasion in the 1980s.

American military operations in Afghanistan were carried out with the approval of the U.N. Security Council and rallied over 30,000 troops from thirty-seven countries to the side of the United States. They were brought together under the U.N. mandate as an International Security and Assistance Force (ISAF) commanded by NATO. Yet despite the military victory over the Taliban, the coalition's success was limited by the primary goal it had set for itself: to eliminate Al Qaeda and kill or capture Bin Laden. Most of Al Qaeda's leaders managed to escape into tribal areas in Pakistan, and this failure to complete the mission had grave consequences in the following years. Internationally, the most charismatic personalities—Bin Laden and Zawahiri—continued to appear in the media, giving a face to the resilience of an armed jihadist network that could mutate at will in order to escape pursuit. Locally, starting in 2005, links between Al Qaeda and the Pashtun tribes along the Afghan-Pakistani border, where many Taliban (most of whom are

Pashtun) had found refuge, allowed the opening of a new front in the holy war against foreign forces.

When Afghans were fighting the Red Army in the 1980s, the strategy of suicide bombing was unknown. But in 2005 there were 25 such attacks in Afghanistan, and 136 in 2006;[2] 2007 saw roughly the same number of suicide operations, and more than 6,000 people lost their lives as a consequence of political violence. This strategy went hand in hand with the kidnapping of foreigners—an Italian journalist and two French aid workers in early 2007 and members of a South Korean evangelical group in July. These stories of carnage and blackmail were very similar to those flowing out of Iraq and cast a shadow on the initial success of the war in Afghanistan. Then on April 27, 2008, President Hamid Karzai barely escaped an assassination attempt at a military parade in Kabul—an attack that was chillingly reminiscent of Anwar Sadat's assassination at the hands of Islamist radicals in October 1981 in Cairo. This operation was a reminder of the capacity of revamped Taliban groups to strike at the heart of the pro-Western Afghan government and a sobering sign of the military and political weakness of the Karzai government.

But for those making the case for a just war in Afghanistan, the most ominous development was taking place half way around the world.

Guantánamo, the Original Sin

In the first weeks after September 11, facing a nebulous jihadist movement whose structure and intentions remained obscure, the United States was understandably obsessed with the need to obtain information that would help identify the enemy, reveal conspiracies, and prevent future attacks. On November 13 President Bush issued an order pertaining to the capture, detention, treatment, and judgment of certain noncitizens suspected of affiliation with Al Qaeda and believed to harbor information that could be useful in the hunt for Bin Laden and his collaborators. These individuals were to be held in locations determined by the secretary of defense, and ultimately they would be judged by military tribunals.

On December 28, 2001, the president received General Tommy Franks, commander of military operations in Afghanistan, at his ranch in Crawford, Texas. During a press briefing, the president replied to a question on the detainees' future in the following words: "One thing is for certain, that whatever the procedures are for the military tribunals, our system will be more fair than the system of Bin Laden and the Taliban. That is for certain. The prisoners that we capture will be given a heck of a lot better chance in court than those citizens of ours who were in the World Trade Center or in the Pentagon were given by Mr. bin Laden." This legal and moral vision of the war on terror—still strongly marked by the emotional impact of September 11 and the tragedy of the thousands who had died—led to the detention camp that was set up on a U.S. naval base in Guantánamo, Cuba.

On January 11, 2002, the camp began to receive its first prisoners. A total of 759 people would eventually be held there.[3] "Gitmo" (GTMO) illustrated the difficulty of using conventional methods to fight an enemy that had emancipated itself from all international conventions. In March 2006, speaking before the American Bar Association Standing Committee on Law and National Security, Philip Zelikow, counselor to the U.S. Department of State, elucidated what he called a "legal policy for a twilight war." As Zelikow saw it, before September 11 the fight against terrorist activities had been waged through recourse to traditional American criminal justice (with the exception of a few Cruise missiles launched on suspected Al Qaeda bases in August 1988 by the Clinton administration). After September 11, with its thousands of victims and billions of dollars in damages, the criteria changed: the United States was now engaged in a war that was more than a war, since it was part of a global struggle against violent Islamist extremists. In this context, the mechanisms of traditional criminal justice were inadequate.[4]

To prevail, it was crucial to identify and target enemy combatants, who, unlike traditional soldiers wearing uniforms, were camouflaged among the civilian population. When combatants were captured, it was necessary to detain and interrogate them and maintain long-term access. This required transporting them to places where they could be held without judicial intervention, under the supervision of the United States or one of its allies. The United States had been operating a naval base at Guantánamo since 1903, through a treaty signed with Cuba long before Fidel Castro came to power. The Castro regime never ratified the agreement and refused to cash the rent checks the U.S. Treasury sent to Havana. Nevertheless, the base stayed open, and before 9/11 it served as a holding camp for boat people rescued while trying to escape from Haiti or Cuba.

Since Guantánamo was not on U.S. territory, only military law applied there, and it was this extraterritorial status that recommended the base as an appropriate location for the detainee camp. There, U.S. military authorities could deal with prisoners captured

during the offensive against the Taliban, carry out summary interrogations and classifications on site, and then detain for further intensive questioning those who seemed to be linked to Al
Qaeda. Guantánamo started out as a clearing house for low-profile
suspects. High-profile prisoners belonging to Al Qaeda's leadership—Khaled Sheikh Mohammed, the mastermind of the September 11 attacks, Ramzi Ben al-Shibh, and Abu Zubayda, for example—were interrogated elsewhere (at Bagram in Afghanistan, on
the British isle of Diego Garcia, and aboard military ships cruising
in the Indian Ocean) without publicity before being sent to Guantánamo for detention.

The detainees in Guantánamo had more than one role to play
in the war on terror, however. Not only did they provide a poten-
tially valuable source of intelligence, but they were also supposed
to symbolize the defeat of terrorists worldwide. By initially holding
suspects who had been captured on the battlefield in Afghanistan,
and later incarcerating other suspects arrested or even kidnapped
in various countries, the planners of Guantánamo sought to put
faces on the terror against which the war was being waged, at a
time when most of the terrorists remained elusive.

Al Qaeda's terrorist activities had taken two forms: attacks
whose perpetrators, in the case of martyrdom operations, disappeared when they blew themselves up, and propaganda messages
broadcast by Internet or television. What was missing between the
suicide bombers and the digital imagery was flesh and blood human terrorists. The prisoners at Guantánamo served this function.
They were the only sample available under lock and key who could
embody the coalition's enemy. Handcuffed and shackled, clad in
bright orange uniforms, their blurred images broadcast in maga-

zines and news reports worldwide, the detainees illustrated the power and reach of the U.S.-led counterattack on terror. The triumphalist pictures of martyrdom operations that Al Qaeda had sent around the world via the Internet were trumped by images from Guantánamo proving that the war on terror was getting results.

Less than three weeks after the camp's opening, President Bush delivered his famous State of the Union address in which he denounced the "axis of evil." As members of Congress and guests applauded, he declared: "The American flag flies again over our embassy in Kabul. Terrorists who once occupied Afghanistan now occupy cells at Guantánamo Bay. And terrorist leaders who urged followers to sacrifice their lives are running for their own." The address went on to announce that the war on terror would not halt with the elimination of the Taliban, since it had "two great objectives." The first was to fight tens of thousands of terrorists worldwide—Hamas and Hezbollah were cited as examples—by shutting down their camps and destroying their underground links. The second was "to prevent the terrorists and regimes who seek chemical, biological or nuclear weapons from threatening the United States and the world." North Korea, Iran, and Iraq were singled out by name as seeking to produce or procure weapons of mass destruction, which they might pass on to terrorists.

In retrospect, this address was the first public presentation of the larger objectives of the war on terror. Playing on the shock caused by the September 11 attacks, President Bush moved quickly to criminalize all his adversaries around the globe as part of a larger agenda to reconfigure power in the Middle East. His rhetoric deliberately fused three categories of behavior—criminal activities carried out by individual conspirators such as the hijackers of 9/11, political resistance carried out by activist parties such as Hamas and Hezbollah, and strategies of aggression carried out by states such as North Korea, Iran, and Iraq. All of these actors—whether individuals, parties, or states—were legitimate targets of Bush's war on terror. The struggle in Afghanistan would be extended to encompass Hamas and Hezbollah, clearly enemies of Israel, and would go on to confront the evil regimes in Iraq, Iran, and North Korea. The rhetorical architecture of the invasion and occupation of Iraq in March 2003 was taking shape.

Within this construction, the reference to Guantánamo, which the president mentioned in the first paragraphs of his address, had major symbolic significance. It proved the administration's resolve to stamp out terror, now broadly defined, and presented a tangible early success: the capture and detention of Al Qaeda activists and sympathizers. Three years after this historic address, Secretary of Defense Donald Rumsfeld was still describing the prisoners at Guantánamo in the same demonic terms: "The kind of people held at Guantánamo," he said, "include terrorist trainers, bomb-makers, extremist recruiters, and financiers, bodyguards of Osama bin Laden, and would-be suicide bombers."[5]

But in fact, the Gitmo prisoners were a motley crew, and their links with Bin Laden's group were often very tenuous.[6] A study carried out by the Department of Defense claimed that most of the inmates were members of Al Qaeda's terrorist network, but another study by legal counsel to some of the prisoners estimated that only about 10 percent of the detainees could yield any information of value. According to Michael Scheuer, a former CIA operative in Afghanistan and the author of two (anonymous) reference works on terrorism, most of the detainees were small fry, sold to or even foisted upon the United States by Pakistani or Afghan warlords, at a price much higher than their going rate on the jihad market.[7] As soon as they arrived at the camp, the detainees were held under harsh conditions and subjected to ruthless interrogation, with the aim of extracting intelligence about Al Qaeda. In January 2002 Rumsfeld described the detainees as "illegal combatants," and as such they were deemed to fall outside international as well as U.S. law. They were not considered to be prisoners of war as defined by the 1949 Geneva Convention, which grants POWs precise legal protection, determines their status, prohibits mistreatment and torture, provides for their release at the end of hostilities, and protects them from being tried unless a competent tribunal has established the likelihood that they have committed crimes. They were incarcerated without being notified of the accusations made against them, and because of Guantánamo's extraterritorial status, they were not eligible to appear before a U.S. court.

The U.S. administration and individual officials, such as former CIA chief George Tenet in his memoirs, denied any recourse to torture but admitted that "severe" interrogation methods, including intense physical and psychological pressure, were used. These techniques drew on explicit instructions written by Rumsfeld and senior officers and eventually leaked to the press.[8] Some British and French detainees released in 2004 published accounts of their experience which claimed that they had undergone continuous mistreatment amounting to torture, especially the use of waterboarding.[9]

By interrogating detainees in this way, the U.S. administration asserted its absolute sovereignty in the definition and conduct of the war on terror, and its prerogative to resort to exceptional measures. According to the philosopher Giorgio Agamben, camps are pieces of territory placed outside the normal legal system.[10] The ability to decree this state of exception with respect to law is the foundation of sovereign power, Agamben argues, and camps are the structure by which the state of exception is durably achieved. The state of exception in Guantánamo was validated by American voters when they reelected George W. Bush in November 2004. His opponent, Senator John Kerry, had not challenged the principle of detention in Guantánamo but was against the use of torture there. The president's supporters lambasted Kerry, arguing that the methods used at the base were the only means of preventing further attacks like those of September 11, by "obtaining information from the terrorists themselves," as John Yoo, one of the administration's legal experts, put it.[11]

Guantánamo had a disastrous effect in the Muslim world and among the United States' European allies, including most human rights advocacy organizations. Rumors of torture and of the guards' blasphemous contempt for the Quran quickly thinned the ranks of those Muslims who might otherwise have supported the war on terror and the democracy project in the Middle East. Instead of isolating jihadists from the mass of the Islamic population, as the war on terror was intended to do, Guantánamo aroused sympathy for the prisoners and outright hostility toward their American guards. The orange uniforms, intended to stigmatize terrorists, came to represent innocent martyrs who were suffering a miscarriage of justice because of their Muslim faith. The jihadists were quick to take the symbolism a step further, turning it into an emblem of revenge: when the young American contractor Nicholas Berg was kidnapped in Iraq in May 2004 and beheaded live on webcam by Abu Musab al-Zarqawi, his executioners dressed him in an orange jumpsuit.

The rest of the world, including much of the West, criticized the United States harshly for incarcerating suspects, interrogating and torturing them, and refusing to allow them to seek justice before an impartial court of law. Bowing to this pressure, around two hundred detainees considered to have no value were released in 2004 and 2005. A good number of them had Western passports and were citizens of countries whose representatives wanted to know why they were being held without due process. On February 20, 2006, four years after Guantánamo was opened, the European Parliament requested that the camp be shut down and that each prisoner be judged immediately by an independent tribunal. Basing their declaration on reports by the International Federation for Human Rights, Human Rights Watch, and Amnesty International, the European body condemned all forms of torture and mistreatment.

Beyond the United States' borders, the base at Guantánamo came to represent one of the main objections to the war on terror, just at a time when the occupation of Iraq hit a dead-end and necessitated, more than ever, closer ties with America's allies and improved relations with civil society in the Arab and Muslim world. But even in the United States itself, the political value of Guantánamo became increasingly unreliable. On June 28, 2004, the Supreme Court ruled that federal courts could determine whether the incarceration of foreign citizens at Guantánamo was legal. Shortly thereafter, the federal court of Washington, D.C., ruled that it was illegal to try a prisoner before a military commission.

On December 30, 2005, in response to this judicial ruling, the Republican-controlled Senate and House of Representatives voted in favor of the Detainee Treatment Act, which deprived federal courts of jurisdiction and referred detainees once again to military commissions. The legal battle continued when the Supreme Court ruled on June 29, 2006, that President Bush had overstepped his authority and that the military commissions were unauthorized by federal statute and violated international law. On September 27 the Republican majority in Congress passed a bill restoring the military commissions and accused the Democrats of weakness in dealing with terrorism.

The Republicans were no doubt motivated by the upcoming November elections in both the House and Senate, hoping that the grand narrative of terrorism would allow them once again to sway public sentiment and win votes. But Guantánamo had ceased to be an effective symbol: the midterm elections of November 2006 confirmed the popular opinion that the conduct of the war on terror had been a failure. Democrats won a majority in both the House and Senate—a defeat for the Republicans that led to Rumsfeld's departure from the Pentagon.

As early as May 2006, the administration had suggested that Guantánamo might close down by the end of 2007, and the vast majority of the detainees—against whom no charge would be filed—might be sent back to their countries of origin, or simply released. On June 11, after three prisoners committed suicide, President Bush announced that he would like to close down Guantánamo. As even he realized by this point, the camp had sent mixed signals abroad, allowing some observers to accuse the United States of "not upholding the values that they're trying to encourage other countries to adhere to." His response to this criticism was to say that "eventually these people will have trials, and they will have counsel, and they will be represented in the court of law."[12] Thus, a little over four years after the camp opened, the political disadvantages of the Guantánamo detention system had come to outweigh its advantages.

The final blow to the whole Guantánamo enterprise came on June 12, 2008, when the U.S. Supreme Court, in a historic decision, ruled that suspects held at the camp had the constitutional right to challenge their detention in U.S. courts. The notion of a "state of exception" that had been the cornerstone of the extrajudicial actions taken against the Gitmo prisoners was now called into question for good—at a time when President Bush was preparing to leave office, a majority in Congress was hostile toward his policies, and his approval rates had plummeted. "The laws and Constitution are designed to survive, and remain in force, in extraordinary times," wrote Justice Anthony Kennedy for the majority in this 5-to-4 decision. "To hold that the political branches may switch the Constitution on or off at will would lead to a regime in which they, not this court, say 'what the law is.'"

Pornography and Torture at Abu Ghraib

When the attack on Iraq began on March 20, 2003, the global war on terror already seemed to have achieved less, in hindsight, than President Bush had predicted in his State of the Union address more than a year earlier. The defeat of the Taliban regime in Afghanistan, at that time, was the only bright spot in an otherwise somber scene. The hunt for Bin Laden and his associates had been unproductive, revealing the disconnect between the Western war machine, adapted for conflicts with conventional armies, and the challenge represented by terrorist activities that seemed impossible to identify and defeat. The Bush administration would have been wise to heed that warning. Bloody attacks worldwide, from Bali to Mombasa, demonstrated Al Qaeda's persistence and the failure of efforts to eliminate it—another clue that the shock-and-awe invasion of Iraq might have a long tail. But in the view of the Bush administration, these events simply provided justification for expanding the war on terror, by showing how grave the threat was and underscoring the need to mobilize any means in order to overcome it.

The invasion of Iraq promised a tangible victory that would make up for the lack of results in the hunt for Al Qaeda's leaders. Equally important, a high-tech defeat of Saddam Hussein's conventional, ineffective army would catapult the United States straight to the last stage of its grand narrative: stabilizing pro-American democratic governments in a restructured Middle East. The shock waves set off by Saddam's overthrow, in this scenario, would blast the jihadist movement to pieces and reveal to the Arab peoples the peaceful benefits of democracy. Iraq would be snatched from the misery it had endured for decades under the yoke of one of the region's most brutal dictatorships.

But shortly after the successful military invasion of Iraq in spring 2003, the situation on the ground began to deteriorate, and during the following year, at a time when the stakes in the war on terror had never been higher, a scandal broke into the news and inflicted major damage on the discourse of freedom and democracy in the Middle East.

Abu Ghraib prison, built near Baghdad in the 1960s, symbolized the tyrannical rule of Saddam Hussein. The prisoners he held there were routinely subjected to brutality, rape, and murder. For Iraqis opposed to the Baathist regime, the prison's very name conjured up the dictator's crimes and provided one of the main moral arguments for overthrowing him. In a speech delivered on April 30, 2004, President Bush expressed his satisfaction that there were "no longer torture chambers or rape rooms or mass graves in Iraq." But for much of the year prior to that address, U.S. jailers in Abu Ghraib prison had not only inflicted brutality and humiliation upon Iraqi prisoners but had also photographed and filmed their acts and posted the images on the Internet.

Ironically, the scandal had already broken out worldwide just two days before the president's speech, when *The New Yorker* and *60 Minutes II* published some of these images.[13] The most graphic of them showed a human pyramid of naked Iraqi men, with a couple of U.S. soldiers posing behind them and smiling for the camera; a naked detainee held on a leash by a female soldier; and a hooded prisoner wearing a burlap sack and balancing on a crate, with his arms spread and electrodes fastened to his hands. That last image—a sort of electric crucifixion—became emblematic of the Abu Ghraib affair. Many other photos and filmed scenes circulated later on, among them images of prisoners smeared with feces or posing naked in a degrading manner. Forced to simulate sexual acts for the camera, their heads covered by hoods or women's underwear, they were staged as feminized bodies posing for porn shots.[14] Stripped of their manhood, the prisoners not only suffered from the guards' cruelty but were also humiliated by the voyeurism to which they were subjected when the pictures were circulated.

In January 2004 a soldier who was appalled by the way some of his army mates were treating the detainees gave his superiors a CD showing images taken between October and December 2003. During that period the insurgency had taken the U.S. forces by surprise, using methods for which the military was unprepared—improvised explosive devices, booby traps, suicide bombings, kidnappings, and beheadings. Pressure to interrogate prisoners in order to obtain intelligence concerning the resistance became especially intense, and the military started to apply the methods of Guantánamo to the situation at Abu Ghraib. Most of the inmates turned out to be merely common criminals who knew little or nothing about the insurgency. Yet the need for rapid, useful confessions in the fight against terrorism encouraged their jailers to "soften them up" before interrogation. The guards to whom this gruesome task was assigned were army reservists lacking sufficient training as interrogators.

The scandalous photographs on the CD made an investigation imperative. The report drawn up after the inquiry was leaked to the press, which was also able to obtain some of the photographs. When the outrages of Abu Ghraib became public knowledge in late April 2004, Rumsfeld—forced to acknowledge the gravity of the matter—made a public apology and tendered his resignation, which the president refused. Meanwhile, seven soldiers and junior officers were court-martialed and sentenced to terms not exceeding ten years in prison; their superior officers were demoted. A final report presented to Rumsfeld in August 2004 by James Schlesinger, a former secretary of defense, concluded that these acts were highly reprehensible but isolated, and blamed gaps in the chain of command for their occurrence.[15]

In remarks made to the United States Army War College at Carlisle, Pennsylvania, on May 24, 2005, President Bush noted that "under the dictator, prisons like Abu Ghraib were symbols of death and torture. That same prison became a symbol of disgraceful conduct by a few American troops who dishonored our country and disregarded our values." In the same spirit, the president expressed his regrets to the Arab world, through the intermediary of the king of Jordan and an interview in the Egyptian daily *Al Ahram*. But these apologies were too little, too late.

According to Fouad Ajami, professor of Middle Eastern Studies at Johns Hopkins University, Abu Ghraib gave anti-Americanism in the Arab world a target and an outlet. Yet in an article in the *Wall Street Journal* in May 2004 he warned: "We should see through the motives of those in Cairo and Amman and Ramallah and Jeddah, now outraged by Abu Ghraib, who looked away from the terrors of Iraq under the Baathists."[16] Ajami made an important point: contrary to many states in the Middle East where torture is practiced with impunity, the misdeeds committed at Abu Ghraib were condemned and a handful of people—most of them very low on the chain of command—were punished. But the United States lost much more than "face" because of the events at Abu Ghraib.

The goal of the Iraq invasion was to sway hearts and minds in the Arab and Muslim world in favor of defeating terrorism and promoting democracy. Sadistic behavior that put a perverse, pornographic twist on torture was contrary to everything the Americans claimed to represent. The mortification inflicted on naked prisoners seemed to mock the insurgency and to function as a sort of exorcism of the danger and violence the uprising had unleashed against the U.S. occupation in the fall of 2003. When those images of sexual abuse were offered up for public consumption in the Muslim world, they sent a clear message that, behind the grand sentiments of the war on terror, the reality of the U.S. invasion was foreign domination and Muslim subjection. From that point on, the United States' claim that it had freed the Muslim world from a cruel dictatorship and emancipated civil society from jihadist barbarity would fall on deaf ears.

The Embargo—a Repressed Memory Resurfaces

Older and deeper problems undermined the U.S. project in Iraq.[17] In planning the invasion, the neoconservatives in Washington were convinced that once the dictator was overthrown, the Iraqi people would greet the Americans with flowers and set about reconstructing a democratic civil society that would become the envy of the oppressed throughout the Middle East. Yet the very notion of an "Iraqi people" had died sometime during the decade-long embargo imposed by the international community after Iraq was defeated in the Gulf War of 1991. When the U.S.-led coalition expelled Saddam Hussein's army from Kuwait, then-president George H. W. Bush did not order the dictator to be overthrown, although he could have done so. The leaders of the Sunni oil monarchies in the Arabian Peninsula, who were settling the accounts of the war and feared that a Shiite government under Iranian influence might come to power if the strongman in Baghdad were to disappear, made their voices heard in Washington, and not for the first time. Coalition forces looked the other way while Saddam Hussein's praetorian guard massacred Shiite rebels in the south.

Instead of overthrowing the dictator, the United States decided to clip Saddam's wings by granting autonomy to the Kurdish regions in the north and imposing a no-fly zone in the south. Most important, in order to forestall the belligerent ambitions of a leader who had invaded two of his neighbors within a decade, it imposed economic sanctions and an embargo on Iraq. The despot and his cronies adapted easily to the situation by organizing a lucrative black market with the assistance of various unscrupulous international agents. It was Iraqi civilians who suffered terrible deprivations as a result of the embargo, not Saddam's relatives and henchmen.

Between the overthrow of the monarchy in 1958 and the embargo of 1991, successive authoritarian regimes in Iraq had bought social peace by investing oil revenues in education, infrastructure, and development. Though divested of freedom and bent beneath the yoke of state terror, Iraqis were still better off, in economic and social terms, than citizens of most other Arab countries, and cultural life flourished—as long as it remained apolitical. According to an Arab saying that was popular in the 1970s, "Egypt writes, Lebanon publishes, and Iraq reads." The war with Iran in the 1980s depleted the country's resources, but the population remained firmly attached to the state. Even a majority of the Shiite conscripts in Iraq had demonstrated loyalty to the regime rather than to their co-religionists in Iran.

The situation was entirely different in 1991 after the Iraqi army invaded and pillaged Kuwait. With the international coalition hot on its heels, the army fled in disarray, and the institutions of the nation-state disintegrated, with the exception of the elite squadrons responsible for protecting the regime. "Bush's strike" (*darbat*

Bush, as the popular expression referred to it) disrupted all the existing social hierarchies. Saddam's state became merely a predator in service to the president's clan. The bulk of the population that could not flee the country joined ethnic, tribal, or religious communities in an effort to obtain food, medicine, and other necessities.

The "Iraqi people" fragmented into Kurds, Arabs, Turkmen, Sunnis, Shiites, Christians, Yazidis, and other clans, sects, religious groups, and tribes that became the centers of identification and social life. In the struggle for survival, these groups excluded fellow citizens who did not share their specific characteristics. In an attempt to divide the citizenry and distract them from blaming the state for their deprivations, Saddam's regime exalted these tribal virtues and initiated "faith campaigns" to encourage public demonstrations of piety, including the veiling of women and the construction of "Saddam mosques." Sunni and Shiite preachers contributed to the social disruption by building their own power bases, as did Kurdish groups, for whom Iraqi society no longer made sense since Arabic was not even taught to schoolchildren in the Kurdish autonomous zone.

For all of these reasons, when Saddam's regime finally fell apart under U.S. bombardment in April 2003, any meaningful concept of social cohesion had long since ceased to exist in Iraq. The neoconservative ideologues in Washington who were planning the country's reconstruction seem to have been shockingly ignorant of this fact. They behaved as though Iraqi society would rise from the ashes of Saddam's fallen regime. By blaming the deterioration of civil society on its leader and then overthrowing him, Washington absolved other parties—the United States, Europe, the Arab countries, and the United Nations—of responsibility for the state of affairs in that country.

The neoconservatives got their fanciful notions from leaders of the Iraqi community in exile, most of whom had left the country before sanctions were imposed. The view of Iraqi exiles depended largely on their memories of a bygone time, when left-wing movements that had no explicit religious or ethnic affiliation had managed to bring ethnic and religious groups together in the name of various progressive, secular ideologies, and when mixed marriages among Sunnis, Shiites, and Kurds occurred frequently in urban centers. The exiles had no concrete experience of the social fragmentation that had occurred because of the embargo, and they did nothing to disabuse their supporters in the Pentagon and the State Department of the notion that the invasion of Iraq would have the same happy ending as the fall of the Berlin wall.

That the state government had collapsed was obvious from the moment Baghdad was invaded in April 2003. But instead of immediately imposing a new order, the victorious U.S. troops gave the population free rein to pillage public buildings, ministries, hospitals, schools, and museums. After a few weeks of catastrophic transition, Paul Bremer took up the position of U.S. civilian administrator of Iraq on May 9, 2003. His first directives demobilized the officers and soldiers of the Iraqi army, liquidated the armed forces, and banned from public office all former Baathists belonging to the party's four highest ranks—around 30,000 individuals. These measures targeted what the occupiers described as "former regime loyalists," many of whom belonged to the ruling Sunni minority and some of whom were members of Saddam's extended family.

In his memoirs, Bremer does not say much about these measures, and one is left to wonder whether they were inspired by de-Nazification in Germany after World War II or by the communist purges that followed the fall of the Berlin wall and the disappearance of the Soviet system in Eastern Europe. At any rate, their consequences were disastrous, and none of the neoconservatives who applauded their implementation at the time has anything to say in their defense today. The cadres of the former regime, suddenly deprived of their salaries and fired from their jobs, entered the armed dissident movement and made up the first wave of insurgents, most of whom were Sunni. They despised the American troops, whom they saw as infidel invaders rather than liberators. The insurgency brought former Baathists as well as Sunni Islamists—from Iraq, initially, and then from abroad under Al Qaeda's auspices—into a single resistance movement much like the 1980s jihad in Afghanistan.

But in Afghanistan there had been few conflicts between Shiites and Sunnis, at least until the Taliban arrived in 1996. By contrast, jihad in Iraq rapidly took on another dimension. In addition to targeting the "crusaders"—the Americans, their allies, and any non-Muslims, including civilians, who were in Iraq—the Sunni insurgents also went after the "heretic" Shiites, who had long been underdogs but who now had taken power away from the ruling Sunni elite, thanks to their numerical superiority in elections and to American support. On the ashes of Iraqi civil society, the occupation planted what Muslim jurists have long feared—sectarian conflict (*fitna*). In Islamic doctrine, this leads to chaos and anarchy, threatens Muslim society from within, and eventually brings about its destruction.

From Iraqi Resistance to Ethnic Cleansing

By late summer of 2003, barely four months after the fall of Baghdad, the Sunni jihadists' opposition to Westerners and Shiites was obvious to observers. On August 19 the U.N. headquarters in Baghdad was attacked in a "martyrdom operation" that killed Brazilian diplomat Sergio Vieira de Mello—the secretary-general's special envoy—and several of his colleagues. Ten days later, in Najaf, one of the holiest sites of Shiism, Ayatollah Muhammad Baqir al-Hakim and many of his supporters were killed in another suicide attack. Al-Hakim had the backing of the United States, despite his position as head of the Supreme Council for the Islamic Revolution in Iraq (SCIRI), a party made originally of Shiite Iraqi POWs who were detained in Iran after 1982 and then freed, trained, and equipped by Tehran. These successive, spectacular operations set the tone for the next two years, as the assassination of foreigners and Shiites reached unprecedented proportions. Then, in spring of 2005, Shiite militias began to retaliate, and these counterattacks intensified after February 2006, when the Golden Mosque in Samarra, one of the holiest mosques for Shiites, was partially destroyed by a suicide bomber.

Within the Muslim world, the invasion and occupation of Iraq—which initially some democratic intellectuals in the region saw as a necessary evil, a means of ridding the Middle East of a bloodthirsty dictator who desecrated Arab and Islamic causes—began to get a very bad press in 2004. Coming in the wake of Guantánamo and Abu Ghraib, the Sunni insurrection received legitimation among nationalist and Islamic groups alike, at least early on. On November 8, 2004, just days after President Bush's war on terror brought him victory at the polls, U.S. forces launched Operation Phantom Fury against the city of Falluja, known to be a refuge for jihadists as well as a detention and torture center for hostages taken by insurgents.

Also in 2004, while suicide attacks of the second intifada were still occurring in Israel, several Islamic scholars of international stature brought together the Palestinian and Iraqi uprisings under the umbrella of a single jihad. Sheikh Youssef al-Qaradawi—a pro–Muslim Brotherhood Egyptian preacher who today lives in Qatar and is well-known for his televised sermons on Al Jazeera's most popular religious program, *Sharia and Life* (*Al-Sharia wal-Hayat*)—was one of the first scholars to offer justification, in 1996, for the "martyrdom operations" launched by Hamas that were claiming victims among Israeli civilians. His argument was that in Israel, where men and women alike serve as army reservists, any citizen is a potential combatant, and therefore by definition a legitimate target for defensive jihad.

Taking it one step further in September 2004, Sheikh Qaradawi—who also headed the International Association of Muslim Scholars and the European Fatwa Council, both based in Dublin— issued a positive ruling in answer to the question whether it was lawful under *sharia* to kill unbelievers who were occupying Muslim territory in Iraq.[18] Coming from a religious scholar professing to occupy the "middle ground" (*wasatiyya*) between the jihadists and the *ulema* (Muslim scholars trained in Islamic law) who were co-opted by the regime, this ruling indicated the degree of support that the insurrection enjoyed among Sunnis and the Islamic imprimatur it could claim worldwide, where over 80 percent of Muslims are Sunnis.

But seen from the perspective of Sunni citizens in Baghdad, the insurgency was something more than defensive jihad. The Sunni rebels were fighting not only foreign troops on Muslim soil but also the nation of Iraq itself, as reshaped by the United States. In this view, the occupiers were intent on giving power to a Shiite-Kurdish alliance that would control the oil fields, most of which were concentrated in the Shiite south and the Kurdish north of the country. Only a continuous state of insecurity could destroy this U.S. plan (not least by terrorizing foreign businesses and investors) and thus deprive the intended beneficiaries of valuable oil revenues. The violence of the Sunni insurgency made it impossible to undertake any prospecting activities, and the wells that were still working were under the control of ethnic or religious militias who were selling whatever oil they could recover on a flourishing black market.

The short-term goal of the Sunni elites who encouraged the uprising went beyond Baathist or jihadist ideology: it was to force the Americans to reconsider their policy of excluding Sunnis from power and from access to oil revenues. This goal was attained in June 2005 when Zalmay Khalilzad—of Afghan, Sunni, and Pashtun origin and a figure appreciated by neoconservatives in Washington—became the new U.S. ambassador to Iraq. He approached the Sunnis to offer them a power-sharing deal and convinced some of them to participate in electoral processes they had boycotted massively in January, when elections to the National Assembly were held. As a result of these efforts, the Sunni population voted in a referendum of October 15, 2005, but was unable to prevent the ratification of a constitution that effectively deprived the Sunnis of most future oil revenues.

The Sunnis voted again, nevertheless, in December's legislative elections. Sunni groups such as the Iraqi Islamic Party—the local branch of the Muslim Brotherhood—that participated in the elections and won seats in the new parliament received a few ministerial positions as a reward. And just like the Shiite and Kurdish ministers, the Sunnis managed their portfolios as though they were communal fiefs, giving their families and tribes positions in government service on a religious or ethnic basis. Still, the violence did not abate in 2006—quite the contrary. The elections had merely confirmed the country's fragmentation. Secular lists of candidates who sought to avoid these splits by referring to ideals that transcended religious and tribal identities received the meanest share of seats. Sectarianism ruled the day, as represented by Sunni or Shiite Islamist parties or by Kurdish nationalists. The process of national dissolution that the embargo had triggered was now pushed one dangerous step further.

Except among the Kurds, the majority of political representatives were Islamists, but unlike the situation in countries where the overwhelming preponderance of the population is Sunni (as in Egypt and Algeria) or Shiite (in Iran), religious discourse in Iraq exacerbated intra-Muslim divisions and gave them an irreversible, existential character. Islamists in Iraq were very different from the Muslim Brothers in Egypt, the FIS in Algeria, or Khomeini's partisans in Iran. In Baghdad, Sunni Islamism represented the apogee of anti-Shiite sentiments, and vice versa. This religious competition was translated into ostensible signs, like veiling, which followed Iranian norms for Shiite women and Saudi norms for Sunnis. Most importantly, each side's desire for armed militias allowed violence to feed off itself, losing any relation to the original objectives of the uprising.

Shiite, Sunni, and Kurdish factions engaged in politics and

gangsterism, seized property by force, and organized rackets in a country where the state was no longer capable of sustaining public order or enforcing the law. Almost exactly the same phenomenon had played out in the civil wars in Lebanon, the former Yugoslavia, and Algeria in the three previous decades. There was a difference here, however: Iraq was experiencing this catastrophe while almost 140,000 soldiers from the world's most powerful army patrolled the streets and crisscrossed the skies. America's inability to quell the cataclysm through military might or sophisticated diplomacy was a shocking revelation not just to surrounding countries of the Middle East but to the entire globe. Terror exploded, uncontrolled, on a daily basis, while the United States stood by impotently, along with the rest of the watching world.

Al Qaeda's Comeback

Instead of contributing to the eradication of Al Qaeda, the occupation of Iraq handed the terrorists a field for action beyond their wildest dreams. Between 9/11 and the invasion of 2003, Al Qaeda had remained disconnected from any social base and incapable of mobilizing the Muslim population. But with the United States' nation-building exercise teetering on failure, Al Qaeda in Mesopotamia, as the group liked to call itself (eschewing the nationalist name of Iraq and preferring instead an old Islamic term derived from classical antiquity, *Al-Qaeda fi balad al-rafidayn*), moved into the breach. It preferred suicide attacks to all other types of operations, because those who blew themselves up at the approach of U.S. forces or in the midst of a Shiite crowd could be turned into emblems of jihadist martyrdom. But if ever there was an ambiguous emblem, this was it, because the vast majority of victims who perished in the hundreds of suicide attacks carried out in Iraq were not infidel Westerners but Shiite Muslims, whom Al Qaeda labeled as "heretics" for the occasion.

The most visible figure of jihadism in Iraq was an interloper—half ruffian and half radical Islamist—who embodied the ambiguity of the insurrection: Abu Musab al-Zarqawi. Born in Jordan in the town of Zarqa (hence his *nom de guerre;* his real name was Ahmad Fadil Nazal al-Khalayleh), he was a smuggler, a tattooed thug, and a convict. But like so many others who skirted the law, from Malcolm X to Khaled Kelkal, he underwent an Islamist awakening in prison, one of the most favorable places for the propagation of that doctrine. Released as part of a general pardon granted on June 9, 1999, after Jordan's King Abdullah II ascended the throne, he joined a jihadist training camp in Afghanistan, then transferred to Iraq via Iran, traveling through the autonomous Kurdish zone, where he helped set up a local Islamist movement. Taking advantage of the chaos after the U.S. invasion, he entered the Sunni Arab zone and offered his services to the insurgency.

During the early stages of his jihad, Zarqawi chose not to submit to Bin Laden's authority. But in October 2004 he paid allegiance to the Al Qaeda founder, and in exchange acquired franchise rights to Al Qaeda in Mesopotamia and the notoriety this branding conferred.[19] Yet Zarqawi did not consider himself constrained in any way by Bin Laden, and under his leadership Al Qaeda in Mesopotamia acquired a new inflection. What Zarqawi took from the Afghan jihad was the ability to merge the local mujahedin with foreign jihadists in order to attack occupying forces—the Red Army in Afghanistan and the United States and allied troops in Iraq—on a given terrain, and in coordination with a complicit civilian population that allowed combatants to move around easily. What he took from Al Qaeda was a preference for spectacular martyrdom operations that could be exploited by the media. Al Qaeda's identification with the suicide bombings of the second intifada was of primary importance for propaganda purposes in Iraq: anti-Israeli suicide attacks had widespread support in the Arab and Muslim world. By creating an equivalence between Palestine and Iraq, images of which were barely distinguishable on Al Jazeera's news bulletins in 2004, Zarqawi aimed to present the two causes as one.

We do not know exactly what part Zarqawi and his henchmen played in stoking the Sunnis' fury after the U.S. invasion, compared with the actions of Baathists who were nostalgic for Saddam's regime or community notables who were defending their particular interests. Whatever the case may have been, the Sunni jihadists now had at their disposal a tool that other elements of the Iraqi insurrection had not mastered well: media communications. Living up to the Al Qaeda brand, Zarqawi and his hooded attendants put on a murderous show for their Internet audience, and this was undoubtedly effective in recruiting violent Sunni jihadists from outside Iraq.

But this brutal behavior soon began to work against the larger interests of Al Qaeda in Mesopotamia. The beheading of civilians in front of a webcam and the perverse enjoyment that seemed to accompany the interrogation and execution of foreign and Iraqi hostages was not well received by Arab television channels. Bin Laden's right-hand lieutenant, Zawahiri—the ideologue responsible for Al Qaeda worldwide—wrote to Zarqawi in July 2005 to warn him that exhibitions of cruelty were more likely to disgust potential sympathizers than to frighten enemies. In a letter that was intercepted and published by U.S. intelligence the following October, Zawahiri wrote that Zarqawi had shown excessive zeal in embracing the local interests of Iraq's Sunnis, to the detriment of global jihad.[20] By turning the massacre of Shiites into a declaration of principles, he made himself vulnerable to reproach from many ordinary Muslims throughout the world, who, with the untutored faith of simple men, considered Shiites an integral part of the community of believers.

Rather than promoting the universal mobilization of the Islamic community, Zarqawi had chosen the short-term, particularistic interests of those in Iraq who provided his group with political cover and a social network. His behavior had embarrassed Bin Laden and his disciples, whose name he was using. But above all, Zawahiri feared a break between the jihadists and the masses, who did not understand the vanguard's actions and were beginning to distance themselves. The 1990s had shown where this could lead in Egypt, Algeria, and Bosnia. Zarqawi had managed to make a place for himself in the Sunni population of Iraq, but by committing atrocities that sickened Muslims around the world, he ran the risk of dragging Al Qaeda's reputation down along with his own.

U.S. authorities tried to calm the insurgency's violence by offering Iraq's Sunni notables a share in the power and material rewards of peace, in return for dissociating themselves from Zarqawi. On February 22, 2006, the leader of Al Qaeda in Mesopotamia attempted to regain the advantage by blowing up the dome of the

Golden Mosque in Samarra. The mosque contains the burial sites of two of the twelve imams of Shiism as well as the entrance to the cave where the twelfth imam, Muhammad al-Mahdi, is said to have disappeared in the tenth century. So-called Twelvers believe that the Mahdi, or messiah, was hidden by God and will return someday to the community of believers, bringing light and justice. Zarqawi's sacrilegious attack on the Golden Mosque so angered Shiite believers that they immediately formed militias to launch unrestrained attacks on the mosques and holy sites of Sunnis. Shiite death commandos captured and tortured Sunnis, whose mutilated corpses were found at dawn in ditches or on garbage dumps. This sharp spiral of violence caused observers to begin to speak of civil war rather than sectarian conflict.

Zarqawi calculated that Shiite counterattacks would cause Sunnis to close ranks behind their most extreme advocates. But the Shiites' growing hatred posed such a threat to the Sunni minority, and the suffering caused by population migrations from dangerous mixed neighborhoods toward homogeneous zones proved so excessive, that some Sunni groups began to regard Zarqawi as the main threat to their survival. They feared becoming victims of a pogrom at the hands of the furious Shiites. Finding himself increasingly isolated, Zarqawi launched a communications campaign to defend his cause. He ran security risks by posing for cameras, weapons in hand, in places that could be identified. Eventually someone betrayed him, and U.S. forces located and killed him on June 7, 2006. Less than a week later, while Zawahiri and Bin Laden were pronouncing audio and video elegies for Zarqawi as the "new martyr of the Muslim *umma*" (world community), Zarqawi's successor was declared. The leader of Al Qaeda in Mesopotamia would be an Egyptian jihadist named Abu Hamza al-Muhajir (or Abu Ayyub al-Masri).

The Americans displayed Zarqawi's corpse on television for all Shiites and Sunnis to see, but his execution did not lead to a decline in sectarian violence—quite the contrary. In the month of July alone, over 3,500 attacks were carried out against coalition forces, Iraqi civilians, and government officials, leading to the highest death toll since the allies entered Iraq. The Baghdad morgue catalogued a record 1,700 corpses for that month, compared with a monthly average of 120 in 2002, just before the U.S. invasion.[21]

Zarqawi's savage journey had pulled many followers in its wake: Iraqis, hundreds of foreign jihadists from Saudi Arabia, Syria, and the Maghreb, as well as a few young Europeans—first- or second-generation converts to Islam. The most famous of these was Muriel Degauque, a bewildered baker from Charleroi, Belgium, who was seduced by a Moroccan Islamist.[22] He married her after she took the veil, and the couple set off for Iraq in an old Mercedes. She blew herself up in a martyrdom operation on November 9, 2005. The jihadists' countries of origin viewed this latest development with ambivalence. On the one hand, they were relieved to see trouble-makers leave; on the other, Iraq provided an exceptional training ground for urban warfare, and those who were initiated there might return to European, American, or Middle Eastern cities to employ their new tactics.

That worry proved mostly unfounded: the vast majority of Europeans who managed to reach Iraq did not return from their journey. The demand for martyrs in that explosive country consumed the available supply.

The Iranian Intrusion

In addition to the rise of Sunni jihadism and civil war, the occupation of Iraq by U.S. and coalition troops had a third consequence that President Bush's neoconservative advisers did not foresee, despite their experience in geopolitical strategy. This was the resurgence of Islamist Iran, embodied in the unlikely figure of Mahmud Ahmadinejad, who was elected president in June 2005.

The Iranians had elected Muhammad Khatami in 1997 and reelected him in 2001. Although Khatami made repeated cultural overtures to the West and preached the "dialogue of civilizations" throughout Europe, the U.S. government preferred to see him only as a smiling face pasted over the despised Khomeinist establishment. As long as disagreements between Iran and the United States were not settled, especially those growing out of the hostage crisis of November 1979, Washington saw any support for Khatami's initiatives as a capitulation that would only strengthen the mullahs' regime.

Rather than seeking a simple behavior change, the United States wanted to bring about regime change in Tehran. To that end, they took as fact any shred of evidence or opinion that supported the theory of a growing split in Iranian society between the educated secularized elites and the religious establishment. They believed that by reinforcing the democratic aspirations of the larger society, they could isolate the regime and force its collapse. In the run-up to the 2003 invasion, some Iraqi Shiite exiles, including Iyad Allawi and Ahmad Chalabi, predicted to their friends in the Bush administration that a ferment of democratic sentiment would indeed swell up not just in Iraq but in neighboring Shiite Iran after the toppling of Saddam's regime. And a plethora of minor facts from daily life seemed to support this view.

For example, in Tehran the well-off classes live in the mountainous north of the city, breathing pure air at altitudes that reach 1,800 meters, while the poor are confined to the southern foothills, at around 1,300 meters. At 1,500 meters and higher, one notices a change in women's clothing. The shapeless black chador worn by poor women at lower elevations is replaced by a different garment: an Islamically correct robe, to be sure, but modified with a shorter hem and a tighter waist to show off a trim figure and perhaps a pair of tight flesh-colored trousers. In full view of the Revolutionary Guards, upper-class women push the obligatory headscarf to the back of their head, uncovering carefully highlighted hair topped with designer sunglasses. Sometimes a small bandage on the nose bears witness to the trendy miracles of recent plastic surgery.

In the early years of the twenty-first century, Iran's secularized urban middle classes deliberately tweaked the Islamic morality preached by the Khomeinists and showed no attachment to the regime—but were still too weak politically to take action. Those who supported it came primarily from the bazaaris and the disinherited—pious urban classes and poor youths who depended for their survival on oil revenues redistributed by the theocracy after the Islamic Revolution of 1979. Near the end of Khatami's presidency, the freedom granted liberal Iranians by the reformists in power alienated these urban youths, who feared that liberalization would deprive them of the social privileges and economic support they received in exchange for backing the mullahs. Included in these benefits were subsidized food and housing and preferential access to university education for the families of the "martyrs" who fell during the war with Iraq.

As the clerics saw their influence over the middle classes frittering away, they took advantage of the American invasion of Iraq to radicalize Iran's foreign policy. Rather than continuing along the liberal path Khatami had opened up, they promised the urban poor massive subsidies for the purchase of consumer goods in return for their support in the elections. In the second round of voting in June 2005, as the reformists split their ballot among several competing candidates, conservative voters chose an outsider, the former mayor of Tehran, Mahmud Ahmadinejad. At forty-eight years of age, the new president was not a "turban" but had emerged from the ranks of the Revolutionary Guards, the Pasdaran. He received popular acclaim after promising a wide-ranging recovery program that would allow Iranians to benefit from oil revenues.

Simply dressed and humble in appearance, the new president benefited from the contribution of a fanatical paramilitary organization, the Basij, and the discreet, belated, but decisive support of the Islamic Republic's supreme leader, Khamenei. The Basij were mobilized in Iran's war against Iraq in the 1980s and became famous for their willingness to seek martyrdom by throwing themselves on Iraqi mines or advancing in human waves, holding hands, their chests bared to Iraqi machine guns. These soldiers—most of whom were very young, having been recruited in schools and indoctrinated on an ad hoc basis—became cannon fodder in the Ayatollah Khomeini's defense against Saddam Hussein's invasion. Each soldier wore a headband bearing the formula "There is no god but Allah and Muhammad is His Prophet" and a chain around his neck with a small metal key to open the gates of Paradise. When the huge numbers of dead made the cost of metal keys prohibitive, they were replaced with plastic ones made in China.[23]

In time, the Basij marched to their deaths wrapped tightly in blankets, so that their bodies would be easier to collect and transform into relics after they had detonated a mine. The Islamic Republic invented this notion of martyrs' relics, and Iran's rulers still use this ritual today to renew their legitimacy. Whenever a mass grave containing Iranian soldiers is discovered, the remains—in coffins draped with the national colors—are honored by the highest authorities and borne in military processions attended by the unquestioning supporters. Then they are sent as rewards to cities the regime wants to favor.

Ahmadinejad had barely been elected before he began to revive the Basij tradition of self-sacrifice and place it once again at the center of official propaganda. "Is there a more beautiful, divine, and eternal art than that of dying a martyr? A nation that knows martyrdom does not know captivity!" he declared on television.[24] By reviving the spirit of martyrdom, the new president was expressing in vivid terms the radicalization he wished to bring about in Iran's foreign policy, reversing course from Khatami's old stories about the dialogue of civilizations.

With U.S. troops bogged down in Iraq and dependent on the good will of the Shiite militias to help quell the Sunni insurgency's murderous attacks, Iran—to Washington's dismay—became a key player in the Iraqi drama. This came about thanks to the influence Tehran exerted over some of the Shiite factions, especially the Badr Organization linked to SCIRI and headed by Abd al-Aziz al-Hakim. This militia was trained, equipped, and funded by Tehran. Sunni insurgents in Iraq despised its members, calling them Safavids, a pejorative label referring to the greatest Persian dynasty. The Sunnis saw the Badr members as an Iranian fifth column that sought to subjugate Iraq, annihilate its Arab character, and reduce it to a religious and cultural annex of Persia.

Ironically, the Sunnis' hatred for Iran and its allies in Iraq did not prevent Tehran from providing the Sunni insurgency with sophisticated weapons to use against the Americans, especially roadside bombs identical to those the Islamic Republic gave Hezbollah in Lebanon. In the south, these explosive devices had defeated Israeli tank patrols and precipitated the departure of Israel Defense Forces (Tsahal) in May 2000, after eighteen years of occupation. By delivering materiel to various armed bands in Iraq, both Shiite and Sunni, the mullahs' regime—and particularly the Pasdaran—turned America's peacekeeping efforts into mission impossible. Iran believed that once the United States was thoroughly mired in Iraq—regardless of which side of the insurgency brought this about—it would be forced to negotiate from a position of weakness and confirm the regional supremacy of the Islamic Republic. This was the dream of the leadership in Tehran, which was determined to turn to its own advantage America's grand narrative of the war on terror, now that the naive Great Satan had eliminated Iran's worst enemy, Saddam Hussein.

Muqtada al-Sadr's Ascent

The Persians' martial art of turning America's strength against itself went undetected during the ingenuous calculations of the neoconservatives in Washington. Victims of their certainty that Iran would be overcome by democratization under the virtuous influence of Iraq's Shiites and America's military presence, the Bush administration blindly and obligingly took out the only power in the region that had stood up to Iran's expansionistic ambitions. The ensuing chaos in Baghdad strengthened the hand of the most radical factions in Tehran, and their influence on Iraqi Shiites increased exponentially, causing scores of them to dissociate from the occupiers.

The January 2005 elections to the Iraqi National Assembly gave a majority to the Shiites, who were allied with the Kurds. Then in March, after long negotiations, the government fell into the hands of Ibrahim Jaafari, leader of the Dawa (Call to Islam) Party. He would be succeeded by another militant of the same persuasion, Nuri Kamal al-Maliki, on May 20, 2006. This Islamist group had been created in 1957 by Shiite activists who followed the organizational methods of the Communist Party, the better to combat it. Among its founders was Muhammad Baqir al-Sadr, who became Ayatollah Khomeini's personal representative in Iraq before Saddam's agents assassinated him in April 1980. The Dawa Party had few militants and no militia of its own, but at first it had the support of the disciples of Muqtada al-Sadr, a relative of Muhammad Baqir.[25]

Muqtada's own father, Ayatollah Muhammad Sadiq al-Sadr, was also killed by the Baathists, after having built up immense popularity during the embargo by bringing supplies and services to suffering Shiite neighborhoods. Muhammad Sadiq advocated the clergy's involvement in the struggles of daily life, and called his movement the *hawza natiqa* (speaking seminary). It stood in opposition to the main seminary of the holy city of Najaf, controlled by Ali al-Sistani, a grand ayatollah of Iranian origin who only spoke on theological questions and had been dubbed the *hawza samita* (silent seminary).

Paradoxically, Muhammad Sadiq benefited from the "faith campaigns" launched by Saddam's regime to co-opt Islamic leaders who had taken responsibility for managing daily life after the Iraqi welfare state collapsed. Saddam (though he had had Muhammad Baqir assassinated) favored the Sadr family because it belonged to an Arab, not an Iranian, lineage, unlike Sistani. To reciprocate, Muhammad Sadiq reestablished Friday prayers, which Shiites hold only when they believe the government is just, since the sermon's invocations are uttered in the government's name. But the exceptional popularity of this ayatollah, who not only delivered rousing sermons but knew the price of tomatoes, ultimately proved worrisome to the dictator, and in 1999 Saddam ordered his assassination, along with two of his sons. Young Muqtada, born in the late 1970s, survived, but none of the Iraqis in exile in the United States paid the slightest attention to him, since advanced age and long years of seminary study are required for preeminence in the Shiite clergy.

Yet as soon as Baghdad fell to the Americans, Muqtada threw himself into the struggle for power in Iraq. The day on which Saddam's colossal statue was pulled down, April 9, 2003, was also the twenty-third anniversary of Muhammad Baqir al-Sadr's assassination. Those who honored Ayatollah Muhammad Sadiq and his son did not attribute this event to the military power of the United States but to miraculous intervention by the Mahdi. They saw the toppling of Saddam's statue on the anniversary of Muhammad Baqir's assassination as an act of divine revenge that signaled the end of days and the coming chaos that would precede the Mahdi's return.

What was particularly striking here was the way in which the two grand narratives fit together. For the administration in Washington, the toppling of Saddam's statue, like that of Lenin before it, announced Iraq's democratization under U.S. hegemony. It was the key indicator that the grand narrative of the war on terror had moved into another phase: the gestation of a democratic society on the ruins of the fallen dictatorship. For the Sadrists, the collapse of the statue announced the imminent return of the messiah after the final defeat of unbelievers and Sunnis, and the ultimate triumph of Shiism on earth and in heaven.[26]

On April 10, at the Najaf sanctuary, Muqtada al-Sadr's gang lynched Ayatollah Abd al-Majid al-Khoei, the scion of one of the main lineages of Sunni clerics, who had returned from exile in London and was a close adviser to the West. Through this sacrilege, Muqtada brutally entered the competition for domination of the Shiite clergy, an extraordinarily presumptuous ambition for a young man. He would try to seize Najaf from Ayatollah Sistani the following year.

After Khoei was assassinated, Muqtada called upon the Shiites of Iraq to undertake a pilgrimage on foot to Karbala, Shiism's holiest site. Each year, on the tenth day of the Islamic month of Muharram, Shiites commemorate the martyrdom of Imam Husayn in spectacular displays of mourning. In 2003 at Karbala, four million people commemorated the anniversary of the fortieth day following Husayn's death, the time when Muslims believe the soul leaves the body permanently and ascends to Paradise. Most of the pilgrims came from the Shiite neighborhood east of Baghdad where

Muhammad Sadiq al-Sadr's enormous popularity was based—a community that by this time had changed its name from Madinat Saddam (Saddam City) to Madinat Sadr (Sadr City).

The pilgrimage to Karbala was the first public manifestation of Shiite devotion on a large scale since the end of Baathist oppression, and as more and more people continued to arrive, it became the greatest human gathering that had ever occurred in the Middle East. The annual pilgrimage to Mecca, controlled by the Sunni state of Saudi Arabia, brings together only 2.5 million Muslims in a good year. For Iraq and the region, the event had important political consequences. It sent a clear message that Iraqi Shiism, led by a young unknown cleric from a prestigious family, had moved into its mobilization phase. This alarmed the Sunni authorities, and it did not augur well for the United States, which—though no one could foresee this in 2003—would be stuck in Iraq long enough to see the Shiites bite the hand that fed them.

Shiism as professed by Muqtada al-Sadr and Mahmud Ahmadinejad is characterized by extreme devotion to the Mahdi, but anticipation of his return is tempered by practical considerations. Ayatollahs stand at the peak of a clerical pyramid whose intermediary degrees are occupied by scholars bearing the title *hujjat al-Islam* (the proof of Islam). The base of the pyramid is made up of mullahs who head their local mosques. The period of time spent studying, the prestige of one's teacher, the exams passed, and the dissertations and treatises written all determine one's progression through the clerical hierarchy—much as they do in Western academia.

The Shiites particularly revere erudition, and at the very top of the pyramid a few great ayatollahs bearing the title *marja al-taqlid* (literally, reference of tradition) were believed to be infallible and were allowed to interpret the Quran. (Nothing quite like this existed among Sunni scholars, most of whom argued that the door to independent interpretation [*ijtihad*] was closed in the tenth century C.E.) Shiite clerics were thought to be responsible for the welfare of the community until the return of the Mahdi and were in a sense his substitutes. They cared for the souls and salvation of believers. Even if the government was iniquitous, their strategy was to pay lip service to it until the imam's return seemed imminent, at which point mobilization against the regime could begin.

These were the principles to which many Shiites adhered before the Ayatollah Khomeini overturned them in 1970. In his view, only the supreme leader (Khomeini himself during his lifetime, and his successors after him, including the current supreme leader, Khamenei) was qualified to be a just ruler, and the faithful must carry out an Islamic revolution in order to hasten the Mahdi's return. To underscore his claim that he himself was the much-anticipated Mahdi, Khomeini encouraged his followers to call him "Imam."

As a general rule, however, the traditional Shiite clergy were in no hurry to see the Mahdi return, since that would cause them to lose their social position and the considerable revenues derived from pious foundations. A corporate entity of sorts with a lot to lose, the clergy sought to temper the messianic enthusiasm of popular faith and channel it through clerical supervision.

Muqtada al-Sadr did not go along with this strategy in Iraq. Not only did he encourage expectations of the Mahdi's return, he did not discourage people from believing that he himself might be the Mahdi. According to tradition, the messiah would appear as a young man and derive his knowledge and charisma from divine inspiration, without having to spend a lifetime studying. Devotion to Muqtada spread very quickly among the masses of Shiites who were inclined toward such messianic beliefs. It was especially widespread on the outskirts of Baghdad and in southern Iraq, where rural exodus and migrations linked with the Iraq-Iran war had swelled the population.

SCIRI and the Hakim brothers, by contrast, were popular in circles linked to the traditional clergy and held a higher rank in the social hierarchy. SCIRI was originally more open to Iranian influence than Muqtada al-Sadr's group was, and its support was based on the loyalty of the large tribes around the oil-rich regions in the south. SCIRI claimed to favor a loose kind of federalism in order to secure as many oil revenues as possible for its own constituency. The Sadrist movement, on the other hand, was expressly pro-Arab and rooted in disinherited urban zones that did not control any oil. It was more inclined to preserve Iraq's unity and at first showed no hostility to the Sunnis. The late ayatollahs Muhammad Baqir and Muhammad Sadiq had called for Sunnis and Shiites to band together in their struggle against secularists, the left, and the West.

In spring 2004, when Israeli forces assassinated Ahmad Yassin, the head of Hamas in Palestine, and his successor, Abd al-Aziz al-Rantisi—both Sunnis—Muqtada's partisans turned out in enormous protest demonstrations, showing solidarity with Arab and Muslim causes that went beyond a narrowly defined Shiite vision of their interests. As a result, in April of that same year U.S. troops had to fight on two fronts: in Falluja against Sunni insurgents, and in Karbala against the band of paupers and outcasts that Muqtada had equipped and dubbed the Mahdi Army. In November, when

U.S. and government troops began their final assault on Falluja, Muqtada sent supply convoys to the besieged jihadists. But when the "heretical" Shiite drivers were killed by Sunni fanatics, cooperation between the two factions faded.

Despite his radical opposition to the U.S. presence, Muqtada encouraged his followers to participate in the three rounds of elections held under occupation in 2005. The mass of voters he mobilized and the number of deputies they elected to parliament gave him a decisive role in nominating the head of the government, turning him into a king-maker of sorts. Nevertheless, Badr cadres controlled the ministry of the interior, and in the name of hunting down jihadists and terrorists who were attacking Shiites, it began to arrest many Sunni suspects, some of whom were later found by U.S. forces. They were starving and had been tortured.

The rise of sectarian tension indicated that Ayatollah Sistani's influence over the Shiites was waning. From his seminary in Najaf, he continued to call for peace, but Badr Organization and—increasingly so—the Mahdi Army remained on the front lines as the violence escalated. They patrolled their respective neighborhoods and created irredentist armed militias. At first, they joined forces against the Sunnis, but soon enough, a mounting antagonism between rival Shiite factions bidding for power emerged.

The year 2008 saw a paradoxical turn of the tables in the complicated relations between Arab constituencies in Iraq and the U.S. occupation forces. On the Sunni side, the weakening of Al Qaeda after Zarqawi's death and the inability of the so-called Islamic State of Iraq to come into being led to a mounting fear that the Shiite militias would subdue them for good once U.S. troops departed. The Sunni community had been the harbinger of armed jihad against the U.S. occupation since the summer of 2003; now it was providing tribal militiamen—the so-called Awakening Brigades (*kataeb al sahwa*)—to fight against jihadists alongside U.S. troops. Trust between the new allies was low and subject to change, yet ironically many Sunnis now saw the U.S. military presence as the only counterweight to mounting Iranian control over Iraq. Former resistance fighters had become staunch collaborators of the Americans. But this change of plans came too late for the Sunnis. By 2008 they did not really count anymore in the contention for power in Baghdad. The big game was now between rival Shiite factions.

The Shiite front did not lack for ironic reversals of its own. In a bid to capitalize on all constituencies opposed to the U.S. presence in Iraq, Muqtada made the surprising about-face of allying with his former rival, the Islamic Republic. Taking up residence in a religious seminary in Iran so as to boost his religious credentials and, on a more down-to-earth level, to protect his life, he unleashed his Mahdi Army against Shiite government officials in Baghdad and Basra. In retaliation, Prime Minister Maliki, also a Shiite, launched—with U.S. and British support—a major military offensive in late March and April 2008 with the aim of eradicating Sadrist control in Sadr City and in the south. But the ill-prepared operation, which claimed hundreds of lives as Shiite factions battled one another in the streets, did not weaken the Mahdi Army's grip on its territories. The struggle ended when the warring parties met in Tehran and reached a cease-fire agreement under the auspices of the Iranian intelligence apparatus. This dramatic show of clout on Iran's part mirrored the disarray of U.S. diplomacy and the limits of American influence in the country it had occupied for five years.

Thus the calamitous U.S.-led occupation of Iraq changed the situation in the world much more drastically than the 9/11 attackers ever did, even though it did not at all fulfill the expectations of its Beltway planners. At a time when the United States enjoyed unprecedented moral standing and sympathy from much of the civilized world, it chose to spend its social capital along with its treasure by taking the lead in an anti-terror invasion with the proclaimed aim of inducing democracy in the Muslim Middle East. Caught up in an insurgency that turned into a full-fledged resistance movement, the U.S. occupation of Iraq lost the support of allies in Europe and lent new life to a jihadist movement that had been unable to mobilize large constituencies since its expulsion from Afghanistan. Islamist militants with no influence in Iraq under Saddam's regime were suddenly able to move freely among Sunnis disgruntled with the occupation and the power grab of Shiite factions. After the jihadists in their turn fell victim to the local Sunnis' disenchantment and fear of a mounting Shiite threat, the Shiite community that the United States had banked on suddenly split ranks, and a significant number of them sided with Iran.

The authoritarian Sunni governments of the region—Saudi Arabia, Egypt, and Syria, which Washington had accused of being too soft on terrorism—enjoyed an ironic reinstatement at the White House as President Bush, at his wits' end, cast aside any concern for democratic principles in a bid for urgent regional support. But in the eyes of the Arab leaders who had been so recently castigated, the military protection previously provided by the U.S. superpower was no longer the huge bargaining chip it once was. It had led to the fiasco in Iraq, with its flailing occupation force, and that in turn had allowed unprecedented Iranian influence to grow in the region, a nightmare that all Arab and Sunni governments shared.

Through some combination of blundering and bad luck in Iraq, Washington had allowed the Shiite card to slip into the hand of the Iranian regime, and this was the biggest, most unexpected loss for the Bush administration. A war game that began with a lot of bluffing about Saddam's WMDs had suddenly turned very real and very dangerous indeed, now that an Iran with nuclear ambitions had a seat at the table.

CHAPTER TWO

MARTYRDOM OPERATIONS
AMONG SHIITES AND SUNNIS

The fourth year of the Iraq War went very badly for its sponsors in Washington. The Republican Party lost its majority in both the House and the Senate as a result of the November 2006 midterm elections, and this stinging defeat forced President Bush to accept the resignation of his embattled secretary of defense, Donald Rumsfeld. On December 6 the Iraq Study Group, co-chaired by James Baker and Lee Hamilton, released its report, which declared the occupation a failure and advocated a radical change in strategy, based on dialogue with Baghdad's neighbors that would pave the way for an allied withdrawal from Iraq. President Bush chose not to follow these recommendations.

But having bet so heavily on Iraqi Shiites and having lost so much as a result, the administration rebalanced its regional investments starting in early 2007, seeking to minimize risks on all fronts. The neoconservative dream of 2003 gave way to a more thoughtful *realpolitik* that included reconciliation with Sunni leaders and with the governments of the Arabian peninsula, which

Washington acquitted of any remaining responsibility for the 9/11 attacks. Iraqi Shiism, on the other hand—once seen by the administration as the epitome of virtue—was now viewed as a shill for the most threatening operator in the region, Iran.

Mahmud Ahmadinejad had raised the stakes relentlessly since his election to the presidency in 2005. In Iraq, he escalated the level of violence by providing weapons not only to Shiite militias but also to Sunni insurgents. Citing Khomeini as his authority, he proclaimed that Israel should be excised like a malignant growth, that it should be wiped off the map. He organized a revisionist exhibition that made the Holocaust the subject of cartoons and caricatures—a digital-age vendetta intended to retaliate for the Danish press's 2005 publication of caricatures insulting the Prophet Muhammad. Enlisting populist regimes like those of Chávez and Morales in South America as well as university students in Indonesia, he promoted Third World demands for nuclear energy, leaving unanswered the question whether it would be used for military or civilian purposes. Access to this energy resource was itself an inalienable human right, he claimed, and not the exclusive privilege of a few dominant world powers.

In forging his alliance of Shiite Islamists and Third Worldists, Ahmadinejad used Quranic parlance to characterize the struggle between oppressors and oppressed—a reversal of the policies followed by Iranian presidents Rafsanjani (1989–1997) and Khatami (1997–2005). Those reform-minded leaders had sought an accommodation with Europe and the United States in order to obtain the advanced technology Iran needed to optimize its petroleum industry and perpetuate the revenues that ensured the mullahs' survival. In contrast with his predecessors, Ahmadinejad aimed to restore

Iran to the revolutionary status it had enjoyed between 1979 and 1989 under Ayatollah Khomeini, who had successfully challenged Washington at every turn—most notably in the American hostage crisis of 1979–1981 which spelled the end of the Carter administration.

Seeing parallels between this earlier crisis and America's current predicament in Iraq, Ahmadinejad hoped to extort concessions from the West that would allow Iran to become a nuclear power and ultimately to dominate the Gulf and its oil reserves. This strategy entailed galvanizing the old revolutionary ardor within the disenfranchised strata of Iranian society that his reformist predecessors had ignored. But it also meant transcending Iran's Persian and Shiite identity by offering aid and comfort to enemies of the United States and the West throughout the world.

The Iranian president realized that he did not have much time to achieve his revolutionary goals. Iran would not be able to endure a protracted standoff with the West because its economic and social margins for maneuver were limited. Revenues from the export of crude oil were offset by the cost of imported fuel for cooking, heating, and transportation, which Iran—lacking refining capacity—had to buy at full price on world markets. This dependence made it vulnerable to a series of increasingly stringent U.N. sanctions designed to force Tehran to drop its nuclear enrichment program. In June 2007 Ahmadinejad imposed gasoline rationing and hiked its subsidized price considerably, a move which took Iranians by surprise and triggered the most serious urban riots since he became president.

In a pallid remake of the Salman Rushdie affair of 1989, when Khomeini issued a *fatwa* calling for the death of the author of *The*

Satanic Verses as a way to distract attention from his costly failure to win the Iraq-Iran war, Ahmadinejad turned up the volume of his rhetoric against the "arrogant" West, hoping to garner Third World support for the inevitable showdown with the "satanic power"—the United States—over the issue of nuclear energy. His language became especially strident on the West's support of Israel, which celebrated its sixtieth birthday in May 2008. Israel was a "stinking corpse," he said, that "has reached the end like a dead rat after being slapped by the Lebanese."

This last reference—a jab at the Israel Defense Forces' defeat at the hands of Hezbollah militants during thirty-three days of battle in the summer of 2006—was especially significant in light of Iran's ambitions for preeminence in the Middle East. For a quarter of a century the Islamic Republic had sponsored this Shiite militant group in its struggles to keep Israel out of Lebanon. Tehran's long-standing support for Hezbollah (the Party of God) placed it squarely on the most active fault line in the region—the one running through Lebanon, Israel, and Palestine.

Tehran on the Fault Line

Iran's influence in Lebanon can be traced back to the early years of the Islamic Republic, and to the Lebanese civil war of 1975–1990. Hezbollah was formed shortly after Israeli soldiers invaded southern Lebanon in June 1982 to destroy Palestinian military bases. Glad to be freed from the heavy military presence of the PLO, the Shiites of Lebanon initially welcomed the Israelis as liberators. But after Lebanese Christians agreed to a peace treaty with Israel that shifted Lebanon into the Western camp, Iran, with the help of the secular Baath regime in Syria, sent detachments of revolutionary guards to activate radical networks that would oppose Israel and the West.

Hezbollah's militants and sympathizers emerged mostly from rural-to-urban Shiite migrants living in the poverty belt south of Beirut. Faithfully following the political and religious line of the supreme leaders of the Islamic revolution—first Khomeini and later Khamenei—Hezbollah quickly became the political voice and military arm of this disenfranchised and dislocated Muslim population. In a 1985 manifesto, the group expressed its intention to bring to account those who committed atrocities during the civil war (especially Christian factions), to eradicate Western colonialism from Lebanon, and to establish in its place an Islamic republic.

The organization's rapid growth during the 1980s gave Khomeini a strong hand in a conflict that drew in all the nations and factions of the Levant (*Bilad al-Sham*)—Lebanese Sunnis, Druze, Shiites, and Christians, Palestinian refugees and the PLO, Syrians, and Israelis—as well as the United States, France, Iraq, Iran, and Jordan. But at the end of this protracted civil war, when the Taif Accords of 1989 were drawn up to reorganize Lebanese institutions, Hezbollah was not recognized. The accords confirmed the decline of Lebanon's Christian community and strengthened the role of the prime minister, an office reserved for Sunnis, but did not give the Shiites representation commensurate with their numbers.

With no seat at the table and little to lose, Hezbollah continued to resist Israel's occupation of a buffer zone in southern Lebanon. In May 2000, after a decade of insurgent attacks, Israel withdrew in what Hezbollah portrayed as an ignominious retreat. Basking in glory that transcended its political and religious base, Hezbollah used its generous Iranian subsidies to provide social assistance in Shiite communities and to invest in new technologies. Its television station Al Manar (The Lighthouse) became one of the most important vectors of radicalization in the region, competing impressively with Al Jazeera, broadcasting out of Qatar.

Iran was not the only regional power to benefit from Hezbollah's successes. The end of Israel's occupation of southern Lebanon also strengthened the hand of the regime in Damascus. Syrian troops had entered Lebanon during the early years of the civil war, initially on the side of the Christians, and would remain there for thirty years. After the Israeli invasion of 1982, Iranian arms and financing were permitted to transit through Syrian-held territory. With the departure of Israeli troops in 2000, Syria's armed forces took charge throughout the country.

After Bashar al-Assad became president of the Syrian Arab Republic in 2001, he was eager to consolidate his power in the region, and Hezbollah became a key ally in the new leader's ambitions.[1] But Bashar overstepped when he forced an extension of the presidential term served by his protégé in Lebanon, Emile Lahoud. This prompted the U.N. Security Council to retaliate on September 2, 2004, by passing Resolution 1559. Proposed by France and the United States, it called for the departure of Syrian troops from Lebanon and for the disarmament of Hezbollah. After Rafiq Hariri, a Sunni Muslim and a former Lebanese prime minister with close ties to the West and Saudi Arabia, was assassinated on February 14, 2005, Syria—suspected of playing a role in his death—was finally forced to evacuate. Hezbollah did not disarm, however, but quickly expanded to fill the void created by the Syrian troop withdrawal. In the same year that Ahmadinejad was elected president of Iran, Hezbollah became the only armed militia in Lebanon.[2]

When Israeli forces retreated in 2000, they did not evacuate Shebaa Farms—a piece of pasture land along Lebanon's southeastern border. According to Tel Aviv, this tract belonged to Syria, but according to Beirut, it belonged to Lebanon and was therefore still under occupation. Using this dispute as an excuse, Hezbollah still considered itself to be officially in a state of war with Israel. The attack in the summer of 2006 was in part an Israeli attempt to enforce Resolution 1559 by knocking out Hezbollah's military capacity, especially its ability to fire missiles into northern Israel. But it was also a broader demonstration that the Israeli leadership, disillusioned by the U.S. occupation of Iraq, was now determined to guarantee its own security, independent of the United States. With Ahmadinejad threatening to wipe Israel off the map and asserting Iran's right to become a nuclear power, Israel believed it could, and must, weaken the Islamic Republic by eradicating the military capability of its protégé in Lebanon. A show of strength would demonstrate the ability of the Israel Defense Forces (Tsahal) to impose the nation's will despite the clouds gathering on the horizon.

The Thirty-Three-Day War

The conflict began on July 12, 2006, after Hezbollah kidnapped two Israeli soldiers on the Lebanese side of the border, and it ended thirty-three days later in an embarrassing military failure for Israel. Imitating U.S. offensives carried out in Iraq in 2003, Tsahal relied overwhelmingly on its air force but was unable to eradicate Hezbollah's missiles, which were buried in a network of underground tunnels and shelters. Israeli planes also battered southern Lebanon's civilian infrastructure, killing scores of noncombatants and forcing a million residents to flee north for Beirut. The goal seemed to be to make the Lebanese population pay a price for Hezbollah's intransigence. But this attempt to cut off the Shiite militia's support at its base was also unsuccessful.

Nine months later the Winograd commission, created by the Knesset, criticized Israel's high command for errors committed during the conflict. Israeli intelligence was also faulted for being unaware of Hezbollah's vast panoply of long-range missiles, supplied by Tehran. These weapons had terrorized the city of Haifa, struck a battleship in the Mediterranean, and destroyed a number of Merkava tanks. The rapid failure of the project in Lebanon led to a vertiginous decline in the Olmert government's popularity at home and weakened Israel in the regional balance of power. Whatever its leaders' original intentions had been, the attack on Lebanon was, ironically, a demonstration to the world that Hezbollah was the only Arab force able to stand up to Tsahal. The outcome of the operation burnished the legend of Hezbollah's "triumph against the Zionists" in a show of strength far superior to that of any Arab leader or even of Al Qaeda. And once again Hezbollah's glory reflected well on its sponsor, Iran.

In reality, Hezbollah's triumph was nuanced. The U.N.-brokered cease-fire was followed by the deployment of a beefed-up United Nations Interim Force in Lebanon (UNIFIL) and by regular Lebanese troops on the border, which made any future attack on Israel by Hezbollah difficult. Yet the symbolic significance of Israel's withdrawal was enormous, especially since on August 14, the day the cease-fire came into effect, the international exhibition of Holocaust cartoons opened in Tehran. One poster bore an image of Nazi helmets emblazoned with the Star of David—particularly meaningful for audiences who for more than a month had seen reports of U.S.-made Israeli planes bombarding civilian buildings in Lebanon and had watched televised images of women's and children's bodies being dragged from the rubble of their homes.

Taking advantage of a propaganda machine that included its own television station, Hezbollah presented its leader, Hasan Nasrallah (whose last name means "God's victory"), as having achieved "victory through God." Even left-wing Arab commentators joined in, drawing parallels between Nasrallah and Che Guevara, who was rumored to be originally from southern Lebanon. In the collective perception of Muslims and Third Worldists around the globe, Hezbollah seemed to have replaced the Palestinian cause as the paramount resistance movement in the Middle East. Unlike the Palestinians, whose image had been sullied by the failures of the second intifada and by fratricidal clashes between Fatah nationalists and Hamas Islamists, Hezbollah managed to successfully brand itself, along with its Iranian protector, as the hero of anti-imperialism worldwide.

Seeing the Shiite leader of Hezbollah being celebrated as a hero throughout the Arab world was worrying to Sunni monarchs and presidents, who feared for their own legitimacy. Two years earlier, in autumn 2004, King Abdullah II of Jordan had warned against a "Shiite crescent" stretching from Iran to Lebanon and passing through Iraq and Bahrain (where Shiites make up a majority of the population) and including the Shiite minorities of Saudi Arabia, Kuwait, and Syria (where the tomb of Sayyida Zaynab, near Damascus, draws Shiites in a major pilgrimage). And in 2006 Egypt's president Hosni Mubarak had told a Saudi-funded television channel in Dubai that Shiites in Arab countries, no matter what their nationality, were loyal to Iran and its ayatollahs above all else. This echoed the old cliché of a Persian fifth column that dated back to Arab-Persian conflicts during the Abbasid period in the early centuries of Islam—a story still taught in school books as a way to buttress the founding myths of Arab nationalism.

The failed Israeli attack on Lebanon also made things more difficult for the United States, which delayed the cease-fire agreement in the vain hope that a few extra days of Israeli bombing would wipe out Hezbollah. Such a flagrant demonstration of the United States' pro-Israel bias, to the detriment of any other regional considerations, revealed to the rest of the world how little the Bush administration cared about the future of Lebanon—a country only recently freed from Syrian hegemony and the sole example of political pluralism in a region where President Bush claimed to support the spread of democracy.

And finally, the Thirty-Three-Day War had repercussions inside Lebanon itself, by weakening the pro-Western camp during the run-up to the 2007 presidential elections. Following the withdrawal of Syrian troops in spring 2005, the Lebanese had been ruled by a pro-Western coalition headed by Prime Minister Fouad Siniora. The government's main support came from three sources: the majority Sunni population, led by the Hariri family, which had ties to Arab governments and to the West; the Druze community under the leadership of Walid Jumblatt; and most of the remaining Maronite Christian leaders, headed by the commanders of the Lebanese forces such as Samir Geagea and Amin Gemayel. This alliance brought together former adversaries who for the previous thirty years had fought one another ferociously.

The same dynamic of shifting alliances had occurred on the other side as well. The opposition that gathered around Hezbollah included the Shiite militia group Amal, which was led by Speaker of Parliament Nabih Berri, against whom twenty years earlier Hezbollah had waged bloody battles for positions in Beirut's southern outskirts. But it also included the Free Patriotic Movement made up mostly of Christians and headed by General Michel Aoun. A Maronite Christian and former prime minister, Aoun had waged an inconclusive battle in 1989–1990 against Syria's military presence in Lebanon, and he was supported in that effort by Saddam Hussein, a sworn enemy of his fellow Baathists in Damascus. Forced into exile, Aoun spent a decade in France, and when he returned to Beirut after the Syrian troops withdrew in spring 2005, he reversed his alliances, moving closer to Syria's new allies, Hezbollah and Amal.

Various factors contributed to Aoun's turnabout. Deprived of their dominant institutional position after the 1989 Taif Accords, all of Lebanon's Christians had sought the protection of various Muslim communities. Notable Christian families close to the West, like the Gemayels, chose to ally with the Sunnis, led by the Hariris, the wealthiest family in Lebanon, who had ties to former President Chirac of France, to the United States, and to Saudi Arabia. General Aoun's support, by contrast, came from less privileged Maronite or Greek Orthodox Christians. Rather than allying with the Sunni majority, Aoun concluded that the best guarantee for the survival of the minority Christian community lay in seeking rapprochement with another minority, Lebanon's Shiite Muslims. He reasoned that, together, the two groups could form a bloc powerful enough to stand up to the Sunni majority in the region as a whole. This bloc would help preserve Lebanon's unique identity as a conglomerate of non-Sunni minorities backed by the Syrian government, which itself was now dominated by members of a heterodox branch of Shiism.

Since Hezbollah was the main voice of Shiites in Lebanon, Aoun's Free Patriotic Movement signed a pact with that group in 2005. This Christian-Shiite alliance was confirmed when Aoun and Nasrallah appeared together at Mar Mikhael Church in Haret Hreik, where the general was born. This once-Maronite village was by this time a crowded Shiite neighborhood situated on one of the sectarian borders of the civil war during the 1970s and 1980s. In the 2005 elections, the majority of Christian deputies sent to parliament were members of the Free Patriotic Movement.

The general was banking on becoming a candidate in the 2007 presidential election, with the backing of his own Christian constituency and also of the Shiites and their Syrian ally. When Hezbollah captured two Israeli soldiers in July 2006, leading to the Thirty-Three-Day War, many in the Lebanese pro-Western government coalition interpreted Hezbollah's move as a political blunder. They predicted that it would be portrayed as a presumptuous provocation on the Jewish state and would bring havoc to Lebanon. But the Party of God managed to inflict losses on Israel that made it appear that Israel had lost the war—at least symbolically, given that Hezbollah's missiles reached Haifa. Refugees from southern Lebanon who had fled to Beirut were returned to their homes after the war ended, and those whose houses were destroyed received cash subsidies from Hezbollah. Consequently, few Lebanese expressed any lasting political resentment against the party that had set the war in motion.

Hezbollah and its allies sought to capitalize on their "divine victory" by imposing their will on the government. In December 2006 they staged major demonstrations which led to the occupation of downtown Beirut by their partisans, who set up tent villages around the prime minister's office. Even though the tents ultimately remained empty, the restored city center—which symbolized the late Rafiq Hariri's attempts to revitalize the country—was blocked until May 2008. Hezbollah and its allies made a number of demands: they asked for a veto right on all government decisions; they were hostile to the formation of the International Tribunal that would judge Hariri's assassination case and possibly incriminate Damascus; and above all they wanted to have the upper hand in the election of the president who would replace Emile Lahoud as of September 2007. The Parliament which would elect the new president could not do so as long as Hezbollah and its allies blocked the process.

This stalemate finally came to an end in May 2008 when Hezbollah troops and allied militias, in an amazing display of strength, stormed the Sunni areas of Beirut and the Druze mountain of Chouf and blocked the airport. Subsequent talks held in Doha, Qatar, by Lebanese factions led to the acceptance of Hezbollah's claim that they had a right to veto government decisions. With this political victory in hand, the Party of God and its allies folded their tents in downtown Beirut, lifted the blockade, reopened the airport, and agreed to the election of a new Lebanese president, General Michel Sleiman, former chief of the army and a neutral personality who could achieve consensus. He was sworn into office on May 25.

The balance of power in Lebanon had shifted in favor of Hezbollah and its Iranian mentor, who had successfully demonstrated that they held the trump card of armed superiority. Nevertheless, their victory must be interpreted with caution. Arms that should have been used exclusively against Israel had been turned against Hezbollah's compatriots, and whatever remained of the party's aura as the embodiment of Lebanese resistance was now blurred by this display of partisanship in local politics. Hezbollah was the dominant power in Lebanon, without a doubt. But the sum total of the Lebanese from all communities who feared or despised it was now a majority, and the Party of God was growing weary of exercising restraint in order to prevent that multifaceted opposition from coalescing.

Throughout 2006 the eyes of the world were trained on the conflict in Lebanon, and Hamas—the religious branch of the Palestinian resistance movement—was no exception. Tehran chose that year to make its presence felt in a movement traditionally reserved for Arab leaders: the liberation of Palestine. This intrusion into Palestinian affairs became clear after the January 25, 2006, elections, when the new government, led by Hamas, was denied the substantial subsidies the European Union and United States had been giving the Palestinian Authority before Hamas took control, as well as customs duties Israel had collected on the PA's behalf for merchandise transiting to Gaza and the West Bank. This blockade was a way to put pressure on Hamas to recognize Israel's existence, to ratify past agreements made by the Palestine Liberation Organization, and to renounce violence.

President Ahmadinejad came to Hamas's financial rescue by pledging $250 million a year to pay government employees' salaries (or, according to another interpretation, to pay the armed groups linked to the Islamist party). But getting the money into the country was not so easy. Since U.S. banks, followed by other global financial institutions, had forbidden any transfer of funds to the Palestinian Authority as long as Hamas was in power, the group's leaders were forced to travel abroad and return via the Egyptian-Palestinian border carrying suitcases stuffed with currency. This conduit was exposed in January 2007 when the Palestinian prime minister, Ismail Haniyeh, returning from a trip to Iran, was intercepted and forced to deposit into an Egyptian bank the stacks of cash he was bringing back.

This was not the first time that Shiite revolutionaries had exercised influence among Palestinians. Islamic Jihad, an Islamist group with the nationalist goal of liberating Palestine, had taken up arms against Israel in the early 1980s. For guidance it referred both to Hassan al-Banna, a Sunni Egyptian who founded the Muslim Brotherhood, and to Ayatollah Khomeini. As for Hamas, although it emerged from the Muslim Brotherhood and constituted the Palestinian branch of that eminently Sunni Islamist movement, it sought to emulate Hezbollah, which had caused Israel to withdraw from Lebanon in 2000. At the root of that success, and therefore of the fascination Palestinian Islamists felt for the Party of God, was a new tactic: the so-called martyrdom operations that Hezbollah pioneered in the Middle East.

The Shiite Origins of Martyrdom

The political figure of the jihad fighter who deliberately puts an end to his own life while killing the greatest possible number of the enemy first emerged in Iran during the Islamic Revolution and then spread to Lebanon under the aegis of Hezbollah. Suicide attacks next jumped from the Shiite to the Sunni population through the vector of Hamas in Palestine, and then were hijacked by Al Qaeda, leading to the events of 9/11. After the U.S. invasion of 2003, suicide attacks were taken up by Sunni insurgents in Iraq, where in a dramatic reversal the Shiite population became the victims of choice for so-called martyrs.

But the grand narrative of jihad through martyrdom—the quintessential discourse of radical Islamists in the early twenty-first century—underwent a major mutation as it passed from Shiites to Sunnis. Shiite suicide missions had never lost their link to the tradition of the founding martyr, Imam Husayn, who was murdered in Karbala (in today's Iraq) in 680 C.E. by troops of the Sunni caliph ruling in Damascus, Yazid. Claiming that patronage, Shiite martyrdom operations targeted only enemy combatants and were carefully organized by the hierarchy of the Revolutionary Guards (Pasdaran) in Iran or by Hezbollah in Lebanon. Sunni suicide bombers, by contrast, targeted military personnel and civilians indiscriminately, not sparing even women and children. The history of this difference is revealing.

After the Prophet Muhammad died in 632 without leaving a male heir, his followers split into two factions over the question of who should lead the young community of believers. One group— later called Sunnis, after the Arabic word *sunna,* which designates the exemplary words and deeds of the Prophet—followed the lead of the great aristocratic families in Mecca. After violent struggles, they had finally accepted Islam and had searched for a way to integrate revelation—and the revolutionary changes it wrought on the customs of the time—within a social order they could continue to dominate. The first three caliphs (or successors of the Prophet) were representatives of these notable families. During their rule, Islam was spread by the sword and the Quran throughout most of the Middle East.

The fourth caliph, Ali, belonged to the Prophet's own family— he was a cousin by birth and, after marrying the Prophet's daughter, Fatima, a son-in-law. Ali wanted to spread the purest message of Islam and ensure that this doctrine would be conveyed by future caliphs within the lineage of Muhammad's descendants— that is, the children from Ali and Fatima's union. His ambitions clashed with those of the Muslim governor of Damascus, Muawiya, a Sunni member of the Meccan aristocracy, who fought Ali and then founded his own dynasty, the Umayyads.

To restore the Prophet's rightful lineage and to resist the Sunnis, one of Ali's sons, Husayn, brought together what would later be known as "the faction of Ali" (*shiat Ali,* hence the term Shiite). In the Iraqi town of Kufa, this small band of believers was betrayed by residents, and as a consequence they were cornered into an uneven battle in nearby Karbala, where they fought against the troops of Muawiya's son, Yazid, the new Umayyad caliph. Husayn was killed, or martyred, along with his followers. His head was sent as a trophy to Damascus. The suffering and death of Husayn became the golden legend around which Shiite religiosity revolved. Every year, Shiites commemorate Husayn's passion on the tenth day (Ashura) of the Islamic month of Muharram, and some believers march in mourning processions, flagellating themselves to make amends for the mistake of Kufa's residents—misled believers who failed to rescue the "prince of martyrs." Shiites reenact the events of the original martyrdom and inscribe it in their own flesh with whips and blades, which leave deep scars.

The Iranian revolution of 1979 transformed these symbolic acts into political action. After Ayatollah Khomeini took power, martyrdom was no longer something to be reenacted. Rather it was operationalized in a real-world struggle to restore the true faith of Shiism. The masses were mobilized, and believers became revolutionaries who took over political and military positions and offered up their lives in imitation of Husayn's sacrifice. In the late 1970s, Khomeini's martyrs stood up to the shah's bayonets, and in the 1980s another wave of martyrs did not flinch when facing Saddam Hussein's invading army. Supplied and financed by the West and the Sunni oil monarchies of the Arabian peninsula, which feared revolutionary irredentism in Iran, Saddam's war machine was far superior to Iranian forces. Facing almost certain defeat, the regime in Tehran pulled teenagers and children out of school and sent them off to blow themselves up on the enemy's minefields, opening breaches in the lines that the Iranian army could pass through unharmed. The organized suicide of tens of thousands of young boys allowed the Islamic Republic to survive Saddam's initial assault and then to stabilize the battle lines before gradually gaining the upper hand.

Mass suicide not only saved the ayatollahs' regime but also eliminated any possibility of a youthful rebellion against the theocracy. As a consequence, the Iranian Revolution fell under the control of the clergy and merchants. But the young men who survived the 1980s returned to the center of power two decades later and in 2005 elected one of their own—Mahmud Ahmadinejad—as president of the Islamist Republic.

When Khomeini's revolutionary ideology took root in Lebanon in the early 1980s, the strategy of suicide attacks went with it. Hezbollah's founding act was a spectacular martyrdom operation that destroyed Israeli headquarters in Tyre in southern Lebanon on November 11, 1982, killing 72 Israelis and 14 Lebanese. Ahmad Kassir, the "pioneer of martyrs" who carried it out, is revered today as a contemporary version of Husayn, and Martyrdom Day in Lebanon is celebrated every year on November 11. The main road in Beirut where Hezbollah's television station was located until the Israelis bombed it in summer 2006 bears his name. On October 24, 1983, a far deadlier double operation was carried out, killing 241 Americans and 58 French and destroying two bases where U.S. marines and French paratroopers were stationed. These troops belonged to the multinational buffer forces that were supposed to protect Palestinians from massacre at the hands of Lebanese Christian Phalangists, but in the eyes of the regimes in Damascus and Tehran they represented Western control over Lebanese land.

These extraordinary suicide attacks, carried out by a handful of determined militants, forced two of the most powerful armies in the world to leave Lebanon for good (the Americans and the French) and a third (Israel) to retreat into the southern border region before being forced to withdraw entirely from Lebanese territory in May 2000. These initial martyrdom operations were quickly reproduced throughout Lebanon by extremist left-wing parties linked to Damascus or Tehran and organized by the intelligence services of these countries. In the years to come, the "poor man's atomic bomb"—suicide attacks—along with the taking of hostages would have an unparalleled impact on the asymmetrical wars of the Middle East, with repercussions reaching into the heart of Europe.

Because its suicide missions were rooted in Shiite martyrology, Hezbollah was able to sanctify the sacrifice of its members as reliving Husayn's immolation. Iconography depicting contemporary martyrs who offered up their lives to expel Israel from Lebanon is still mingled today with portraits of the traditional imams of Shiism in a sacred litany of political activism. In the neighborhoods and villages where Hezbollah holds sway, walls and lamp posts are plastered with photographs framed in yellow (Hezbollah's trademark color) showing young men, now dead, with sweet smiles, their gaze turned to heaven. These suicide bombers take their place in a hierarchy of martyrdom that permeates all of Shiite society in Lebanon. The top twelve martyrs are called *istishhadi mujahid* (jihad fighters aspiring to martyrdom) and represent the most morally exalted type because they, like Husayn, deliberately sought death. Then come 1,281 *shahid mujahid* (martyred jihad fighters), who were killed while fighting the enemy during the eighteen years of Israeli occupation. Next are simple martyrs (*shahid*), killed by Israel without participating in combat. And finally there are "national martyrs" (*shahid al-watan*), which include all Lebanese—Christians as well as Muslims—who were killed by Israelis.[3] This taxonomy of martyrdom, with its levels of achievement, allows Hezbollah to present itself as the vanguard of a civil society of willing victims.

Hezbollah's social and symbolic interpretation of martyrdom

operations is best understood in the context of the grand narrative elaborated during the Islamic Revolution. According to Shiite doctrine, legitimate martyrdom can take place only within a jihad approved by a jurist-theologian who wields supreme religious authority—Khomeini and then his successor, Khamenei—to whom the party pledges allegiance. As Sheikh Qasim, Hezbollah's principal ideologue, defines this jurist, he is the "guardian of Muslims"; he not only rules Iran but also "defines general political commandments for all Muslims, wherever they may live." Shiite martyrdom is not intended to quench the thirst for earthly victory, however. In the words of Qasim: "The act of jihad bears two fruits: martyrdom *and* victory. The martyr earns martyrdom, while the community and its freedom fighters gain victory."[4]

Although martyrdom operations send their perpetrators to certain death, those Shiites who order these missions make the point that martyrdom is different from suicide (which Muslims consider a grave sin), and indeed represents "the supreme manifestation of self-sacrifice, a form of confrontation with the enemy that follows the clear, legitimate rules of *sharia*" (Islamic law). Martyrdom operations are the absolute, exclusive, infallible weapon of those who believe in Islam and jihad: "The enemy's only weapon is to threaten life, and it only works against those who seek life. In consequence, it is futile to fight those who believe in martyrdom."[5]

Adapting Martyrdom Operations to the Sunni Milieu

Submission to the authority of the Islamic Republic's supreme leader was of course unacceptable to the Sunni majority of Muslims worldwide, and the Islamic Revolution did not spread beyond the Shiite populations of the Middle East, the Indian subcontinent, and the Diaspora—a bitter reality that Ayatollah Khomeini had to face during his own lifetime. Hezbollah, by contrast, managed to transcend this sectarian divide and to transmit to the Sunni world the concept of suicide attacks as "the essence of jihad."

Prior to Hezbollah's influence, Sunni Islamists had made the guerrilla version of jihad that triumphed in Afghanistan the quintessential mode of holy war against the enemies of Islam. They revered the sacrifice made by combatants who fell while fighting the Red Army, exalted them as exemplars, and invoked the rewards promised to the martyr and his family. These ranged from the miraculous preservation of musk-scented corpses to direct access to Paradise, where black-eyed virgins awaited. But during the entire decade of Soviet occupation (1978–1988), Afghan jihadists had never resorted to suicide attacks, for two reasons.

First, the number of combatants, particularly foreign fighters, was limited, and losses had to be minimized. In the multitudinous Shiite population of Lebanon, by contrast, martyrdom plucked individuals from anonymity and granted them heroic status while guaranteeing financial recompense for their families. Second, Sunni doctrine and history never elaborated a tradition of deliberate self-sacrifice. Fighters who died as martyrs on the battlefield or who assumed great risks to wage jihad did not determine the circumstances of their death: its time was chosen by God, who took back life as he had granted it, when he wished. A great martyr who perished in exceptional circumstances against a multitude of enemies stood the same chances of surviving as anyone else, since only God decides the outcome of a battle. The Sunni tradition has no emblematic figure comparable to Husayn, and the prohibition on suicide or on any act resembling self-destruction was strongly reiterated until the mid-1990s. In all his sermons and written works, Abdallah Azzam, the Palestinian "imam of the Afghan jihad," celebrated martyrs killed by the enemy but never those who deliberately killed themselves.

In its rise to power among Palestinians, Hamas cast aside these Sunni reservations about self-destruction. The first martyrdom operation attributed to Hamas was carried out in Israel near the Mechola settlement in the Jordan valley on April 16, 1993, over ten years after Hezbollah had begun using this tactic in Lebanon. The perpetrator, Tamam Nabulsi, was a member of the Izzeddin al-Qassam Brigades, Hamas's military wing. The operation had been poorly prepared, however, and the only person killed was Tamam himself, though a few others were wounded. But this crack in the dike soon gave way to a flood of Sunni suicide attacks, in large part because Sunnis have no clerical hierarchy to guide extreme actions and put an end to them when it so chooses. Consequently, once Palestinian martyrdom operations got going, they became far more numerous than the twelve celebrated by Hezbollah, even though the first failed attempt is rarely mentioned.

Hamas—also known as the Islamic Resistance Movement—was an offshoot of the strictly Sunni Muslim Brotherhood. It was born during the first intifada, a Palestinian uprising that began in December 1987. This protest entailed strikes, boycotts, barricades, and acts of civil disobedience, but what caught the attention of news media around the world was stone-throwing by Palestinian youths against the tanks and soldiers of the Israel Defense Forces. These guerrilla tactics were inspired by the feats of the Afghan jihad and by various anticolonial uprisings such as the Algerian war of independence against France (1954–1962). Hamas's goal in the "war of the stones," apart from fighting Israel, was to contest the control of Fatah (the largest faction within the PLO) over the larger Palestinian liberation movement and over the political representation of Palestinians in any future state.

The first intifada allowed audiences worldwide to see images of Palestinians portrayed as victims and Israelis portrayed as tormentors, and in that sense it was a symbolic success for the Palestinian liberation movement. But by spring 1993 the uprising was dying out. Although Hamas had received a tremendous boost from the intifada, five years of rebellion had resulted in innumerable deprivations and a considerable decline in the living standards of the Palestinian population. An agreement between Israel and the PLO appeared to be in the offing, and Hamas could not mobilize the masses to resist it. The Madrid conference on Middle East peace, held in December 1991, allowed initial contact to be made between Israelis and Palestinians, under pressure from the United States. In 1992 a Labor victory in Tel Aviv that made Yitzhak Rabin prime minister and a Democratic victory in Washington that elected Bill Clinton paved the way for the Oslo Accords, signed in September 1993. This agreement allowed for mutual recognition between Israel and the Palestinian Authority, led by Yasser Arafat.

For the Palestinian Islamists, the "Oslo betrayal" was a death threat. At the moment when the PLO laid down its weapons, Hamas took up armed struggle in order to survive politically. Their Izzeddin al-Qassam Brigades professionalized Islamist violence against Israel, despite the exhaustion of Palestinian society. These brigades were named after Sheikh Qassam, who had declared jihad on the British mandate in Palestine during the period between the two world wars and was killed in combat in November 1935. In that spirit, on December 17, 1992, the brigades kidnapped a border guard on Israeli territory; his body was later found bearing knife wounds. This qualitative leap in aggression provoked the Rabin government to arrest 415 Islamists and deport them to Marj al-Zuhur, a snowy mountain peak in southern Lebanon, in the zone controlled by Hezbollah. There, the Palestinians saw for themselves, on the ground, the impact of suicide attacks carried out by the Party of God. Martyrdom operations had forced the Israeli army to evacuate Beirut and hunker down in a security zone along the border.

In addition to members of Hamas, the deportees in Marj al-Zuhur included about fifty activists who belonged to Palestinian Islamic Jihad, also a Sunni group but one inspired by the Islamic Revolution in Iran. While Hamas competed with Fatah for political control over a future secular Palestinian state, Islamic Jihad considered armed struggle in Palestine to be an integral part of the global Islamic Revolution. In 1988 the organization's top leader, Fathi Shiqaqi, had defended bombings in which the perpetrator died, and the group's militants had joined Hezbollah in carrying out military actions against the Israeli presence in Lebanon.[6] That Hezbollah's methods and doctrine inspired Islamic Jihad is evident in the emblem of the Palestinian group's armed wing, the Jerusalem Brigades (Sarayat al-Quds), which imitated Hezbollah's logo: the group's name in Arabic calligraphy, topped by an assault rifle held up by the letter *alif,* which was transformed into a fist raised skyward.

During the same period, Yahia Ayyash (known as "the engineer"), the top man in the Izzeddin al-Qassam Brigades, recommended the use of human bombs in order to make the cost of occupation of Palestine unbearable for Israel, against whom the stone-throwing was no longer effective. Thus, suicide attacks made their appearance in the Palestinian Islamist movement as a replacement for milder tactics that had stalled, at a time when Arafat was entering "shameful" negotiations with the "Zionist entity." Because guerrilla warfare, as practiced in Algeria, Egypt, and Bosnia at that time, was not an option in a society exhausted by five years of intifada, Hamas's leadership concluded that suicide attacks, as pioneered by Hezbollah, were better suited to derailing a peace process that a majority of Palestinians now supported.

Palestinian martyrdom operations acquired their legitimacy gradually, in contrast with the foundational acts of Hezbollah. The first phase began in April 1993 and ended in November 1998, after critical arrests were made by the Israelis.[7] It took place against the backdrop of the Oslo Accords, and it did little more than slow down the dynamism of the peace process, since a majority of Palestinians did not approve of suicide attacks in those years.[8] Still, the concept of martyrdom operations became anchored in the imagination of Sunni jihadists worldwide, and during this first phase they were used in a few specific contexts. A first series of attacks came in response to the massacre of over thirty Palestinian Muslims who were praying at a mosque in Hebron on February 25, 1994; the killer was Baruch Goldstein, an Israeli settler. In operations that began in April and continued into the summer, several dozen Israeli civilians were killed. These attacks were initially justified in the name of revenge against a sacrilegious crime, but their main goal was to force Arafat to recognize Hamas as a political player. In May Arafat was scheduled to sign the Cairo Accords, which would regulate the transfer of sovereignty over evacuated territories to the Palestinian Authority.

In January 1996 Israel assassinated "engineer" Ayyash, the principal designer of Hamas's martyrdom operations, and in retaliation three particularly deadly operations in February and March murdered over 60 Israeli civilians in the span of a few days. One consequence of this mayhem was that in May 1996 Israelis elected as prime minister Binyamin Netanyahu, who promised a firm policy on terrorism. He erected innumerable obstacles to the peace process and made things difficult for the Palestinian Authority, fulfilling Hamas's deepest wishes in that regard. Islamist martyrdom operations continued as the Palestinian population faced the closure of territories where they had previously lived and grew increasingly disillusioned about the prospects for peace.

Controversy among the Ulema

The great armed combats that jihadists had waged since the beginning of the decade—the war in Bosnia, which had ended in failure with the Dayton Accords of December 1995 and the expulsion of foreign combatants; jihads in Egypt and Algeria, which were overwhelmed by public opposition after the massacres of civilians in autumn 1997—had not included suicide attacks. Egyptian or Algerian jihadist groups saw themselves as a vanguard that worked to gain a foothold in society by fighting the government and its agents, and shifted to actions against civilian opponents only when they failed to get a satisfactory response.

Hamas followed a different logic. By the time it began martyrdom operations in the mid-1990s, it already had important networks of solidarity and mobilization that had been created during the first intifada. Hamas was able to recruit many candidates for martyrdom from a mass of sympathizers who were dissatisfied with the Palestinian uprising's failure and hostile to the compromises Arafat had worked out with Israel in the framework of the Oslo Accords. But unlike Hezbollah, which officially struck only military targets, Hamas and Islamic Jihad chose soft targets that claimed civilian victims. These operations on public streets or in shopping malls were easier to carry out and guaranteed vast media attention.

The PLO at first was hostile to suicide attacks because of its own political considerations. It had built up a large base of support among humanistic left-wing activists in Europe, and to a lesser extent in the United States, after winning the battle of symbols during the first intifada. This support, which had great political value, might be lost if the Palestinian cause came to be identified with the massacre of Israeli civilians.

Hamas's suicide attacks in February and March 1996 led to an anti-terrorism summit in Egypt. The Palestinian Authority solicited Sunni religious authorities to condemn martyrdom operations as suicide attacks, forbidden by religion, and to proscribe the killing of civilians. Hamas petitioned these same authorities to make martyrdom operations a part of legitimate jihad and to confer the glory of martyrdom on their perpetrators. But recognizing how dangerous the loss of civilian lives might be to its cause, Hamas addressed a memorandum to the summit's participants in which it deplored the death of "certain innocent victims," which it attributed to unavoidable "collateral damage." The particularly difficult circumstances Palestinians were experiencing under Israeli occupation left no alternative to armed resistance, they claimed.[9]

The opposing Palestinian factions then requested *fatwas* (legal opinions) from high-ranking religious leaders to approve or prohibit suicide operations. In Sunni Islam every jurist (*alim;* plural *ulema*)—and, today, even self-declared cyber imams—can render autonomous opinions on questions submitted to him. The influence or authority of those opinions is based on a changing balance of power in which access to mainstream media and doctrinal prestige both play a large role. Nevertheless, the grand mufti of Saudi Arabia, Sheikh Ben Baz, a Sunni, declared he was opposed to martyrdom operations, as were several eminent figures from the kingdom's Wahhabi establishment, among them Sheikh Ben Othaymin, as well as the Syrian Sheikh Nasr al-Din al-Albani. For these *ulema* the Islamic prohibition on suicide permitted no exceptions. In response to a question regarding his opinion on "those who blow themselves up to kill a group of Jews," Ben Baz replied: "This is not allowed, for those who do so are killing themselves, and God said 'Do not kill yourselves,' while the Prophet, peace be upon him, said 'He who kills himself will be tortured on judgment day.'" On the other hand, the sheikh reminded his audience that combatants who waged armed jihad and died in battle were blessed.

This long-standing distinction between martyrs who willingly take their lives and martyrs who die in combat represented an attempt by the Saudi religious establishment to ensure that the government remained the sole authority in applying Islamic law and also that uncontrolled groups would not resort to exceptional actions that threatened to destabilize the Saudi kingdom. Also, beyond the Palestinian question, these Wahhabi sheikhs were thinking of the threats made by Osama Bin Laden, whose declaration of war against the Saudi government was issued in September of that same year. The concept of self-sacrifice, if allowed to stand, might destabilize the entire political and religious order of a kingdom that, from the 1970s on, had used oil revenues to establish large support networks within a population whose religious views were grounded in a rigorous variant of Sunni Islam dating back to the eighteenth century.

Two high-ranking Sunni religious dignitaries from outside Saudi Arabia spoke in favor of martyrdom operations but limited the application of such attacks.[10] The first, Sheikh Tantawi—then grand sheikh of Al Azhar, the Islamic university in Cairo, the authority of which is recognized throughout much of the Sunni world—welcomed martyrdom operations if their aim was to defend religion, the community of believers, and the nation against oppression in the case of overriding necessity (*idtirar*). In such circumstances, he argued, those who blew themselves up could not be considered as having committed suicide. Rather, they were "martyrs who gave their blood and soul on the path to God," in the legal framework of jihad.[11] This favorable opinion was in line with sentiments expressed by a segment of the Egyptian population, which was very hostile toward a peace treaty with Israel.

A year later, in response to Jewish religious figures who asked him to forbid martyrdom operations, Tantawi said that these constituted a legitimate form of defense which expressed the extreme circumstances to which Palestinians were reduced by Israeli oppression. He did not give further details, but encouraged the Palestinians to defend themselves "by all the legitimate means offered by Islam and morality, without oppression or aggression."[12] When Israeli authorities objected repeatedly to the Egyptian government, citing the sheikh's official function and the peace treaty that binds the two countries, Tantawi's views became more restrictive. After he was appointed mufti of the Egyptian republic, and especially after September 11, 2001, he expressed a far more negative opinion regarding the legitimacy of suicide attacks in general.

The most coherent and durable position taken in support of Palestinian martyrdom operations was expressed by Sheikh Qaradawi, one of the most charismatic figures on the Arab and Muslim media scene. Called upon in 1996 to determine whether these operations were to be considered jihad or terrorism and whether those who carried them out were achieving martyrdom or committing suicide, the sheikh opined that these operations fell under the category of "legitimate terrorism" (*al-irhab al-mashru*) and were "the most glorious form of jihad in God's path."[13] "As the Quran indicates in the words of the Almighty: 'Against [the unbelievers] make ready your strength to the utmost of your power, including steeds of war, to strike terror into [the hearts of] the enemies of God and your enemies.'"[14] It was, the sheikh maintained, "wrong to consider these acts as 'suicidal,' because these are heroic acts of martyrdom" committed by *fedayin*. In Arabic, this term designates those who are willing to sacrifice their lives for a supreme cause. "Jihad combatants are fighting the enemies of God with a new weapon that destiny has placed in the hands of the disinherited [*mustadafun*] so that they may resist the omnipotence of the powerful and the arrogant [*mustakbirun*]."

Employing the rhetoric of the Islamic Revolution, the sheikh cast Palestinian society as an emblematic victim for which martyrdom operations were a legitimate means of defense. As for killing Israeli civilians, that was moderated by the fact that Israel is a "military society" where women serve as reservists and are therefore members of the enemy army. As for children or old people, if they die it is not because they were targeted explicitly, Qaradawi argued; they were collateral damage. His *fatwa* was accompanied by quotes from prestigious Muslim religious scholars belonging to different schools of Sunni interpretation.

Even though Qaradawi's opinion applied explicitly to the Palestinian situation, it could—and would—be extended by analogy to other cases where Muslims might be called upon to defend their land or their honor in dire circumstances—the definition of which was growing more and more elastic. The *fatwas* of Tantawi and Qaradawi constituted the first public religious approval of suicide attacks to emerge from a conservative, nonextremist Sunni milieu. Sheikh Tantawi belonged to the Azharite establishment, and Sheikh Qaradawi had been a member of the Muslim Brotherhood and in 1996 was the figurehead of a centrist Islamist movement known for its willingness to compromise with the modern world. Like Tantawi, Sheikh Qaradawi modified his position after the September 11 attacks, from which he wanted to distance himself, by insisting that his *fatwa* applied exclusively to situations where an enemy was waging war on Islam.

The stakes in this scholarly debate were high indeed. To what extent could eminent religious figures establish a legitimate relation between a society's victimization and its recourse to martyrdom operations? These religious leaders from Saudi Arabia, Syria, Egypt, and elsewhere recognized that the grand narrative of Muslim martyrdom had taken hold in the Sunni world, and they understood the importance of controlling its evolution, if only to ensure that Shiite jihadists or Sunni extremists like Bin Laden and his sympathizers would not appropriate it.

In this turbulent context, 1996 was a pivotal year. First, the appearance on the air of Al Jazeera—the all-encompassing Arabic-language news channel—allowed every home with a satellite dish to follow live images and commentary produced in Israel and Palestine, as well as *fatwas* issued by religious scholars. Arab television audiences now entering the age of globalization could decide for themselves whether the Palestinian resistance constituted a unique case for the legitimacy of suicide attacks or a model for militant resistance elsewhere. It is impossible to overstate the extraordinary impact of Al Jazeera in keeping the grand narrative of martyrdom alive for its tens of millions of viewers starting in the late 1990s. It did so by positing a plot line in which the violence at the heart of modern Middle Eastern history is attributable to the creation and legitimation of the state of Israel. Al Jazeera claimed as its mission the exposure and denunciation of the lies which brought that state into existence.[15]

The extreme freedom of speech tolerated on this channel represented a break with the heavy propaganda favored by all state-run television, which was dedicated to praising His Excellency Brother President or His Most Pious Majesty. It opened up a space which the voice of Arab society rushed to fill, in a rich, disorderly clamor that Al Jazeera quickly channeled into programs displaying paroxysms of antagonism and confrontation. In the West, television stations tend to broadcast images to viewers' homes that underline deviations from the norm (accidents, violence, warfare, and so on), the better to celebrate a normally reconciled universe. Evening news-viewing constitutes a sort of daily high mass aimed at glorifying the underlying social order. In contrast, Al Jazeera presents violence and animosity as the essence of a perverted world order, and its programming strives to incriminate and expose its endless injustices. The blockbuster programs that focus on that essential and foundational conflict, reenact it, and unleash the strongest disagreements—*The Opposite Opinion* (*Al-ittijah al-muakkes*), with the Syrian journalist Faysal al-Kazem, or *More Than One Viewpoint* (*Akthar min rai*)—enjoy the highest audience ratings in the Arab world. From the perspective of the governments that allow these broadcasts to be heard, this verbal violence fulfills the theatrical function of catharsis in the Aristotelian sense: it neutralizes the expression of disorder and emotion that would destabilize the ruling governments if translated into reality.

But flowing like a river beneath all the on-air arguments about tactics and interpretation is the unifying problem of Israel's existence, which all commentators perceive as the fundamental cause of discord in the region. And no struggle better exemplifies for Al Jazeera's audience the unbearable injustice that brought the state of Israel into being than the Palestinian conflict. The brutality of Israeli repression and the heroism of Palestinian resistance are, for Al Jazeera, the criteria against which the world's disorder is measured. Unlike Arab propaganda programming that for the most part ignores the "Zionist entity," Al Jazeera invites uncensored interviews with Israelis and also with Western experts on the Arab world, especially those who speak fluent Arabic. These interviewees give the Other a face and a powerful voice, which just makes opposition to them all the more urgent.

In the language of Al Jazeera, any Palestinian, Lebanese, or

Arab killed by Israelis is a martyr, while Israelis killed are simply counted. A news item referring to three martyrs and five dead, with no further explanation, means that three Arabs and five Israelis were killed. But what really sways public opinion are the images on the screen. Audiovisual media allow easy equivalence between Palestinian martyrs killed by Israeli bullets and Palestinian martyrs who blow themselves up in an Israeli pizza parlor. On television, there is little distinction between an Al Qaeda martyr in New York who flies a plane into the World Trade Center and a Sunni martyr in Baghdad who blows up a tank in the middle of a Shiite crowd. In the logic of television space-time, similar images have similar causes. The postmortem hagiographies and pious films and images organized around the prerecorded last testaments of suicide attackers are identical no matter what the outcome.

Al Jazeera's explosive debut in 1996—the year when some high-ranking Sunni *ulema* were justifying suicide attacks on Israel and Bin Laden was broadcasting his first "declaration of jihad against the Americans occupying the land of the two holy sanctuaries"—was an important vector in the transmission to the Sunni Muslim world of the new grand narrative of martyrdom. This task would eventually migrate to the Internet and to a proliferation of sites specializing in the glorification of the feats and atrocities of armed jihad.

Bin Laden's declaration, issued in September while he was hiding out in Afghanistan, applied essentially to Saudi Arabia, but it mentioned the occupation of Palestine as the main source of suffering imposed on the Muslim world by the "Zionist-crusader alliance." He paid homage to Sheikh Yassin, the founder of Hamas, and praised an attack on an American base in Khobar, on Saudi territory, the previous June. Bin Laden would take the logic of self-sacrifice to its extreme conclusion on 9/11, substituting it for a losing strategy of guerrilla jihad in Bosnia, Algeria, and Egypt. At a time when martyrdom operations in Palestine were beginning to acquire legitimacy among Sunnis, he was already considering ways to capture that legitimacy for his own benefit.

Al Qaeda Goes Global, While Sharon Takes a Walk

The first spectacular suicide missions that can be attributed to Al Qaeda—although the organization did not claim responsibility for them at the time—took place simultaneously on August 7, 1998, and targeted the U.S. embassies in Nairobi, Kenya, and Dar es Salaam, Tanzania. Both attacks involved a car bomb. In Nairobi, over 4,500 people, mostly Muslims, were wounded and 213 died (among them 12 Americans). In Dar es Salaam, 85 were wounded and 11 died (none of them American). In contrast with the martyrdom operations carried out by Hezbollah or Hamas, which presented acts of self-destruction as sacrifices made by a specific victimized society, Al Qaeda sought to use the grand narrative of martyrdom to confront the West, and the United States in particular, on a global rather than a local scale.

On February 21, 1998, Bin Laden, Zawahiri, and the leaders of a few radical Islamist groups from the Arab world and the Indian subcontinent signed a declaration announcing the creation of a World Islamic Front against Jews and Crusaders. The front called on all Muslims to kill Americans and their allies, civilian and military, in any country where that proved possible. It declared the

Arabian peninsula to be under U.S. occupation because of the presence of American military bases, from which the United States was waging war on Iraq.[16] (And indeed at that time, while Iraq was under international embargo, the United States and its allies were conducting selective air strikes on Iraq in order to put pressure on Saddam Hussein.) Another aim of the U.S. occupation, according to the declaration, was to facilitate the colonization of Palestine by the Zionists and to sow divisiveness among Arab states, the better to rule them. "All these crimes and sins committed by the Americans are a clear declaration of war on God and His messenger"— hence the obligation to defend Islam with armed jihad. The double suicide attack of August 7, 1998, was the concrete expression of this imperative.

In carrying it out, Bin Laden and his acolytes followed the logic of Sheikh Qaradawi, who had stated that since Israel was at war against Muslims, neither the blood nor the possessions of its citizens were off limits. The sheikh, however, had explicitly limited his opinion to the Israeli case. The World Islamic Front extended the category of aggressors to include the United States, with its global reach, and reasoned that if martyrdom operations were allowable against Israel, by analogy they were also permitted against the interests of the United States anywhere in the world. This implied equivalence between Israel's oppression of the Palestinians and the United States' oppression of Iraq echoed sentiments that were widespread in the Muslim world during the late 1990s. The embargo against Saddam Hussein's regime had sent nutrition and hygiene into a steep decline among the Iraqi civilian population and proved especially harmful to children. By declaring the embargo and air strikes to be attacks by infidels on Muslim people and their land, Bin Laden and his henchmen hoped to turn the suffering of Iraqis to Al Qaeda's benefit and give religious legitimacy to the organization's political objectives.

But in 1998 martyrdom operations against U.S. citizens around the world were not embraced by Muslims as a legitimate way to protest the Iraqi embargo. A year earlier, the massacre of 59 tourists in Luxor, Egypt, and of ordinary citizens in Algeria, carried out by (or attributed to) armed militant groups, had caused popular revulsion. The "collateral deaths" of innocent civilians posed a huge obstacle for radical Islamist movements. That most of the hundreds of Kenyans and thousands of Tanzanians wounded or killed in Al Qaeda's August 7 suicide attacks were themselves Muslim was especially unacceptable. One of the organizers of Al Qaeda's attacks claimed that the intention was to carry out the massacre during Friday prayers, so that only "bad" Muslims who were loitering in the streets instead of attending mosque would be killed. But this argument was much too specious to sway people who were not already within the circle of Al Qaeda sympathizers, and later on the "spilling of Muslim blood" would become a major source of controversy within jihadists' ranks.[17] For both of these reasons, Bin Laden's first attempt to appropriate the grand narrative of martyrdom for his own purposes did not have the anticipated results. But it served as a practice run for the September 11 attacks, which were carried out in the far more propitious climate of the second intifada.

When this uprising (also known as the Al Aqsa intifada) broke out in late September 2000, martyrdom operations quickly became the quintessential act of resistance for Hamas. They allowed the

Islamist organization to tilt the balance of power in its favor, to the detriment of the Fatah nationalists and Arafat. The political and economic situation in the autonomous Palestinian territories had been deteriorating in recent years, and Arafat's own popularity was eroding in the face of persistent Jewish colonization and corruption within his own entourage. When Ariel Sharon (who was at that time part of the Israeli opposition to the Labor government led by Ehud Barak) provoked Palestinians by parading along the Haram al-Sharif (which Jews call the Temple Mount) on September 28, 2000, Arafat saw an opportunity to stir up unrest and distract attention from his leadership failures. He hoped that the uprising, if controlled and channeled against Israeli soldiers and settlers, would put pressure on Barak to renegotiate the 1993 Oslo Accords on terms that the Palestinian masses would view favorably.

To Arafat's dismay, the rising violence of the Palestinians allowed Sharon—campaigning on a war platform—to be elected prime minister in February 2001. He attuned his policy with the mind-set of the neoconservatives surrounding President George W. Bush, who had taken office the previous month. Sharon abandoned the negotiation process dictated by Oslo in favor of force and unilateral measures imposed on the Palestinian population, which he hoped to beat into submission. Arafat's initial strategy of guerrilla warfare not only failed to soften up the hard-line Israeli government, it did not obtain even the slightest concession.

Facing Israel's overwhelming military superiority, Hamas and Islamic Jihad saw in martyrdom operations the perfect alternative to Arafat's tactics. As Palestinians sank ever deeper into misery and the infrastructure of their society deteriorated, the population began to support suicide missions, which it had rejected in the late 1990s.[18] To a television audience following the daily torment on Al Jazeera and Al Manar, suicide bombings became an understandable and legitimate expression of resistance to Israeli oppression. The thirty suicide attacks carried out between the beginning of the second intifada in September 2000 and the attacks on New York and Washington just one year later were almost all the work of Hamas and Islamic Jihad. They quickly made martyrdom operations the hallmark of the second uprising—just as boys throwing stones had been the hallmark of the first. Telethons broadcasting from the Arabian peninsula began to raise funds for the families of suicide bombers.

Because the Oslo Accords had diminished Arab-Israeli antagonism and raised hopes for a two-state solution to the Palestinian question, the disillusion that followed upon the failure of the peace process polarized antagonists as never before, transforming a language of conflicting interests and negotiated settlements into an existential struggle. By the beginning of the millennium, jihadists had only to invoke the word "Palestine" in order to stigmatize Israel and its Western supporters as oppressors of Muslims. Transcending the suffering of local Palestinians, the word became synonymous with martyrdom—a legitimate response of the Islamic community, whether Shiite or Sunni. The grand narrative of martyrdom became part of their self-representation, and martyrdom operations were now seen as the best way to bear witness to the reality of oppression, and the only way to inflict meaningful harm upon Islam's powerful enemies. Suicide attacks—once an exception—were on their way to becoming the norm.

September 11, 2001, and the Road to Iraq

In the attacks of 9/11, Al Qaeda adapted Hamas's methods to its own global jihad against the West. Aware of the growing support for Palestinian martyrdom operations, Bin Laden expected to glean sympathy from the Muslim world for his spectacular suicide operation on American soil. The massacre of innocents in New York and Washington would be justified to the Muslim populace by drawing an analogy with the now-legitimized killing of Israeli civilians. But unlike the Africans killed in Al Qaeda's 1998 suicide attacks—hundreds of anonymous dead that neither the jihadists nor the media were interested in as individuals—the civilians who perished in the World Trade Center and Pentagon soon had faces, families, and former lives. Through twenty-four-hour television coverage, audiences on every continent came to identify with the victims, and this commiseration led to the condemnation of terrorist actions around the world.

Reactions in some parts of the Muslim world, however, were contradictory and confused. Condemnations issued by institutions and official bodies hastened to exonerate Islam of any responsibility, preferring to see the perpetrators as abnormal extremists or (even better) agents from outside Islam who sought to sully the religion and its causes—Palestine liberation being first and foremost—in order to provoke Western reprisals. But here and there, outbursts of joy made their way to the Internet and television, and the popularity of Bin Laden grew, even though he had not yet taken official credit for the operation. From his headquarters in a mountain cave in Afghanistan, he had managed to strike a historic and unprecedented blow at the world's only superpower. Feelings and expressions of pride in this accomplishment often coexisted—sometimes in the same person—with a widespread belief that neither Al Qaeda nor any Muslim had participated in this unjustifiable massacre of civilians. These incoherent interpretations rejoiced at the blows dealt to the United States without taking responsibility for them. Frequently, such denials were accompanied by accusations directed against Mossad (Israel's secret service) and even at the CIA or the U.S. Secret Service, which were alleged to have ordered the attacks. Conspiracy theories abounded as to the mysterious instructions said to have been issued to Jews employed in the Twin Towers, warning them against going to work on September 11.

Bin Laden might have expected Sheikh Qaradawi's past opinions about suicide missions against Israelis to provide his operation with a safe harbor in Islamic law. But the sheikh quickly issued an irrevocable condemnation of the attacks on the World Trade Center and Pentagon. Since the United States was not at war against Muslims, he reasoned, there was no cause for jihad or martyrdom operations. The nineteen hijackers had therefore committed suicide—an act prohibited in Islam—and would not find a place in Paradise. To preserve the legitimacy of martyrdom operations against Israel, Qaradawi and other *ulema* understood that it was absolutely necessary to dissociate the two kinds of operations from one another; otherwise, they would both go down together, under pressure from world opinion.

Perhaps coming to recognize this risk himself, Bin Laden did not claim responsibility for the attacks on the United States at first—even though he did not hide his approval, calling them a "blessed double raid" on October 7, 2001. But that all changed in April 2002, when a broadcast by As-Sahab (Al Qaeda's media branch) was released to Al Jazeera. It showed the prerecorded testaments of some of the hijackers, accompanied by commentary that identified the United States with Israel. It also harangued the *ulema* who had permitted the killing of Israeli civilians in martyrdom operations but had then denounced suicide attacks against the United States. The declaration went over Sheikh Qaradawi's argument step by step (without naming him), making the point that since the United States was Israel's principal supporter, it was just as much at war against Islam as Israel was. Those who approved of attacks carried out by Palestinians therefore had to acquiesce to the attacks of September 11. If they refused, they ran the risk of contradicting themselves: "Who can allow the branch to be killed and forbid the killing of its root and support? All those who authorized martyrdom operations in Palestine against the Jews must authorize them in America."[19]

Al Qaeda's belated acknowledgment of responsibility for September 11 and the argument it put forward to justify the attacks were broadcast in a context where, after a moment of pause, violence between Israelis and Palestinians had reached a new peak. In April 2002 Israeli air strikes and tanks hit the refugee camp at Jenin, which supposedly sheltered bomb-making workshops. The attack was soon perceived in the Muslim world as a slaughter, and the emotions aroused by this brutality gave September 11 some sort of retroactive legitimacy. Jenin bore witness to the fact that the Palestinians' agony was still the paradigm against which any other martyrdom operation must be measured, and the ultimate criterion by which to measure it.

Enthusiasm for self-sacrifice reached such a level that candidates for martyrdom presented themselves spontaneously to

Hamas and other Islamist groups, in contrast with the long and rigorous selection process that had prevailed before. This profusion of candidates turned out to be a military and political handicap, since activists who were poorly prepared might back down at the last minute or miss their target or be arrested by Israeli authorities, who would learn new details about the militants' tactics. But the abundant supply of volunteers demonstrated the unprecedented intensity of the popular commitment to Palestinian liberation. Nonreligious movements like the Marxist Popular Front for the Liberation of Palestine (PFLP) and particularly Fatah were forced to resort to suicide operations themselves or risk being marginalized.

The Al Aqsa Martyrs' Brigades, an ad hoc group at the fringe of Fatah, gained particular distinction by claiming the first martyrdom operation to be carried out by a woman, Wafa Idris, on the afternoon of January 27, 2002. That very morning, Arafat had addressed Palestinian women as an "army of roses that can crush Israeli tanks." The impact of this woman's sacrifice was immense, and Arafat did not hesitate to take credit for it. Idris became the heroine of the entire Arab world. An Egyptian academic compared her to Jesus Christ, whom Muslims revere as one of the prophets preceding Muhammad: "From Mary's womb, a martyr was born who triumphed over oppression, while Wafa's body became a bomb that ended desolation and reawakened hope."[20]

This description of the social function of sacrifice echoes René Girard's well-known remarks in *Violence and the Sacred* regarding the way in which sacrifice restores harmony to the community and strengthens social cohesion.[21] In Girardian terms, the Egyptian academic was making the case that the body of Palestine was initially torn apart by the creation of Israel and then dismembered by the Israeli occupation of the territories before being shattered by Jewish settlements. Rising antagonism between Fatah and Hamas ripped the social fabric, while misery and chaos increased inexorably. Sacrifice was perceived as restoring symbolic harmony to the Palestinian people, but also (moving from the microcosm to the macrocosm) strengthening the Muslim community as a whole, the community of believers (*umma*) that was torn asunder into rival nation-states, first by colonialism and then by imperialism.

This siege mentality, echoed even in moderate Islamist literature, provides the frame of reference within which martyrdom operations function as sacrificial rites. A woman's womb, which under favorable circumstances carries hope for new life in the form of a child, is turned into an engine of death by the desperation of Palestine. Symbolic hyperbole on this scale allowed Sheikh Yassin, Hamas's mentor, to issue a *fatwa* authorizing the participation of women in Islamist martyrdom operations. There was one detail to work out, however. Female martyrs could not receive the same sort of reward as their male counterparts in the hereafter, since recompense in the form of male virgins would be a scandal from the perspective of religion (and a mediocre recompense from the perspective of the libido). In a bid to establish some kind of equal pay for equal work, the sheikh stated that unmarried women would have the best of husbands in the afterlife, while those who were already married would soon be joined in Paradise by their earthly spouses.

During the three years after 9/11, while the United States waged its war on terror, militant groups carried out 94 martyrdom operations in Israel and Palestine before they hit an intractable obstacle: the separation wall that Israel built between itself and the West

Bank, starting in 2002.[22] This forced Hamas to declare a "truce" in 2005 and redirect its efforts toward political participation. When Sharon unilaterally evacuated Israeli settlers from the Gaza Strip in the summer of that year, Hamas attributed his "retreat" to the effectiveness of five years of suicide attacks. This claim allowed Hamas to win a majority of seats in the Palestinian elections in January 2006.

But what had been good for Hamas was not necessarily good for Palestine. The second intifada, with its profusion of martyrdom operations, had spelled disaster for the Palestinian population. In addition to suffering unspeakable misery, they were now deprived of the political infrastructure that had been so patiently built through the Oslo peace process, and they could no longer look to Yasser Arafat for leadership, for he had died in a French hospital on November 11, 2004. In June 2007, after months of fighting between Hamas and Fatah, the territory over which Palestine had been granted limited self-rule in the Oslo Accords was split into two political entities. Hamas alone controlled the Gaza Strip, while the West Bank fell under the aegis of Fatah. Far from restoring the unity of a torn nation, self-sacrifice and martyrdom had led Palestine to a state of existential fragmentation. Whether the Palestinian Authority created by the Oslo Accords had any political future at all remained unclear, and the notion of a two-state solution—Israel and Palestine—which seemed so close to realization in the mid-1990s, became less and less viable with each passing year of the millennium, as the tentacles of Israeli settlement reached into every corner of the West Bank.

As fragmented as Palestine had become by 2007, Hamas could claim one enduring credit: its grand narrative of martyrdom operations against civilians had achieved legitimacy throughout the Muslim world, both Shiite and Sunni, as the best means to resist oppression. It was no longer an exception limited to Palestine but a model that could be reproduced in any arena of conflict, including Iraq. But there, as in Palestine, the logic of jihad through martyrdom had caused *fitna* (discord) within the Muslim community. The radical Islamists' strongest weapon was co-opted by Sunni insurgents and then turned back against the Shiites who invented it. Shiite Iraqis became the main targets of the increasingly bloody suicide missions perpetrated by Sunni martyrs.

Posing as the defender of his co-religionists, Mahmud Ahmadinejad stepped forward to blame not just Sunni jihadists but also the West, especially the satanic United States and its Zionist ally. But the interests of the Iranian president extended far beyond fragmentation in Iraq. At stake were control of the Gulf's oil resources and dominance in the Middle East. In the coming apocalyptic battle over those tangible assets, the theocratic grandstander in Iran seemed intent on taking martyrdom operations to a new level, knowing very well that a nation willing to risk everything—including nuclear annihilation—would not be ignored.

CHAPTER THREE

THE THIRD PHASE OF JIHAD

In December 2004 a text that was remarkable for its length and unusual for its style and content began to circulate on jihadist Internet sites. Titled *Call to Global Islamic Resistance* and over 1,600 pages long, it was written by a radical Islamist activist born in Aleppo in 1958: Mustafa Sitt Mariam Nassar, better known by his *nom de guerre* Abu Musab al-Suri ("the Syrian").[1] He had made jihadist headlines in the mid-1990s as London editor of *Al Ansar* (*The Partisans*), a photocopied weekly put out by Algeria's Armed Islamic Group (GIA).

At the age of eighteen, while Suri was studying in Aleppo to become an engineer, he joined a radical Islamist organization, the Fighting Vanguard, a paramilitary offshoot of the Syrian Muslim Brotherhood. Wanted by Syrian security services, he sought refuge in Jordan, then in Iraq, where governments hostile to the regime in Damascus offered facilities to Muslim Brothers in exile. He put his engineering skills to use by training supporters of jihad, and in February 1982 he witnessed the bloody failure of the uprising in Hama instigated by the Brotherhood against the government of Syrian President Hafez al-Assad. Suri blamed that organization's strategic shortcomings for the Hama bloodbath, and this conflict led him to exile in France, where he continued his engineering studies. In 1985 he joined relatives in Spain and set up an import-export business. Because he married a Spanish woman, Suri possessed a precious European passport that allowed him to move freely and work at leisure for global jihad.

Suri had read the Egyptian Islamist ideologue Sayyed Qutb, who radicalized the Brotherhood's thought and was hanged by the Nasser regime in 1966, and he began to write notes on the failure of the Syrian Brotherhood's experience. Seeing in the Afghan jihad the concrete realization of his hopes, he traveled to Peshawar, where he grew close to Abdallah Azzam, the "imam of jihad," who was assassinated in November 1989. He cultivated relations with Bin Laden and Zawahiri and attended the first meetings of Al Qaeda, which was created in 1988. In Afghanistan he also met an Algerian, Qari Said, who went on to play a preeminent role in launching jihad in Algeria starting in 1992.

After the Red Army's evacuation in 1989, the Afghan jihad sank into a quagmire of internecine warfare among mujahedin chiefs. His expectations disappointed, Suri returned to his adopted city of Granada in 1992. His legitimacy as an "Arab Afghan" and his reputation as a thinker and strategist preceded him. But in a period before the widespread use of the Internet, his influence was confined to the circles of activists who could read the few copies of his works printed in Peshawar.

Following on the heels of the Syrian debacle and the Afghan disappointment, Algeria came to represent the promised land for radical Islamism. Suri placed his talents in the service of the GIA, working out of London from 1994 to 1997. While there, Suri associated with another prominent figure in London's Islamic community (nicknamed "Londonistan" by insiders), Omar Othman, also known as Abu Qatada al-Filastini ("The Palestinian"). Abu Qatada was jailed from October 2002 to March 2005 and then again—this time for life—after the July 2005 suicide attacks on the London transportation network. His involvement would give rise to a re-evaluation of British leniency toward radical Islamist ideologues residing in the U.K.

Back in 1996, bloody purges inside the Algerian organization and the spiral of massacres that followed put an end to Suri's collaboration with *Al Ansar*. It concerned him that his publication had lent the prestige of Afghan jihad veterans to the legitimization of the GIA's activities. Furthermore, the religious extremism of his comrade Abu Qatada troubled Suri, who was more of a political ideologue in the style of Qutb than a theologian. Still, copies of the bulletin, sent by fax at great cost from London to mosques in France and Algeria and read avidly by all those who were following the political strife in Africa, significantly widened the militant intellectual's readership. In fall 1996, when the Taliban took power, he departed London for Afghanistan.

The Taliban's conquest of Kabul coincided with Bin Laden's return to Afghanistan in the summer of 1996. Suri acted as public-relations intermediary for the Al Qaeda leader, organizing his first major interviews with the international press and launching his media career. In the Taliban-run nation Suri saw at last a real-life Islamic state. He took charge of a training camp named Al Ghuraba (The Foreigners), where he may have trained a large number of young Westerners—the children of immigrants or converts. He also devoted a great deal of time to writing profusely, not only as the chronicler of the radical movement's activities in the 1980s and 1990s (in *My Experience with Algerian Jihad*) but also about jihad geopolitics—an interest that gave rise to his 2004 magnum opus, *Call to Global Islamic Resistance.*

Although Bin Laden's media project was originally Suri's idea, Suri believed that Bin Laden's intoxication with television was a politically risky habit. In his view, after the failures of jihad in Egypt, Bosnia, Algeria, Kashmir, and Chechnya, the way out of the impasse for Islamism in the late 1990s was not spectacular martyrdom operations that would draw global attention to the organization. He favored instead harassing the infidel West and its apostate Muslim cronies "from below," via autonomous terrorist cells that engaged in smaller, more targeted activities. This, he argued, would progressively widen the circle of sympathizers and make it possible to create counter-societies that would eventually put an end to the regimes in power.

If this strategy was to succeed in the midterm, however, sanctuaries for training future activists must be established. The Taliban emirate, and even Londonistan, were archetypes for places where jihadists could receive ongoing technical and especially ideological instruction that would allow them to create cadres capable of making concrete decisions about local opportunities for action. Suri expressed his opposition to the August 7, 1998, attacks on the U.S. embassies in Nairobi and Dar es Salaam, carried out on Bin Laden's instructions, because he was concerned about their consequences for a jihadist movement that was still incapable of defending itself against the American superpower. The precision of U.S.

missiles launched in reprisal on various training camps in Afghanistan alarmed him, and he fully approved the Taliban's advice to
Bin Laden to lay low.

From Suri's point of view, the attacks of 9/11 were a disaster. Bin
Laden's hubris had led him to provoke America by attacking its
economic and political centers, and the result was the eradication
of the jihadists' Afghan sanctuary. This delayed global jihad for
many years. Bin Laden's reliance on television to broadcast the au-
dacity of radical Islamists and to galvanize the masses seemed to
Suri to put the organization at excessive risk. Suri himself suffered
the consequences of this new adversity: he was forced to flee U.S.
carpet-bombing of the Taliban emirate on which he had pinned all
his hopes, and in his haste he left behind some of his writings.
Wandering between Pakistan, Iran (where he was placed under
house arrest by the mullahs' regime), and the Islamist zone in Iraqi
Kurdistan (where he may have found temporary refuge with Abu
Musab al-Zarqawi, whom he had met previously in Afghanistan),
he put most of his energy into completing his major work, which
he published online in December 2004. The United States put a
price of $4 million on his head and captured him in Pakistani Bal-
uchistan in autumn 2005.

The Three Phases of Jihad

During a quarter century of intellectual and militant activities,
Abu Musab al-Suri passed through three phases of the jihadist
movement. The first began with a radical critique of the Muslim
Brotherhood's political strategy in Syria (by Suri) and in Egypt
(by Zawahiri) and was advanced by the discovery—aided by Az-

zam and the experience of Afghanistan—that a military solution was necessary for the creation of an Islamic state. This first phase took place before the advent of Al Jazeera or the Internet, when printed materials circulated slowly via traveling "Afghan jihadists." It culminated in the evacuation of the Red Army from Kabul on February 15, 1989. The defeat of the Soviets was in one sense a Pyrrhic victory, however, because the mujahedin commanders in charge of Afghanistan immediately starting tearing one another to pieces.

The second phase of jihad began with the 1990s (when Suri was in his thirties and Zawahiri in his forties), and its early years were marked by a succession of unsuccessful guerrilla wars inspired by the Afghan experience. But it ended with a spectacular martyrdom operation designed to overshadow the multiple failures in Egypt, Bosnia, Algeria, Kashmir, and Chechnya: the attacks on New York and Washington of September 11. Phase two was led from two centers: Londonistan during the first half of the 1990s, which corresponded to the period of guerrilla war; and then Kandahar and Kabul, starting in the summer of 1996 after the Taliban took control in Afghanistan. The period from 1996 to 2001 represented the highpoint of Al Qaeda's growth and influence. With the spread of fax machines, ideas moved at greater speed than they had in the 1980s. But it was especially the launching of Al Jazeera in autumn 1996 that allowed Islamist doctrines and strategies to circulate rapidly and widely. The growth of the Internet just a few years later created a new, polycentric base that did away with borders, censorship, and physical space altogether.

Just as Azzam had been emblematic of the first phase of the jihadist movement, Bin Laden and Zawahiri embodied the second.

They believed that September 11 heralded a linear, triumphal jihad that would lead to the end of time and the Islamization of all humanity. The strategy of 9/11 was elaborated by Zawahiri in his work *Knights under the Prophet's Banner,* which was made public in December 2001, the year he turned fifty. By this point, Zawahiri was a mature man chronicling a series of political and military defeats that made him understand the necessity of a radical change of scale. With the "blessed double raid on New York and Washington," the clock of universal jihad was turned back to year zero. Past failures were erased, and time could now move forward irreversibly toward a plausible, ultimate triumph for Islam over unbelief.

Zawahiri repeated this scenario in his many televised and online declarations over the following years, as did Bin Laden during infrequent appearances. They relentlessly interpreted every event (or nonevent) on the jihad front—attacks, wars, and even Hurricane Katrina and the earthquake in Kashmir, both in 2005—as plot lines in a grand narrative leading to the apotheosis of Islam and the defeat of infidels. In this second-phase version of the end of history, there would be no third phase: fate was sealed and the future was secured. And yet, just as the strategy leading to September 11 had been built on an assessment of the defeats of the early 1990s and a willingness to move beyond the template of guerrilla warfare, the third phase was built on a critique of the 9/11 attacks and a desire to transcend this strategy of media-based spectacular martyrdom operations.

The 2004 critique of "the engineer," Abu Musab al-Suri, was explicit, while that of "the butcher," Abu Musab al-Zarqawi, head of Al Qaeda in Mesopotamia, was more implicit, but they had much in common. According to Suri, the negative rebound effects of the

9/11 attacks were greater than their positive consequences. Sanctuaries in London and Afghanistan were dismantled, and military, police, and financial pressures on Al Qaeda became so great that the jihadist leaders who had not already been arrested or killed were on high alert. Mass mobilization beneath the banner of jihad, which the miraculous events of September 11 were supposed to hasten, had not come about. The undeniable rise in Islamic consciousness that followed the attacks was of no benefit to Al Qaeda specifically. Instead, its enemies within Islam—the Muslim Brotherhood and especially the despised Shiites of Iran, Iraq, and Lebanon—were the ones who profited. Everywhere in the Sunni world, parties that had emerged from the Brotherhood or were linked to it had been "misled" into participating in elections or even believing in democracy, rather than waging jihad. "Apostate" ruling regimes from Turkey to Algeria and Egypt to Saudi Arabia had been co-opted to various degrees, with Washington's blessing.

As for the Shiites, the hated Iranian regime had benefited from its support of Hezbollah in Lebanon and Hamas in Palestine, but Tehran seemed to receive greatest payback from its meddling in occupied Iraq. There, in Suri's view, secular Kurds and "heretical" Shiites had taken control of the government and laid claim to the country's gigantic oil reserves, despite the "heroic" resistance of the jihadists under Zarqawi's leadership. In contrast with the self-satisfied speeches Zawahiri made on television and the Internet, Suri and other jihadists of the third phase saw the world as still dominated by the forces of evil. From their perspective, the unbelieving West, supported by its local allies and now clearly aware of the danger it faced after the hasty, premature operation on September 11, had concentrated its considerable resources on the task of eliminating the Muslim vanguard, which was paying a high price that had mortgaged both the present and the future.

In order to avoid catastrophe, Suri called for "global Islamic resistance." But this resistance movement could no longer find sanctuary in London or Afghanistan, nor could it deploy the sophisticated means that had made the 9/11 attacks possible. The centralized hierarchy of the second phase had been destroyed in the wake of the attacks on the United States. According to Suri's analysis, it was now necessary to create and train cells whose members—bound by a common global ideology of belief in jihad— could wage war against the West and its apostate Muslim allies through independent harassment operations that they could plan and execute themselves, without help from headquarters. These cells would have autonomous financial means and operational capacities and would not depend on a weakened central command.

Neither Suri nor Zarqawi believed that jihad was in a "consolidation phase" (*marhalat tamkin*), as Zawahiri and Bin Laden did, but rather in a "phase of weakness" (*marhalat istidaf*). For Muslims familiar with early Islamic history, these notions referred to the Prophet's political and military career. When he was too weak to wage war on unbelievers, he journeyed from Mecca to Medina (a flight known as the *Hegira*), in order to prevent the small community of believers from being wiped out. He continued the battle through small clashes and other limited-impact encounters. When he felt sufficiently strong, he launched an attack on Mecca, emerging victorious.

For contemporary jihadists obsessed with this legendary model, the main difficulty lay in choosing a moment for attack that would ensure victory rather than lead to defeat. Zawahiri's triumphalist rhetoric in his December 2001 *Knights under the Prophet's Banner* was aimed at galvanizing militants and sympathizers among Internet and television audiences, and convincing the virtual Muslim community that victory was nigh and the decaying West was about to crumble under the blows of jihad. Suri's austere, more realistic *Call to Global Islamic Resistance* of 2004, in contrast, presented jihad as a defensive act aimed at establishing new sanctuaries in combat zones that could escape the authority of the dominant forces of unbelief, and at wearing down adversaries until the final, decisive attack could be launched.

This is one way to interpret the "Islamic resistance" led by Zarqawi after the United States occupied Iraq: its aim was to create "liberated" pockets like the town of Falluja in 2004, or even to represent them symbolically, as in the proclamation of the so-called Islamic State of Iraq in autumn 2006. Zarqawi was killed four months before this virtual legal entity was declared, but it found support in Sunni bastions like Anbar province, where the U.S. army, Iraqi government forces, and Shiite or Kurdish militias ventured only rarely. Zarqawi may have pledged allegiance explicitly to Bin Laden and made use of the brand name Al Qaeda in Mesopotamia, which brought media attention to his actions.[2] But there was no love lost between Zarqawi the butcher, whose idea of a good time was to decapitate hostages in front of a webcam, and Zawahiri the geopolitical strategist, who considered action in any local arena as subordinate to a global jihad that was on the verge of triumph. Zawahiri's reproaches to Zarqawi bore witness to the divergence between his own universal view and that of a local fighter, who had built his military division in haste within Iraqi Sunni enclaves, as close as possible to their particular fears and forms of vengeance.

To summarize: two forces underlay the logic of jihad in the post-9/11 period. One, expressed in Bin Laden's video appearances but especially in the writings and speeches by the omnipresent Zawahiri, deployed a triumphalist grand narrative. Through its numerous manifestations, it sought to place each event in a trajectory that was bringing Islam ever closer to a heralded victory over unbelief. Zawahiri's discourse during this period, especially starting in September 2005, was essentially a second-phase message retooled to address the critique of Suri and Zarqawi. In contrast with Zawahiri's videos produced somewhere in the mountains of Pakistan, the critique of the third-phase jihadists emerged from attacks and battles on the ground in the Middle East, in other parts of the Muslim world, and in Europe. It presented itself as a "resistance," but its spokesmen wound up either in jail (Suri) or dead (Zarqawi), and those who survived to fight another day were incapable of giving public meaning to its actions via the media.

The events that have unfolded beginning in the summer of 2001 are located at the intersection of these two lines of force. The conflict of interpretation between Zawahiri/Bin Laden on one hand and Suri/Zarqawi on the other revolves around the question of whether the triumphal global narrative of spectacular martyrdom operations, opened on 9/11, is the only meaningful form of jihad, or whether a more difficult but more productive form of resistance rooted in the small successes of local groups is the wave of the future and the way to an ultimate victory.

Zawahiri's Triumphalist Message

Zawahiri's numerous declarations between 2005 and 2008 are accessible on jihadist websites, and excerpts have appeared on news reports worldwide. Generally videotaped in front of a background cloth featuring a rifle or a machine gun (the symbol of armed jihad), these repetitive and widely available statements have little news value and are mentioned by large media organizations (including Al Jazeera) only when a precise threat against a particular target makes them seem like a scoop. The uniform message conveyed in Zawahiri's invectives—though they vary in style from the dogmatic stiffness of a Friday sermon to the clipped urgency of breaking news—constructs history as a discourse of heroic Islamic truth pitted against the countless lies of the "Zionist crusaders."

This reiterated message works especially well in his commemorative pronouncements, which are numerous. For example, after Zarqawi was killed by U.S. bombs in June 2006, Zawahiri delivered a eulogy that situated Zarqawi's battles as being in Al Qaeda's service (even though Zawahiri had previously denounced Zarqawi's modus operandi).[3] In another example, at the beginning of 2007 he gave a sort of State of the *Umma* speech clearly designed as a counterweight to the U.S. president's State of the Union address. When a political event occurs that seems to contradict his grand narrative, Zawahiri strikes while the iron is hot to rectify any potential discrepancy.[4] To take just one case, when the Shiite sheikh Nasrallah, secretary-general of Hezbollah, became the spokesman of the Arab street following the Thirty-Three-Day War with Israel, Zawahiri issued a videotape that replaced the traditional rifle in the background with pictures of the September 11 "martyrs." The message: Hezbollah's glory was a mere distraction from the true story of Sunni jihad.

On September 11 of every year since 2001, Zawahiri has given an assessment of jihad in a mock interview with a "journalist" from Al Qaeda's own As-Sahab Productions. The television format of these commemorations is aimed at Muslim audiences who stumble across them on YouTube or ogrish.com and would be put off by an extremist speech for militants.[5] The videos include professionally translated English subtitles, convenient for the many Muslims of the Indian subcontinent who do not speak Arabic—an inexhaustible potential reservoir of recruits for jihad. English also allows the videos to defy the "Zionist-crusader alliance" in its own language, the better to expose the "truth of the battle between Islam and unbelief," to quote the title of a speech posted in December 2006. Following Al Jazeera's example, many of As-Sahab's videos are preceded by a selection of clips and images to attract Internet users and press attention.

A review of the two years between Zawahiri's fourth commemoration of September 11 in 2005 and the sixth in 2007 reveals how "Dr. Ayman" integrated every opportune event into the grand narrative of triumphant jihad. His videos during this period were designed to curse unbelievers, to demonstrate the failures of their vain crusade against the Islamist vanguard, and to combat the upsurge of Shiite competition. But they were also intended to counter the growing critique that Zawahiri's 9/11 mind-set was out-of-date for a struggle that had entered a new phase.

The "interview" of September 11, 2005, titled "Four Years after the Raids on New York and Washington," was meant to show that "the Americans and their crusader allies" had undertaken a "global war against Islam and Muslims" since September 11, but that "the new crusades are unsuccessful, like the previous ones."[6] With this introduction, Zawahiri cleverly exploited the belief of many Muslims who, without adhering to jihadist ideology, reacted negatively to the war on terror, seeing it as an attack on Islam. Their suspicions were confirmed by President Bush's use of the word "crusade" when evoking the reprisals planned by the United States after September 11. While in English the word "crusade" designates a cause in the generic sense (much as the word "jihad" in contemporary Arabic signifies any virtuous struggle), to the ears of Muslims "crusade" is a loaded term.

To demonstrate his point about the crusaders' lack of success, Zawahiri began by speaking of Afghanistan, where the war on terror in 2001 had eliminated the Taliban regime, dismantled Al Qaeda, and undertaken a hunt for its leaders. By the summer of 2005, by contrast, the Karzai government barely controlled Kabul, and Karzai himself "cannot leave his office; if he goes to Kandahar he might be assassinated." Afghanistan's so-called elections had been rigged with the U.N.'s consent, he said, since the international organization "belongs to the crusader kingdom, ruled by the Caesar in Washington who pays the salaries of Kofi Annan and his ilk." Rather than being defeated, as the Americans claimed, the Taliban had simply "fallen back to the villages and the mountains, where the real power is."

As for Iraq, it was ruled by "a government put in place through scandalous elections, which half the people boycotted" (a reference to the March 2005 vote for the Constitutive Assembly that gave an absolute majority to Shiites and Kurds because many Sunnis did not turn out to vote). This had led to "an independent state in the north [Kurdistan], infiltrated by Jewish intelligence services and divided between two treacherous parties [the PKK and the PUK], which kill each other at the slightest provocation and agree only on secularism and waging war on Islam beneath the American flag. If Saladin [the ruler of Kurdish origin who defended Muslim lands against the Crusades], God bless him, were there, he would have fought and killed them." "Thank God, the declarations of the Americans and the British after the blessed raid on London [July 7, 2005] have shown the truth of their defeat," since they announced their intention of leaving Iraq "in order to calm the terror of their population."

The "blessed raid" of 7/7 in London was dealt with in a separate address on September 1, 2005. As-Sahab included a clip that showed Muhammad Siddiq Khan, the main perpetrator, presenting his prerecorded testament. In the accent of his native Yorkshire, Khan declared: "This is a war, and I am a fighter."[7] Against a background of images featuring the attacks on New York, Madrid, and London, as well as jihad in Iraq, Palestine, and Chechnya, Zawahiri explained that the London attack was "a slap to Blair, the arrogant crusader." Contrary to Blair's false claim that he had destroyed three quarters of Al Qaeda's members, the organization was still the "base of jihad" (a play on words in Arabic). Indeed, "it is expanding, propagating, gaining in strength and, thank God, it has become a popular vanguard organization that can stand up to the new Zionist-crusader campaign and defend all the land usurped from Muslims." Along the same lines, "The jihadist movement is making intense progress; it reached its peak with the raids on New York and Washington, and it is currently waging historic battles in

Iraq, Afghanistan, Palestine . . . and even at the heart of the crusaders' land, in London."

The mock-journalist then asked Zawahiri what he thought of the belief, expressed by many analysts, that "Al Qaeda has been destroyed as an organization, but remains as a message and a strategy." He replied by presenting a radiant vision of Al Qaeda, which "thank God is acquiring new members and better means, and carrying out new operations. Suffice it to count those it has undertaken since the American crusade on Afghanistan—besides its giant operations in Afghanistan and Iraq, and, the most recent to date, the blessed raid on London."

The remainder of the interview, conducted in a manner that was more militant than professional, went over the cause of the attacks on the U.K., exhorted the Muslim population of Pakistan (where Bin Laden and Zawahiri were probably hiding) to rise up against President Musharraf, denounced Muslim *ulema* who preached without calling on the faithful to take up arms, and claimed that the Israeli withdrawal from Gaza the previous month had been achieved "through martyrdom and sacrifice," not through "negotiations and concessions." This was an indirect warning to Hamas not to abandon armed struggle in favor of participation in elections. Finally, Zawahiri concluded by lambasting the United States' stated desire to propagate freedom throughout the world.

The primary aim of this September 11, 2005, interview was to demonstrate that, notwithstanding the views of Suri and some jihadists—among them Bin Laden's own son, Hamza—the raid of 9/11 was the right choice for Al Qaeda. The "base of jihad" was growing ever stronger, as was the Islamist movement, because of this strike at the "distant enemy" in New York and Washington.

But Zawahiri's videotape was equally valuable for what it left unsaid in 2005. It failed to mention Ahmadinejad's victory in the Iranian presidential elections the previous June, a sign of increased competition from the Shiites. Nor did Zawahiri refer directly to internal conflicts within the jihadist movement, although a debate was raging about the methods Zarqawi was using in Al Qaeda's name in Iraq. Those methods had earned Zarqawi a letter that same summer—intercepted and published in the fall by U.S. intelligence—in which Zawahiri chided the leader of Al Qaeda in Mesopotamia for issuing multiple declarations against the "heretical" Shiites, as well as massacring them and slitting the throats of Western hostages on webcam. Zarqawi ran the risk of cutting the jihadist vanguard off from the Muslim masses, which did not yet understand such operations. In a quasi-Maoist variation on a phrase attributed to the second caliph of Islam, Omar Ibn al-Khattab, Zawahiri wrote, "You must not throw people into the sea before you have taught them to swim."

In the absence of popular support, he continued in the letter, "the Islamic jihadist movement will be plunged into darkness, far from the distracted, fearful masses. The battle between the jihadist elites and the arrogant authorities will be confined to the shadows of prisons, far from people and the light of day . . . This is exactly what the secular and apostate governments, as well as their allies, seek to achieve. They want to isolate the jihadist movement from the Muslim masses. Our strategy must therefore aim to rally these masses and never wage the combat far from them." Popular support was especially crucial in the case of Iraq, since it is at the heart of the Middle East. An Islamic state in that country would make the destruction of Israel easy. True, the Shiites, as their history demonstrates, are heretics who fought Islam and embraced the Americans in Iraq, "as even [former Iranian President] Rafsanjani admitted." Making the battle against them a priority, however, could endanger the struggle for Israel's destruction, which is the major aim of jihad in the region. The Shiites' turn would come later. Zawahiri considered Israel's eradication to be the primary item on the jihadist agenda, and the elimination of the Shiites to be secondary.

Expelling the Americans from Iraq would come about inevitably in the midterm, he noted, and would be followed by "the establishment of an Islamic authority or emirate, which must be developed until it grows into a caliphate, extending over as many territories as possible in the Sunni region, in order to fill the vacuum left by the Americans' departure, and before an un-Islamic force has the chance to fill that vacuum." Such an emirate would spearhead the jihad to destroy Israel. Indeed, just one year later an Islamic State of Iraq would be declared, but it would not be what Zawahiri advocated, since its priority was war on Shiites and Kurds.[8]

In October 2005, when a devastating earthquake hit Pakistan, Zawahiri invited himself into the global discourse of charity work. In a declaration broadcast by Al Jazeera, he disputed the monopoly that Western, or even Christian, nongovernmental organizations held over humanitarian aid and called on all Muslims and Islamic NGOs to mobilize their resources and help the Muslim population of Kashmir, despite the obstacles "American agents" and "Musharraf's army, a branch of the CIA," had erected to prevent him from joining his brothers in their time of trial.[9] With this abrupt entrance into the charitable arena, he posed as the charismatic leader of all Muslims worldwide, interpreting even natural catastrophes as part of God's plan to ensure the success of Al Qaeda's grand narrative. The oxymoron of a humanitarian terrorist organization was a news scoop of sorts, and many Western television stations broadcast excerpts of his announcement.

Al Qaeda between a Western Rock and a Shiite Hard Place

In January 2006 Zawahiri turned against the Arab League and the Islamists who ran for elections, accusing them of helping President Bush hide his inevitable defeat in Iraq.[10] The Arab League (whose first secretary-general in 1945, Azzam Pasha, was Zawahiri's maternal great-uncle) had organized a meeting in Cairo in late 2005, bringing together representatives of Iraq's various political and religious groups to prepare a "reconciliation conference." Taunting the U.S. president in familiar, condescending terms, Zawahiri said: "Bush, admit it: you've been beaten in Iraq, you're losing in Afghanistan, and you'll soon lose in Palestine, with God's help and power . . . Today, I congratulate and bless the Islamic community for the victory of Islam in Iraq. See the U.S., thank God, begging to get out of Iraq, and pleading for negotiations with the mujahedin."

But Zawahiri reserved his most caustic tone for the Arab League, "that old deaf-mute, which is trying today to strip all meaning from the sacrifices" made by the insurgents in Iraq, in order to find a way out for the United States. "Suddenly, life returned to it, and the blood of American power flowed through its arid veins." But in Zawahiri's view, elections in the Arab states represented a last gasp for breath, which the Muslim Brothers and other traitors to the cause of jihad were assisting. In Egypt, the Muslim Brotherhood won 20 percent of seats in Parliament (when they were allowed to run and win), while in Saudi Arabia "the United States gave its blessing to the farce of so-called municipal elections"—the first ever held in that country. And in Egypt, Washington "allowed the Brotherhood to obtain a quota that had been agreed on before-hand."

Zawahiri continued: "This is a game that consists of tricking Muslims, to turn their attention away from their basic rights: to govern according to *sharia*, to free themselves from occupiers, and to demand accountability from their rulers." Zawahiri claimed that his opinion coincided with that of most independent analysts and NGOs, which remained skeptical about the impact of cosmetic de-mocratization designed simply to satisfy the Bush administration. Then he shifted, concluding with references to the necessity of Is-lamic consciousness-raising among the masses, despite the obsta-cles erected by the West.

Despite this tirade against the Arab League's participation in elections, Zawahiri was more preoccupied with an election he did not mention, one that seemed to run against the grain of his rea-soning: the vote on January 25, 2006, in Palestine that brought Hamas to power. In later declarations Zawahiri would do all he could to show that this political victory was ephemeral, but in fact the Islamist movement in Palestine—which was keeping Al Qae-da's global jihad at arm's length while waging a nationalist strug-gle—seemed to demonstrate that armed conflict could not be an end in itself, and indeed could be combined with a strategy for democratic participation.

On January 13, 2006, the U.S. Air Force bombarded a village on the Afghan-Pakistani border where Zawahiri was hiding out. He escaped miraculously, and three weeks later he appeared in a new video message, dressed all in white like a martyr.[11] He cited relevant Quranic verses and reminded his listeners that he was ready to return to God, but only when God decreed it—not on the schedule of the arrogant "Washington butcher," whom he addressed casually: "Hey, Bush, you're not only a liar and a loser . . . but I want to ask you: Who's going to leave Iraq and Afghanistan, you or us?" This statement, placing Al Qaeda on the same footing as the world's superpower, along with the dramatic special effects and solemn tone of this speech, earned it a primetime slot on Al Jazeera. It received over four minutes of airtime on the evening news, with commentary by the channel's female star, the Algerian anchor Khadija Bengana, who wore a green headscarf for the occasion.

On March 6, 2006, the scandal surrounding caricatures of the Prophet Muhammad, which had been published the previous autumn in a Danish newspaper, aroused intense emotions in the Muslim world. Arab leaders voiced protests and recalled their ambassadors to Copenhagen; citizens boycotted Danish products; in Syria and Lebanon Danish diplomatic or consular buildings were burned. In these crowd (if not mass) movements, Al Qaeda—which in Zawahiri's narrative was supposed to represent the vanguard of the Muslim masses—had been conspicuously absent, while Ahmadinejad was on the front line. Zawahiri had to scramble to avoid being outmaneuvered by the heretical Shiite but also by "apostate" Sunni states seizing the opportunity to pose as "defenders of wounded Islam."[12]

Zawahiri's tack was to situate the caricatures in a more general context: that of the intellectual crusade being carried out by the West to sully Islam. He recalled numerous examples, ranging from Salman Rushdie's *Satanic Verses* to the inconsistency of French laws. "In France, a Muslim father doesn't have the right to prevent his daughter from behaving immodestly because the law protects her; but that same law punishes her if she covers herself [with a headscarf] at school." Faced with such threats to Islam, demonstrating or setting fire to an embassy before returning to one's daily routine was not enough: it was necessary to inflict heavy economic losses on the West, along the lines of the raids on the United States, Madrid, and London. It was necessary to expel the enemy from Palestine, Iraq, and Afghanistan, to strike down corrupt apostate governments, and to call for pure *sharia* to be applied everywhere. But Zawahiri had stepped onto unfamiliar terrain in this video, and he came across as uncertain, downplaying the importance of the Danish caricatures on the one hand and on the other suggesting that the only adequate response was something on the scale of 9/11.

On March 31, 2006, Zawahiri returned to the commemorative format to celebrate the fourth anniversary of the "victory at Tora Bora," where U.S. forces, despite their enormous firepower and intelligence-gathering capacity, were unable to track down Bin Laden in the Afghan mountains.[13] On April 12 he marked the third anniversary of the invasion of Iraq, which had provoked Al Qaeda in Mesopotamia to carry out over eight hundred successful martyrdom operations.[14] Unfortunately, noted Zawahiri, this victory was tainted by the treachery of those Muslims who were willing to conclude agreements with the crusaders, explicitly disobeying the injunctions pronounced in the Quran: "O you who believe! Take not the Jews and the Christians for your friends and protectors: They are but friends and protectors to each other. And he amongst you that turns to them [for friendship] is of them. Verily God guides not a people unjust."

On the videotape in which he recited this verse, Zawahiri was filmed from above, which made him appear older. His face was drawn, and his gaze seemed to follow the prompter wearily, as he stumbled on his words several times. Usually very careful to speak in classical Arabic, Zawahiri let himself go and spoke in Egyptian dialect. Most of this declaration (twelve out of sixteen minutes) was devoted to upbraiding Arab leaders, but especially Pakistan's President Musharraf, for having allied with the crusaders against the Muslims. Zawahiri promised them an unhappy end, although his warning applied mainly to Iraq's Sunni leaders and tribal chiefs. U.S. Ambassador Zalmay Khalilzad had approached them in an attempt to dissociate their interests from those of Zarqawi and his henchmen and to lead them away from jihad in return for a role in a legitimate government.

Zawahiri's denunciation of this scheme had the character of a premonition. The notorious head of Al Qaeda in Mesopotamia—having become known around the world for his beheading of hostages and others—was killed by U.S. forces on June 7, probably after the Sunni tribal chiefs who had been protecting him gave him away. Zarqawi's corpse, displayed on television, newspapers, and magazine covers, confirmed to friends and foes alike that he was indeed dead. As the "unbelievers" clamored about their success in taking Zarqawi down, Zawahiri sought to put this event in context by demonstrating that it did not constitute a setback to the imminent apotheosis of jihad. While covering the "prince of martyrs" in compliments, however, he emphasized the differences between himself and Zarqawi, notably with regard to the struggle against the Shiites. He believed it was urgent for Shiite and Sunni combatants to find common cause; if this was not done soon, Zawahiri feared for the future Islamic State of Iraq—which he prayed for and hoped to control more closely than he had controlled Zarqawi.

Zawahiri's eulogy was broadcast by Al Jazeera on June 23, fifteen days after Zarqawi's death, and it began with a declaration that was curiously out of sync with the publicity the event had already received: "We announce to the Muslim *umma* that Abu Musab al-Zarqawi—soldier among soldiers, the hero among heroes, imam of imams, martyr (in our evaluation)—is dead." He seemed to be suggesting that only when Zawahiri pronounced these words in Al Qaeda's name was Zarqawi elevated to martyrdom and his death inscribed in the grand narrative of triumphant jihad.[15]

Zawahiri continued, "What struck me, when I learned the fatal news of Abu Musab—may God have mercy on him—is that those who announced it were Nuri al-Maliki and Zalmay Khalilzad. I felt that this declaration itself summed up most of the characteristics of the battle between crusaders and Muslims in Iraq. Zalmay Khalilzad, the Afghan apostate who abandoned his religion, emigrated to America and threw himself at the feet of the Zionist fundamentalists, affiliating himself with [Paul] Wolfowitz. And Nuri al-Maliki, [who] bought and sold Islam to reach power. He and others like him made agreements with the crusading invaders, before, during, and after the invasion. He renounced the sovereignty of *sharia*, and forbade anyone from resisting the invasion, but he fought the mujahedin under the banner of Bush the crusader."

It is significant that Prime Minister Maliki was not denounced here as a Shiite nor called a heretic, as he would have been in any of Zarqawi's speeches. Instead, Zawahiri referred to him simply as a religious charlatan—like the Sunnis who collaborated with the United States. Zawahiri enjoined Al Qaeda's combatants to continue their struggle until victory or martyrdom, and to die, if it came to that, like the heroes of early Islam, Ali and Husayn (references no doubt designed to pacify the Shiites) and contemporary Islamist martyrs from Qutb to Azzam and the leaders of Al Qaeda who had fallen in battle.

Just two weeks later, the first anniversary of the attacks on the London Underground allowed Zawahiri to erase Zarqawi's death by delivering another of the annual commemorations that kept time for the jihadist movement as regularly as a metronome. The video, broadcast on July 7, 2006, starred the "martyr" Shehzad Tanweer, who was Muhammad Siddiq Khan's companion.[16] Standing in front of the same faded purple cloth as Khan and wearing a similar red-and-white checked Palestinian *keffiyeh* fastened by a bandanna, he painstakingly recited Islamist clichés in his prerecorded testament. Then Zawahiri, a machine gun displayed behind him, decreed that the young man was hungry for martyrdom. The next person to appear in the video was Adam Gadahn, a Jew from a well-off California family who converted to Islam at the age of seventeen and was known as Azzam the American. With winks and a bright white smile, like a West Coast lawyer in a black turban and a *jellaba*, he condemned U.S. soldiers who had gang-raped a young

Iraqi woman and then killed her, along with her family, to hide traces of their crime—thereby demonstrating the ignominy of the Iraqi occupation. (This crime was investigated and punished by court-martial.)

Barely had Zawahiri's anniversary celebration of 7/7 occurred than a major event took Al Qaeda by surprise: the war between Israel and Hezbollah, which lasted from July 12 to August 14, 2006. During the fighting, the Shiite leader Nasrallah, a consummate orator, became primetime entertainment for viewers of Al Jazeera, making Bin Laden, Zawahiri, and Company look somewhat threadbare and tacky, barely able to do more than rant away on B-grade videos while Hezbollah mobilized popular support for armed resistance and aroused the enthusiasm of Muslims throughout the world. On July 27 Zawahiri tried to meet the challenge by showing that, whatever the vicissitudes of the "Zionist Aggression against Lebanon and Gaza" (as the video clip was titled), the battle waged by Al Qaeda was more important. The clip included the voice of the newly minted martyr, Zarqawi, who was not identified but whose sluggish diction and delusional tones were easy to recognize. He reminded listeners that "we are fighting in Iraq, but our eyes are set on Jerusalem"—in other words, the major struggle was being waged in Iraq, under the aegis of Al Qaeda in Mesopotamia, not in Lebanon.

Zawahiri, dressed in gray, appeared in front of three iconic photographs that were intended to cut Hezbollah's operation down to size: Abu Hafs al-Masri, an Egyptian policeman who became one of Al Qaeda's top military leaders and was killed in Afghanistan during the U.S. attack in autumn 2001; Mohamed Atta, commander of the 9/11 attacks; and the Twin Towers themselves, in flames. Waxing ironic about Israel's emotional reaction to the kidnapping of three soldiers (two by Hezbollah and one by Hamas) at a time when ten thousand Palestinian prisoners were being held in Israeli jails, Zawahiri pointed out that behind Israel's retaliation was the entire Zionist-crusader alliance, which was financing and fueling a war on Islam that threatened every Muslim.

"How can we remain silent, when we are the children of Islam's heroes?" he demanded, mentioning Ali and Husayn. He also spoke of Youssef Ben Tashfin (a Malikite Berber emir who beat the Spaniards in the eleventh century and founded Marrakesh), Saladin (the Kurdish sultan who beat the crusaders), Saad (who defeated the Persian Safavids), and Mehmet Fatih (Mehmet the Conqueror, the Ottoman sultan who conquered Constantinople). "This great civilization, which . . . destroyed Byzantium to exalt God's name has once again set out to conquer the world since September 11, 2001. In a training camp run by Al Qaeda in Kandahar, Afghanistan, a year or so before that date, after a talk Commander Abu Hafs had given on Palestine, Mohamed Atta, the hero, got up and asked: 'How can we fight the Israeli enemy?' America knows the rest of the story very well."

Zawahiri drew out the tale slowly, suggesting that the liberation of Palestine would come about only if all the interests of the countries that support Israel were under attack everywhere—in other words, through Al Qaeda's method rather than Hezbollah's. "The Muslim *umma*, whose ranks produced nineteen martyrs, can easily produce twice that number," he threatened. It is possible that this was an allusion to an attack planned for the following month in which hijackers carrying liquid explosives were supposed to blow up ten airliners traveling between Britain and the United

States. The plot was foiled, but had it been successful it would have confirmed Zawahiri's claim.

In the meantime, he insisted, the two central battlefields were Afghanistan and Iraq. All Muslims had to help expel American forces from those countries—especially from Iraq, where the creation of a jihadist Islamic emirate would allow fighters to transfer the war to the border with Palestine, via Jordan, and to meet with jihadists on the inside in order to destroy Israel. Returning to the words of Zarqawi highlighted on the broadcast, Zawahiri called on the "disinherited and oppressed" (using the vocabulary of revolutionary Shiism) to rise up, overcome tyranny and injustice, and reclaim their rights. The presentation was awkward but very clear: without ever once mentioning Hezbollah or Hamas—the two organizations that everyone in the Middle East was talking about—Zawahiri sought to rechannel the events taking place in Palestine and Lebanon for the benefit of jihad and the historical narrative represented by Al Qaeda.

Zawahiri's exercise in jihadist rhetoric of July 27, 2006, did not have the desired impact on the enormous popularity that Hamas and Hezbollah continued to enjoy on the Arab street. Zawahiri had to go back to work in early September to restore Al Qaeda's credibility—especially given that the planned airliner attacks in August were disrupted. No fewer than four videos were broadcast by As-Sahab Productions during the month commemorating the fifth anniversary of the "blessed raids" of 9/11. Two episodes, each over half an hour long, put together the chronology of the preparations and the attacks—yet another reminder to viewers that 9/11 was the seminal event in the resurrection of jihad and the *umma*.

The clips had about the same production quality as historical documentaries made by Al Jazeera. They began with the destruction of the Ottoman Empire, recounted the creation of Israel and the history of Arab nationalism, and concluded with the sublime achievements in New York and Washington. The future hijackers were shown practicing the way they would slit the throats of passengers and reading their prerecorded testaments in monotonous voices, exalting Islam and threatening unbelievers with the worst imaginable punishment. In the background were the smoking towers. Nothing was really new here, apart from the fact that these images had been brought together in a vernacular televised version.

In a 48-minute clip dated September 2, 2006, and dubbed "Invitation to Islam," Zawahiri gave the microphone over once again to Azzam the American (Adam Gadahn).[17] In a sermon that borrowed gestures and expressions from Protestant televangelists, the neat, plump, bearded 26-year-old, wearing a white turban, exhorted his compatriots in particular—and Westerners in general—to convert to the only religion whose scripture had not been falsified. If they refused, they would bear the unhappy consequences of their perseverance in error. Al Qaeda's media blitz culminated on September 29 with a new video where, among other themes, Zawahiri called on Pope Benedict XVI, whose comments on the Prophet had aroused controversy in the Muslim world, to convert to Islam.[18] Here again, faced with an expression of opinion that Al Qaeda had neither encouraged nor anticipated, Zawahiri attempted to make himself its interpreter.

Among these numerous, lengthy, often boring declarations, which the Arab and Western media broadcast only infrequently and whose audience seemed to be mainly jihad aficionados, the most important was an interview lasting 105 minutes. Conducted by an As-Sahab "journalist," it was titled "Hot Topics" (*Qadaya Sakhina*) and commemorated the fifth anniversary of September 11.[19] Zawahiri was filmed standing before shelves of religious books bound in garish colors, which evoked the library that a pious scholar might put together from the many Islamic book fairs held in the Middle East. He gave a sweeping overview of the various hot topics facing the community at war, but for the first time he seemed to adopt a defensive posture.

His interviewer impersonated a sincere Muslim, enthusiastic about jihad and wondering about recent troubling developments. This pretext allowed Zawahiri to play the pedagogue, dealing once again with the questions of Lebanon and Palestine in the context of global jihad but without mentioning Hezbollah and Hamas. Nor did he say a word about Ahmadinejad, although the Iranian president was on everyone's mind in late summer 2006, after having taken the lead in the ideological struggle against the United States and its allies. What seemed to give Zawahiri the greatest cause for joy was Afghanistan, where the Taliban was now regrouping and engaging in suicide attacks. Zarqawi's death in Iraq had been a setback, he said in Egyptian dialect, but the transition to power of his successor, Abu Hamza al-Muhajir, had been successful, and the creation of an Islamic State of Iraq that would invade corrupt Jordan and meet up with the Palestinian fighters to annihilate Israel was imminent.

As usual, he called on the jihadist vanguard to mobilize the community and strike at the crusader enemies on their own territory. *Sharia*, he claimed, makes no distinction between civilians and military personnel; it distinguishes only combatants from noncombatants. And "combatants" includes all voters and taxpayers in Western countries, even those who oppose their government's policies: democracy, after all, puts collective responsibility on all its citizens. His interviewer seemed to wonder whether the jihadists in Iraq were isolated from the larger Islamic movement. Zawahiri was quick to insist that this was not the case, since Al Qaeda in Mesopotamia had always sought to widen its alliances in its fight against the American superpower.

The Kurds in particular—"the rock of Islam, on which the Crusades broke" (a reference to Saladin) and "the writers of brilliant pages in the history of Islam"—were invited to join the jihad and reject the secular parties that put Kurdistan "in the service of the Jews and the Americans." As for the Shiites, Zawahiri did not insult them—indeed, he did not even mention them. Only the "government forces" in Iraq were accused of sowing discord among Muslims. Al Qaeda proposed an alliance among "all those combating the Americans."

Finally, the interviewer, presumably giving voice to the concerns of the average Muslim, expressed apprehension that the jihadists' strategy might be unrealistic: after all, the masses had supported the Islamist parties that ran for office. "But they are even more supportive of Sufi brotherhoods or football clubs," replied Zawahiri. That is why the jihadist vanguard is the only entity qualified to speak for the community's conscience, and why it must remain steadfast in times of trial. The Egyptian Gamaa Islamiyya and the Algerian Salafist Group for Preaching and Combat (GSPC) had pledged allegiance to Al Qaeda, Zawahiri claimed (though the Gamaa denied it), and a new jihad front had opened in Somalia.[20] From the south and the west, jihad was surrounding the infidel nations, and especially those of Europe, as the attacks attributed to Al Qaeda in the Islamic Maghreb would show.

A message in late November was addressed to U.S. Democrats, whose party had been victorious in the 2006 midterm elections. Zawahiri informed them that they were not the ones who had defeated the Republicans. Rather, it was the "vanguard of the Muslim community in Afghanistan and Iraq." If the Democrats did not order a troop withdrawal from these two countries and stop supporting Israel, they would meet the same fate. "You must understand that a new phase in the history of the world has begun!" he exclaimed. "The time of Abd al-Aziz Ibn Saud's sons is past. The grandchildren of *sharif* Hussein, Sadat, Mubarak, and Arafat have had their day. Now is the time of Khaled al-Islambuli [Sadat's assassin], Abdallah Azzam, Commander Abu Hafs, Khattab [the Saudi leader of the Chechen jihadists], Mohamed Atta, Muhammad Siddiq Khan, and Shehzad Tanweer [the two perpetrators of the suicide attacks on London]—may God have mercy on them!" This new era had begun on September 11, 2001, and the "martyrs" of jihad were its heralds and witnesses.

The clearest "truth" in this November 2006 video was aimed not at the Democrats but at the Muslim community, and its purpose was to discredit the Shiites. According to Zawahiri, Hezbollah and its sponsor, Ahmadinejad, claimed to champion the Muslim community, but they were merely usurping the new era Al Qaeda had brought about. "If jihad against the Jews in Lebanon is allowed, how can jihad against the Americans in Afghanistan and Iraq be forbidden? Why is cooperating with the Zionist enemy treason in Lebanon, while cooperating with the crusader enemy in Iraq and Afghanistan is called progress and security? . . . If Imam Ali—may

God honor him—or al-Hasan and al-Husayn (may God be pleased with them) were in Iraq and Afghanistan, would they have joined the crusaders in invading Muslim lands? Would they have cooperated with them, and fought the mujahedin, who are defending themselves? Would they have run for office in governments appointed by the crusaders and blessed by the U.N.? Would they have obeyed Bremer, Tommy Franks, and Lakhdar Brahimi? . . . Is this the same religion for the sake of which Imam Ali and al-Husayn . . . sought martyrdom?" A true Islamic martyr, Zawahiri seemed to say, must combine the character of Imam Husayn in the seventh century with that of the Yorkshire Pakistanis who carried out Al Qaeda's operation in London on 7/7.

After the usual imprecations against the *ulema* who legitimize heads of government, and praise for Turkish Muslims who protested the visit of Pope "Benedict the Charlatan," Zawahiri offered the Islamic State of Iraq—finally proclaimed on October 16, although no one paid much attention apart from jihadist websites— a very restrained salutation, indicating that he probably did not control its destiny in the way he had hoped. He concluded by sending encouragement to the Islamic courts in Somalia (who were guarding the "southern front" of the Muslim community) and to the Algerian GSPC (who were watching over the "western front").

In December 2006 Zawahiri made a 51-minute speech, "The Truth about the Fight between Islam and Unbelief," on the occasion of the eighty-ninth anniversary of the signing of the Balfour Declaration.[21] In this 1917 document the British promised to establish a national home for the Jews in Palestine (or, as Zawahiri described the event, "Someone who did not own the holy land of Palestine gave it to someone who did not deserve it"). Britain has earned special animosity from Muslims, he said, because from the time of the Balfour Declaration, when it also encouraged the Hashemites and the Sauds to stab the Ottoman Empire in the back, to its current military presence in Iraq and Afghanistan, it has always conspired against Islam. Without saying so explicitly here, Zawahiri's comment suggests that he condoned the attacks on Britain carried out between summer 2005 and summer 2007. He went on to reiterate that Al Qaeda was the only organization with a solution to the Palestinian tragedy. All of its political adversaries had failed—as would Hezbollah and Hamas, along with those other Muslim groups that had gone adrift in pointless elections. Only the expulsion of the "crusader forces" occupying Afghanistan and Iraq provided hope for a victorious jihad.

Zawahiri Calls for Unity

Declarations Zawahiri made in 2007 maintained the momentum of the previous year. In January, fourteen minutes were devoted to "The Just Equation," an ironic reaction to the "surge" President Bush announced that would dispatch twenty thousand additional troops to Baghdad.[22] Zawahiri suggested that the United States should send its entire military force, because the dogs in Iraq were hungry for more corpses. The "just equation" referred to the equivalence in force between the Americans and the jihadists, despite the apparent disproportion in numbers. The jihadists, because of their faith, were determined to wreak revenge and inflict irreparable damage on the West.

This triumphal vision was repeated in "Lessons and Deeds of the Year 1427 A.H. [2006]," a 40-minute video produced by As-

Sahab and accompanied by a fixed image of Zawahiri.[23] The "lessons" in this video repeated the same "facts" as his earlier sermons, leaving out everything in the preceding year (including the emergence of Shiism as a political factor in the Middle East) except those elements demonstrating that Sunni jihadists were marching to victory everywhere around their two bastions of strength, Afghanistan and Iraq. These emirates were led, respectively, by Mullah Muhammad Omar (to whom Zawahiri reiterated his allegiance) and Emir Abu Mohamed al-Baghdadi (to whom he sent his salutations).

In May a new speech, 67 minutes long, predicted inevitable defeat for the United States in Iraq, based—Zawahiri claimed—on American sources.[24] At the end of that month, he issued a eulogy for the commander of the Taliban, Mullah Dadallah, a martyr who had been killed by "cowards" after having kidnapped two members of a French NGO.[25] It was reminiscent of the funerary oration Zawahiri had pronounced for Zarqawi the previous year, was illustrated by images that plunged the audience into the atmosphere of Afghanistan, creating a link between the jihad waged in the 1980s against the Red Army and the battles of the twenty-first century. It also predicted that the current jihad would be as successful as its predecessor.

On June 25, 2007, shortly after Hamas militias routed Fatah troops from Gaza (giving the lie to Zawahiri's dire predictions regarding the consequences of Hamas's reckless participation in the January 2006 elections), Al Qaeda's ideologue appeared on alhesbah.org, one of the main jihadist forums, in a 25-minute audio message titled "Forty Years after the Fall of Jerusalem."[26] True to form, he situated the event in Al Qaeda's grand narrative, his aim being to correct Hamas's "errors" and show the true path to the liberation of Palestine. Jerusalem fell in the Six-Day War of June 1967, he explained, because Arab rulers had strayed from God's course onto that of nationalism. Today's Palestinian leaders, such as President Mahmoud Abbas, had become agents for U.S. interests. Hamas would triumph only if it adhered strictly to jihad and abandoned illusions of elections and nationhood, which it had embraced in Gaza under "Zionist-crusader" pressure.

Zawahiri believed that the concessions made by the Palestinian Islamist movement's leaders—such as declaring to Moscow that Chechen resistance was a Russian domestic affair, and announcing that they sought cordial relations with the West—were wrongheaded. He urged all the Islamist community's forces to mobilize with the mujahedin of Hamas, who would triumph if they refused to compromise. The West, intoned Zawahiri, was not to be feared: "America has been beaten in Iraq, in Afghanistan, and in Somalia. It has been bled dry. There is no way out for it, and it will be defeated in Palestine, with God's permission."

A few days later, on July 7, As-Sahab posted online Zawahiri's most comprehensive video to date.[27] Over 90 minutes long, it was titled "Nasihat Mushfiq." The word *nasiha* means advice and was used here to signify the advice that a wise and solicitous (*mushfiq*) legal scholar might give the ruler or the community. Victory was on the horizon, Zawahiri began, but history teaches us that it is always in such circumstances that the enemy—attempting to delay an inevitable defeat—multiplies his plots. The worst of such conspiracies would aim at dividing the jihadists. Thus, the recently proclaimed Islamic State of Iraq was facing challenges, even within the ranks of the jihadists themselves (including one of the main groups of Sunni combatants, the Islamic Army of Iraq), who questioned its legitimacy and qualifications and did not seem to take it seriously. Zawahiri's task here was to establish Al Qaeda's credibility as the sponsor of this embryonic state.

Recognizing that errors had been made on all sides, he called for unity, which has always been rewarded by God, and then he painted a vast historical and geopolitical panorama involving all those who claim that Al Qaeda is the United States' main enemy, indeed that it is the *zeitgeist* or Hegelian "spirit of the times." American journalists and politicians were roped into the project via edited televised excerpts from Samuel Huntington, Henry Kissinger, and various neoconservative polemicists, which were dubbed in Arabic and subtitled in English. Cleverly, Zawahiri developed Al Qaeda's mobilizing myth by presenting it just as the Western media would—in Arabic, with English subtitles—but with the difference that Arabic was put into the mouths of English-speaking Westerners.

Most of the demonstration, however, consisted of very long passages taken from programs produced by Al Jazeera in which Arab intellectuals, who were not members of Al Qaeda and therefore could provide an "objective" analysis, presented the organization as the quintessential motor force of international relations, and the only leverage Arabs and Muslims had in their bid to recover their special destiny to control the world's progress, which was fixed for them by divine revelation. The two principal orators Zawahiri drew upon were Abd al-Bari Atwan, editor-in-chief of the Arab nationalist daily *Al-Quds al-Arabi,* published in London, and Abdallah al-Nafisi, a British-educated Kuwaiti academic with radical Islamist sympathies.

Atwan's commentary constituted a blessing from the anti-imperialist and anti-Zionist school, arguing that Bin Laden and his followers had grown increasingly powerful since September 11 and had come to embody, in a different form, the same ideals that had motivated the Arabs in the second half of the twentieth century. Nafisi, speaking at a conference for Islamist movements organized by Al Jazeera and held in Doha, Qatar, in June 2006, praised Al Qaeda on two counts. First, unlike the Muslim Brotherhood, it had never sought political compromises for the sake of financial reward. Second, through the attacks Al Qaeda had carried out, it had turned the violence exported by the "central" states (the United States and western Europe) toward the "periphery" states (from Vietnam to Iraq and Palestine) back against the central states, in order to make them pay the price and repent.

Zawahiri concluded that there was no alternative to Al Qaeda. Hamas and the Arab nationalists had compromised with the West, while Iraq's Shiite leaders had gone astray. All of these approaches were part of a losing strategy, and all of these causes were subsumed in a single battle that had come to structure the world: jihad, which would strike ever harder at the distant enemy before putting paid to the nearby enemy and establishing *sharia* on earth, to humanity's greatest joy.

A Questionable Bin Laden Offers a "Solution"

Around the sixth anniversary of September 11, As-Sahab sent its fans a special treat: a double message from Osama Bin Laden himself. He had not been seen since the fall of 2004, during the campaign that led to President Bush's reelection, when he had broadcast a message to the American people. At that time, he was filmed standing at a pulpit and wearing ceremonial robes like an emir from the Gulf. His appearance three years later, after rumors had circulated that he was ill or dead, guaranteed that his declarations would command a vast audience, which Zawahiri's frequent appearances no longer could.

The first video was dated September 7.[28] Dressed, as previously, in sand-colored robes, a blurred figure resembling Bin Laden, his beard and mustache dyed black, read a text in the languid tones and hoarse voice that people had come to associate with the leader of Al Qaeda. For all but 4 of the 41 minutes, the figure read his text standing perfectly still, while scenes from September 11 passed in the background. Entitled "The Solution" and subtitled in both English and Arabic, this speech was addressed to the American people. It adhered to the spirit of the declaration Bin Laden had made in 2004, but especially to the various speeches Zawahiri had delivered on the same themes; indeed, it was a sort of anthology.

The September 7 message deliberately tried to appeal to modern secular reasoning. It borrowed the vocabulary of protest used by the counter-globalization movement and the extreme left wing, and its referenced authorities were Noam Chomsky, the American linguistics professor and activist, Michael Scheuer, former head of the CIA in Afghanistan (both virulent critics of U.S. involvement in Iraq and of Bush's policies), as well as a "European thinker" who remained unnamed but was clearly the French demographer Emmanuel Todd, who had predicted the collapse of the Soviet Union and who, in a more recent book *After Empire,* envisaged the end of the United States' global domination.

In a second speech on September 11 itself, Bin Laden addressed militants and Al Qaeda sympathizers. Showing only a still image taken from the September 7 video and soberly titled "Preface to the Testament of Abu Musab al-Shehri" (a reference to the Saudi subject who was the youngest of the nineteen 9/11 hijackers), it employed classical jihad rhetoric to exalt martyrdom and repeated platitudinous imprecations against Jews and Christians. By dissociating the messages intended for his outsider and insider audiences, Bin Laden—or the virtual character who stood in for him—formulated two versions of the grand narrative of jihad through martyrdom, one profane and euphemistic, the other sacred and virulent.[29]

In the September 7 speech for Westerners, parts of which were quickly made available on YouTube, the Bin Laden figure began by demonstrating that freedom and democracy are false values. These ideological illusions mask the real interests at play in the war on Iraq, which are those of CEOs in major corporations and financial institutions. The neoconservatives have claimed that continuing the war on Iraq is the only alternative to facing a holocaust (in Arabic *muhraqa,* sacrifice by fire). But, Bin Laden pointed out, "the morality and culture of the holocaust is your culture, not our culture." The Jews were persecuted by Europeans, not by Muslims; indeed, Jews "would have been saved by taking refuge with us" had the persecution occurred closer to Muslim countries. That Jews found refuge in the Arab world after the Spanish Inquisition is evidenced by the large Jewish community in Morocco. (Bin Laden seemed to believe that the Moroccan Muslim community was as large in 2007 as it had been before the end of the colonial period.)

As for Christians, he went on, they have been living among Muslims for fourteen centuries, as demonstrated by the presence of millions of Christians in Egypt. It is really Americans and Westerners who are keen on exterminating the human race, not Muslims. No further proof of this was needed than the sixty-second anniversary of the bombing of Nagasaki and Hiroshima, which had just been commemorated, or the extermination of Native Americans, not to mention the million orphans and 650,000 dead claimed by the war on Iraq.

A blurry Bin Laden then harangued American voters to stop the war in Iraq. In November 2006 "you elected the Democratic Party for this purpose, but the Democrats haven't made a move worth mentioning . . . [Why] have the Democrats failed to stop the war, despite them being the majority?" His answer was that capitalists were the real decision-makers, who controlled politicians by bankrolling their election campaigns. When John F. Kennedy wanted to end the war in Vietnam, the "owners of the major corporations" grew angry. Shortly thereafter, Kennedy was assassinated—"and Al-Qaeda wasn't present at that time," Bin Laden remarked, adding that the corporations were the primary beneficiaries of JFK's death. In passing, he also mentioned that "Donald Rumsfeld and his aides murdered two million villagers" in Vietnam, although in fact Rumsfeld opposed that war and traveled to Vietnam during the 1960s with a team of congressmen to investigate U.S. military and economic assistance programs there.

American citizens bore responsibility for the Iraq War because they had reelected Bush in 2004: "This innocence of yours is like my innocence of the blood of your sons on the 11th—were I to claim such a thing," said the indolent voice, whose irony was out of character for Bin Laden. "The leader of Texas" did not follow the "sober advice" given by Chomsky, who spoke out on "the manufacturing of public opinion," and the American people now had two options. The first was "to continue to escalate the killing and fighting against you." The second, which was the occasion for a long elaboration, entailed consciousness-raising which would result in America's mass conversion to Islam.

This change of faith would require Americans to realize that democratic ideology disguised the interests of rampant capitalism, where major corporations used globalization to turn the entire world into their fiefdom. Global warming caused by capitalist factories, "insane taxes," and real estate mortgages were ruining the American people, who must come to understand that only one "methodology" could bring about emancipation from capitalism: Islam. Secular laws only made "the rich richer and the poor poorer," continued Bin Laden. Americans claimed to believe in God "so much so that you have written this belief of yours on your dollar." But the separation of church and state, as well as working on God's earth while disobeying his orders, was "manifest polytheism."

The sacred texts of Judaism and Christianity—the Torah and the Gospels—had been altered and sold by men of knowledge "for a paltry price." The Quran, on the other hand, had been "safeguarded . . . from being added to or subtracted from by the hands of men." The jihadists adhered to it scrupulously, and this was the reason for their success. If Americans wanted to know why they had failed, Bin Laden advised them to "read the book of Michael Scheuer in this regard." Furthermore, a "European thinker" (Todd) had announced the end of the American empire, after having predicted the collapse of the Soviet empire. Because Bush had fallen prey to the same blind arrogance and vanity as Brezhnev when he refused to see that his policies were leading the USSR to ruin, the United States would ultimately crumble in the same way.

His clinching argument targeted Christians and, strangely, taxpayers. Jesus and his mother, Mary, are mentioned dozens of times in the Quran, he pointed out, and the source of the Quran is the same as that of the Bible: God. After the monks betrayed Christianity, God's message culminated with Islam. Islam is the solution, as the title of his speech indicated. And as an added bonus, there are no taxes in Islam, only alms set at 2.5 percent of revenue.

This odd speech was to some extent a "greatest hits" remix of Zawahiri's typical proselytism among non-Muslims. But the solicitude of Sunni jihadists toward the "oppressed" who suffer from the economic consequences of globalization—wage workers, pensioners, and people of modest means being the main victims—was a new theme. Bin Laden was advertising Islam as an alternative "solution" to socialism—the twentieth century's favorite version of messianism—through Marxist-flavored rhetoric that bore little relation to his earlier confirmed speeches.

Al Qaeda did not hold exclusive rights to this left-Islamic mixture, of course. The Islamic revolutionists in Iran as well as Tariq Ramadan—a Swiss Muslim academic and activist whose grandfather, Hassan al-Banna, founded the Muslim Brotherhood—had also adopted it. Their versions found a receptive audience in the West among various Third-Worldist intellectuals, social-democrat officials like Ken Livingstone (mayor of London from 2000 to 2008), and the notables of Rotterdam who finance the chair at Erasmus University that Ramadan now holds. Shiite Islamists and Ramadan accommodate the vocabulary of democracy, believing that it is compatible with Islam, as the Iranian elections and calls by young Muslims for European citizenship show. Al Qaeda's grand narrative, by contrast, denounces democracy as "false consciousness" or "ideology" in the strict Marxist sense, meaning that it is an illusion intended to placate the masses. It must be transcended—in the past by communism and in the present by Islam.

At first glance, Bin Laden's speech seems disconnected from his organization's terrorist rhetoric and practices of the previous decade. The human afflictions that concern him include global warming, the high cost of real estate mortgages, and particularly the U.S. subprime crisis that ruined small-town midwesterners. But in the 2007 context of an America whose certainties had been smashed by four years of misadventure in Iraq and by elected decision-makers who had deceived them at every turn, a space had opened up for the inanities of a digital Bin Laden. The many anguished reactions of the American media to this September 11 message were evidence of how seriously they took this speech.

The Management of Barbarism

The question of whether the Bin Laden shown on screen in September 2007 was "real" circulated endlessly in cyberspace, and what this discussion revealed about Al Qaeda's grand narrative was significant. The prophecies of Zawahiri and Bin Laden were repeatedly announced with the help of the networks and the Internet, which guaranteed their presence in the virtual world. But the only "proof" of Al Qaeda's responsibility for real-life attacks in London and elsewhere consisted of the prerecorded testimony of "martyrs" and the videotaped claims of the masterminds. If the "Bin Laden" of the September 2007 video was not real, Zarqawi's barbaric methods in Iraq, by contrast, left no doubt about reality or responsibility.

Whereas Bin Laden and Zawahiri are the scions of well-known families—Saudi in the first case and Egyptian in the second—Ahmad Nazzal al-Khalayleh emerged from the lower strata of Jordanian Bedouin society. He was a member of the Bani Hasan tribe, which boasted an illustrious lineage but had joined the working class when it settled down in the town of Zarqa (which gave Abu Musab his *nom de guerre*). In the early 1990s, in Peshawar, Zarqawi met one of the most important jihadist theoreticians of the time: a Palestinian from Jordan, Abu Mohamed al-Maqdisi, known for his 1984 work *Millat Ibrahim* (*The Community of Abraham*), a modern reformulation of the most intransigent strain of Wahhabism. His argument culminated in a virulent indictment of the Saudi royal family, which he accused of impious behavior in his second book, written in 1989: *Al-Kawashif Al-Jaliya fi Kufr Al-Dawla Al-Saudiyya* (*Flagrant Evidence of Saudi Unbelief*). Maqdisi was also the creator and webmaster of the site that boasts the largest online collection of jihadist works, Al-Tawhid wal-Jihad (Monotheism and Jihad, at www.tawhed.ws).

The two men met in a Jordanian jail, where they spent the second half of the 1990s together. During these years behind bars, through contact with the master, Zarqawi—a former felon and jihadist strong man—became an Islamist figure. Pardoned when King Abdullah II ascended the Jordanian throne in 1999, he traveled to Afghanistan, where he was accepted in circles around Bin Laden, but without enrolling as one of his followers. Then he moved on to the Islamist camps of Kurdistan and became known as emir of a jihadist group after the U.S. invasion of Iraq. Zarqawi gave his group the name of his mentor's website, Monotheism and Jihad, on the occasion of an address he delivered at the time of the group's inauguration. It was broadcast on January 4, 2004, and titled "Join the Caravan [of Jihad]"—a title copied from a 1980s work in which Azzam called on Muslims everywhere to join the Afghan jihad.[30] Zarqawi, whose education and demeanor were somewhat rustic, probably did not write the wordy text, stuffed with quotes from the Quran and salafist tradition. The author was probably the "*sharia* officer" of his group, Abu Anas al-Shami, a recent graduate of the Islamic University of Medina, who would be killed in a raid on Abu Ghraib prison the following September.

"God, as You cut the emperor, Caesar, to pieces, cut King Bush to pieces, scatter and terrorize the Americans, make them loot for the Muslims. God, damn the tyrants of the Arabs and the Persians, count them, kill them, may none escape, by God, Amen!" Thus ends Zarqawi's fairly conventional jihadist text. Another document that was supposed to remain secret was seized from one of Zarqawi's messengers by Kurdish combatants. Dated February 15 and addressed to Bin Laden, this text is of dubious authenticity, but it is featured in the complete Zarqawi archives, which his disciples collected and posted online during the week following his death.[31] The missive, an offer of cooperation with Bin Laden, was remarkable for its violent anti-Shiite (and to a lesser degree anti-Kurdish) tone—one of the important ways in which Zarqawi deviated from the norm established for public consumption by the jihadists in their battle against the "Zionist crusaders." Such curses were present in all his public declarations, even after he pledged allegiance to Bin Laden on October 17, 2004, and turned his Mono-theism and Jihad group into Al Qaeda in Mesopotamia (*Tanzim Al-Qaeda fi Bilad Al-Rafidayn*).[32]

Zarqawi intoned this litany until his last breath. In the first week of June 2006, just before his death on June 7, he recorded a series of four talks consisting of insults and accusations directed against the Shiite "heretics" (*rawafid*) and echoing all the clichés of salafist po-lemics accumulated over the centuries.[33] The Shiites supposedly worship Ali, Husayn, and the twelve imams, which makes them idolaters and not monotheists. They shower abuse on the first ca-liphs and the Prophet's companions, he claimed. Shiites accuse Aisha, the prophet's young wife, of adultery. And so on. They are "Christian seeds planted by Jews in the land of the Magians [Zoro-astrians]," according to an imam whom Zarqawi cited. And today, they are the agents of the eternal "Safavids"; wearing the uniforms of Badr (which Zarqawi dubbed *ghadr,* meaning treachery) Orga-nization or those of the National (*watani,* which Zarqawi trans-formed into *wathani,* meaning pagan) Guard, they massacre and imprison Sunnis.

Zarqawi's anti-Shiite obsession earned him reproaches from his master, Maqdisi, in a letter written in summer 2004 and titled "Zarqawi: Assistance and Reprimands, Hopes and Pain."[34] The let-ter was revived in an interview with Al Jazeera the following sum-mer. In Maqdisi's opinion, the systematic massacre of Shiites, and in general suicide attacks that killed Muslim women and chil-dren, were not within the framework of legitimate jihad, which should concentrate on "the crusader occupiers." According to the pious commentators on his collected-works website, Zarqawi per-sonally participated in two "live" beheadings: the American journalist Nicholas Berg in May 2004 and the American contractor Eugene Armstrong in October 2004. Preceded by a recitation of Quran verses that he claimed justified his actions, these beheadings were described as follows: "Here, Sheikh Abu Musab, may God have mercy on him, decapitated Nicholas Berg, and after the decapitation your brothers the mujahedin hung the corpse of this infidel mule from one of Baghdad's bridges, that it might serve as a lesson for the other mules of his species, and testify to the honor of Muslims." In the case of Eugene Armstrong, whose liberation Zarqawi had unsuccessfully tried to negotiate in return for the liberation of jailed Sunni women, the theme of purity was highlighted: "Here, the sheikh decapitated the impure American with his pure, immaculate hand, to serve as a lesson to all those who might be insensitive towards this religion, and to avenge the [wounded] dignity of the believers held in the crusaders' prisons. God is greater, may God be praised!"[35]

The only people Zarqawi was likely to convince with this hallucinatory rhetoric were the assassins who immediately surrounded him. Dragged unwillingly into a spiral of daily massacres, Muslims in Iraq and elsewhere did not identify with him personally and were far from enthusiastic about his actions. His attempt in November 2005 to extend the Iraqi jihad to his native Jordan ended in a public relations catastrophe: he sent a couple to blow themselves up in big hotels in Amman, on the occasion of "apostate" weddings. The woman, called Omm Omeira, faltered at the last minute and was arrested and shown on television, a belt of explosives under her Islamic veil. This added to the consternation of Jordanian society, which was already traumatized by the suicide attack her husband successfully carried out. Until then, Jordan, whose population is mainly of Palestinian origin, had a high rate of approval for "martyrdom operations"—provided they targeted Israel. According to a poll by the Pew Research Center, that rate collapsed from 85 percent in 2002 to 57 percent after November 2005.

This growing gulf between the global vision of jihad advocated by Zawahiri and the initiatives carried out on the ground by Zarqawi began to pose a problem for the propaganda efforts of Al Qaeda's leaders—even if Zarqawi's pledge of allegiance to Bin Laden had left him some margin to determine his actions on site. On April 24, 2006, when Zarqawi began to realize that Sunni tribal leaders were abandoning him and the trap was about to close, he broadcast a video of his "declaration to the people," a sort of rallying cry.[36] He appeared bare-faced and dressed in black like a gangster, with a belt of explosives around his waist, and seemingly under the influence of some drug: his eyes were unfocused and his manner of speaking was flat and impersonal. It was fortunate for Al Qaeda that he was killed shortly thereafter on June 7, because his death allowed the global jihadist movement to turn him into a martyr who, from that point on, would be remembered only for his feats of war against the Americans. While Al Qaeda went about diligently sanitizing Zarqawi's legend, his successor, Abu Hamza al-Muhajir, to whom Zawahiri gave his approval, stayed busy mopping up after "the butcher" and purging the organization of his controversial tactics.

On October 15, 2006, the Consultative Council of Mujahedin in Iraq, a body that claimed to bring together not just members of Al Qaeda but all jihadists, and in whose name Zarqawi had signed his last video, declared the creation of the Islamic State of Iraq, an important stage of jihad that Zarqawi had anticipated. Its commander of the faithful was Abu Mohamed Al-Baghdadi, whose *nom de guerre* suggested that he was a native of Iraq. This appointment implied that the foreign jihad combatants had joined the local nationalists and that Al Qaeda was now running a "liberated Sunni territory" analogous to the autonomous Kurdish state in the north and the quasi self-ruled Shiite provinces in the south.

A series of video recordings posted on the Internet sought to give this imaginary construct the appearance of an institution.[37] An official spokesman with his face blurred, sitting ramrod-straight at a desk next to a computer, announced—in the usual manner of authoritarian Arab states—the composition of the government, in which Abu Hamza al-Muhajir had been appointed minister of war. A mock state-run television channel, The Voice of the Caliphate, produced a parody (involuntarily) of the traditional Arab news, where an anchor, his face hidden by a *keffiyeh* and his voice distorted, praised the jihad combatants and denounced crusaders, apostates, heretics, traitors, and saboteurs. Since the fall of the Baathists, Iraqi television viewers had had access to dozens of new-generation international and national channels, among them Al Jazeera and its many imitators. It is hard to imagine what they made of this incongruous, not to say grotesque, production reminiscent of information broadcasts during Saddam Hussein's regime.

The sectarian anti-Shiite line taken by the Islamic State of Iraq caused dissent even within the Sunni jihadist movement. The Islamic Army of Iraq, an underground Baathist militia that had kidnapped or killed several foreign journalists and led many attacks on U.S. forces, invoked Bin Laden's authority so that those who claimed to act in his name would stop making threats and killing not only Shiites in general but also Sunni figures who did not find favor in their eyes.[38] The "management of barbarism" turned out to be more difficult than anticipated, and the masses were just as unenthusiastic as before about following the self-proclaimed vanguard of the Islamic community. Meanwhile, the Iraqi civil war was moving inside the Sunni camp, pitting tribes who had joined the Americans against those who supported Al Qaeda. Spectacular suicide attacks on civilians were the result.

Suri's Call to Global Islamic Resistance

Abu Musab al-Suri's 1,600-page *Call to Global Islamic Resistance*, posted online in December 2004, was an attempt to resolve the growing contradiction between Zarqawi's erratic resistance movement at the local level and Zawahiri's global media triumphalism. This voluminous work echoed conventional Islamic literature in deploring the collapse of Muslim values. It drew up a depressing balance sheet of the community's present situation and sought to restore Islam's former grandeur by mobilizing its living forces. Suri's work followed a methodology pioneered by the principal modern ideologue of radical Islamism, Sayyed Qutb. In the years that preceded his execution by Nasser's regime in 1966, Qutb produced a manifesto describing how an Islamist vanguard should seize power. It was titled *Maalim fil-Tariq* (*Milestones* or *Signposts on the Road*), and it analyzed the world in the 1960s using the concepts through which traditional Islamic scholars understood revelation. These concepts posited the pre-Islamic period as a time of "ignorance" (*jahiliyya*), in contrast with the Islamic era, which opened with the mission of God's messenger in the early seventh century

C.E. According to Qutb, the twentieth century was a time of return to *jahiliyya*, and the Islamist vanguard, emulating the Prophet, had the responsibility of destroying this ignorance in order to build a new Islamic state on its ruins.

Qutb's work had a decisive influence on jihadists during the second half of the twentieth century. They translated its fairly general statements (the author's execution having prevented him from elaborating his ideas more precisely) into concrete action. Qutb had directed his wrath principally against the governments of the Muslim world, which he felt had forgotten true Islam, and his followers concentrated their attacks on those "nearby enemies." This ran counter to the priority set by the same Arab governments, which was to fight Israel. Qutb's strategy of fighting enemies within Islam and delaying the battle against the "distant enemy" of infidels led most jihadist movements to failure in the 1990s. Under Western pressure, Arab states had followed the path of the "Oslo peace" and accepted the existence of Israel. By targeting America first—the quintessential distant enemy—Al Qaeda reversed the order of priorities and sought to end the cycle of jihadist defeats and of accommodation with the West. Following 9/11, Zawahiri used Internet and satellite television to make himself into the propagandist and zealot of this salutary reorientation.

Unlike Zawahiri's *Knights under the Prophet's Banner* of December 2001, Suri's massive work echoed shades of Qutb from forty years before. He lamented the fact that the Muslim community's moral, religious, and political decadence had not allowed the "great feat" of the "nineteen brave knights" to trigger the final battle between Muslims and unbelievers. He paid homage to Bin Laden for having found the right path, but observed nonetheless that the concrete consequences for the Muslim world in general and its jihadist vanguard in particular were catastrophic in the short term. Suri's dark tale focused on the imbalance of power between the global coalition of "Zionist-crusader" unbelief, headed by the United States, Israel, and Britain, and the alienated, disoriented Muslim world, in which the jihadists—hunted down and martyred in the tens of thousands—no longer had training bases and had to find other outlets for the "global Islamic resistance" he invoked throughout his work.

Like Qutb, who began *Milestones* by declaring that "today, humanity is on the edge of a precipice," Suri started his text with a disillusioned observation: "Concretely, as the twenty-first century of the Christian era begins, the Islamic community is being subjected to an American Zionist crusader western invasion [*ghazu*] combined with the complete alliance and cooperation of ruling regimes and the forces of hypocrisy in the Arab and Islamic world with the infidel invaders. Many cadres from the jihadist movement have been eliminated, and many of its bases have been destroyed in the military and police offensive of this alliance . . . The jihadist movement's survival is under threat, as is the perpetuation of its legal and doctrinal heritage. Similarly, the Islamic revival [*sahwa*] is undergoing intellectual and legal decline because of the maneuvers of the hypocritical palace *ulema* and the mistakes made by its defeatist leaders. This decline threatens its bases and militants, and endangers the community's belief, identity, and existence."

He continued: "I believe that due to these circumstances, kernels of resistance will be born anew in this living community, but they will be scattered and nothing will be able to bring them together—neither thought nor doctrine nor identity. The only thing that will do so is the goal of repelling the attack . . . Because so many leaders and cadres who had been systematically trained over a long period have now been martyred, most of the remaining jihadist resistance groups have lacked in political, legal, and intellectual training programs that could have served as a reference for them . . . For all these reasons, I am writing this book, in the hope that it will be, with God's permission and assistance, a guide [*sifran*]."[39] The cover of the book identified it to the reader as "your handbook [*dalilak*] on the path of jihad."

Qutb—a literary man by training and taste, educated during the efflorescence of Arabic literature in the 1920s and 1930s—had written *Milestones* as a text that any Arabic-speaking graduate would find easy to read. Its only shortcoming was its lack of specificity. Suri, a professional engineer and terrorist, wrote haphazardly and repetitiously, in the fashion of the general logorrhea that has struck Arabic-language texts ever since words were placed in the service of authoritarian governments during the 1960s and 1970s, when Suri was a student. His *Call to Global Islamic Resistance* is a difficult read.

It tries to be a sort of universal history of the clash between the eternal good of Islam and the unbelief of Americans and Zionists, who take their place on an axis of evil beginning with the misdeeds of the "crusader" Christians and the Jews. Both groups falsified their sacred texts, which proclaimed that Islam would come to place a seal on revelation. Judaism and Christianity are, in other words, the culmination of a global plot described ad nauseam here, using all the clichés known to anti-Semitism. But the text is quite interesting in the numerous passages where the author stops trying to be a theoretician and recounts his personal experience during the quarter century when he was one of the main activists of global jihad, starting with his youth in Syria in the early 1980s and ending with his time as an itinerant jihadist after September 2001. The text concludes with lessons for the present time.

To make this massive work more accessible online, Suri divided it into nine books and a conclusion, each of which can be downloaded independently. Every modern graphic-design tool—various font styles, sizes, and colors, Excel tables, and illustrations—has been employed to make this e-book a didactic instruction manual written by a practical engineer. The work is accompanied by numerous videos accessible on jihadist websites in which Suri, dressed in salafist garb with a long red beard, is giving a lesson in front of a whiteboard. With multicolored markers in his hand, he speaks in fairly casual Arabic mixed with Syrian dialect, his phrases punctuated by the question *"Fihimt?"* ("Got it?") for the virtual student body following his jihad practicum as a remote-learning module.

The eighth book, "Theories for the Call to Global Islamic Resistance," and especially its chapter 4, "Military Theory," are, as the author himself notes, the heart of the work, "the essence and summary of our thought." Reflecting on his personal experience in jihadist ranks, he distinguishes between three "schools" of jihad in the early decades: the centralized pyramid; the open front; and "individual jihad with small terrorist cells." The first two led to failure because they gave a foothold to infidel enemies, who then proceeded to eliminate the combatants. It is the third school of jihad that Suri develops theoretically and defends here as the most reliable route to Islamic victory on earth.

To validate terrorism as the main mode of action, he refers—

like Sheikh Qaradawi and most exegetes—to verse 60 of sura 8 in the Quran, "Spoils of War," which advises Muslims to gather all their forces "to strike terror into [the hearts of] the enemies of God and your enemies, and others besides." This, according to Suri, constitutes "praiseworthy terrorism," and jihadists must be proud of it, rather than allowing themselves to be intimidated by Western polemics, especially since September 11 and the beginning of the war on terror. "Terrorism is a religious obligation, and assassination is a prophetic tradition," Suri insists, citing a member of the Muslim Brotherhood who was one of his military instructors from the time he was waging jihad in Syria. Individual jihad carried out by small terrorist cells is the only strategy that can ensure global Islamic resistance in the disastrous balance of power that has prevailed since September 2001. It is no longer necessary to move to an "open front," like Afghanistan or Iraq, because, writes Suri, the whole world is now a battlefield. Today, jihadists must become members of terrorist cells wherever they live, in their immediate environment—that strategy will yield maximum returns on investments of time, energy, and resources.

The best example of this, according to Suri, is the series of attacks carried out in Spain in March 2004. The author knew the country so well that he was accused of having inspired the attacks, and he wrote of the operation in the heat of the moment as he was putting the finishing touches on his text. Carried out with the limited means of a local cell, the Madrid attacks wounded around 1,700 and caused around 200 deaths. This carnage produced three political consequences that were very beneficial for the global Islamic resistance: the defeat of Prime Minister José María Aznar, a faithful ally of the United States; the replacement of Aznar's administration by a socialist government, which rapidly pulled Spanish troops out of Iraq; and an incentive for all the other countries with soldiers in Iraq to withdraw them, for fear of experiencing similar attacks.

In calculating the ratio between cost and benefit, Suri wrote, it is preferable, in Muslim countries, to kill liberal intellectuals who are known in the West, since assassinating them will be newsworthy and will spread fear. Heads of state are less preferable, because their security forces make them more difficult to hit, and in any case they have no moral authority. This was the strategy followed by the GIA in Algeria for a time, when Suri was advising it from London in the mid-1990s. One of its branches had specialized in assassinating academics, journalists, and writers, described as "sons of France, who had suckled her poisonous milk."

Such resistance could not be waged by groups with a pyramidal hierarchy because repression of the few at the top could dismantle the entire structure too easily. Rather, it had to be undertaken by flexible networks of well-trained jihadists, or even isolated individuals indoctrinated via specialized websites. Suri called his strategic vision *nizam la tanzim*—a method, not an organization—in contrast with the strategy Al Qaeda had implemented. According to the method, brigades specialized in ideology were supposed to help train preachers, who would be the contacts for individuals making up a third circle, the active brigades. Each cell would be secret and independent from others, but their anticipated proliferation, thanks to emulation and information communicated by the Arab media and the Internet, would allow them to become a form of resistance for the masses, not just for the elite. Al Qaeda had been unable to move beyond its hierarchical beginnings, according to Suri.

What Suri did in his text was to develop a theory of action and then attempt to rationalize it with a method. Depending on opportunity, brigades or individuals should take control of a zone where the forces of oppression have reduced their garrisons—as in the Palestinian camp of Nahr al-Bared in northern Lebanon in 2007—or even carry out actions with nothing in common apart from inspiration. A number of jihadist or similar armed feats undertaken since Suri published his *Call to Global Islamic Resistance* can be interpreted in light of his advice, whether or not the perpetrators were directly inspired by this work. A sample list would include the assassination of the video artist Theo Van Gogh, stabbed by a Dutch-Moroccan Islamist in Amsterdam on November 2, 2004; the failed attacks in London on July 21, 2005, carried out by apprentice jihadists from the Horn of Africa (an attempt to imitate the 7/7 attacks); the "doctors' conspiracy" in Glasgow and London in June and July 2007 (involving attempts to blow up booby-trapped cars); and the email from a young French courier of Algerian origin to the webmaster of Al Qaeda in the Islamic Maghreb, offering to plant bombs in eastern France in spring 2007.

On January 4, 2008, a discussion on the Islamist Internet forum Shabakat al-Ikhlas al-Islamiya (Islamic Devotion Network) aroused strong emotions in France.[40] A blogger hiding behind the pseudonym Murabit Muwahhid (Monotheistic Combatant on the Jihad Front) called for attacks on Paris, possibly through "martyrdom operations" or hostage-taking like the Chechen attack on the Douma Theater in Moscow of October 23, 2002. In exchange, he speculated, it would be possible to demand "the liberation of Muslim prisoners in the Maghreb" or of "Palestinians jailed by the Jews." In the same vein as Suri, he advocated the creation of small groups that could hone their martial skills discreetly at gyms, on beaches, or in forests. Clearly unfamiliar with the situation in France, he had accessed basic information about Paris on the Arabic Wikipedia site, including a map of the Metro.

Other participants with such evocative sobriquets as Abu Kandahar or Seifallah (Sword of God) answered him, applauding his project of attacking the capital of unbelief, but wishing to spare Muslims living in France, or fearing that the Muslim Brothers or other lukewarm Islamists would see such operations as a pretext to renew their allegiance to the French. One blogger suggested that the perfect target would be the financial center of La Défense, west of the capital, and provided a list of the tower blocks and their respective heights. The fact that such threats are primitive and display ignorance of their target does not mean that no danger exists. But it does indicate that the nocturnal ruminations of individual jihadist bloggers from the Middle East are a far cry from the efficiency Al Qaeda demonstrated on September 11.

In Suri's classification, these dispersed attacks are part of an initial phase, which he calls the war of attrition, aimed at destabilizing the enemy. In the second phase, which he calls equilibrium, cells would systematically attack the army or the police, hunt down and execute its chiefs, and seize zones to liberate. During the third phase, the war of liberation, cells based in the newly liberated zones would conquer the remaining territory, while, behind enemy lines, assassinations and attacks would continue in order to complete the destruction of the world of unbelief. The first phase—which, in late 2004 when the author was finishing his text, he claimed the world was currently experiencing—requires only light weaponry and explosives. The second requires mortars, missiles, and sophisticated explosives. The third requires war weaponry that will make it possible to enter the decisive battle against the "Nazi" armies of the "crusader-Zionist coalition."

Unlike Zawahiri, who saw victory on the horizon, Suri did not underestimate the difficulty of the battle, especially the challenge of convincing the masses, which had been alienated from true Islam by Western culture, to take up the duty of fighting a very long-term jihad everywhere on earth. Fearing for his own survival and freedom, he repeatedly asked God to let him see the wonderful outcome of this jihad, but he entertained few illusions that it would occur during his lifetime.

Suri's existential angst, along with the frightening vision of a near future when the state of barbarism would be combined with a war of all against all, resulted in an astonishing conclusion. The rationalist engineer—who threw physics, Arab nationalism, Third World ideologies, Qutb's Islamism, and French and Spanish essays and novels into the jihadist blender of his mind—turned into a prophet of the apocalypse at the end of his magnum opus, much like the authors in the Arab world who flood the displays of sidewalk vendors with predictions about the end of the world, the return of the messiah, and torture in the grave.

As if he had shell-shocked himself with his practical, all-too-human theories of how to take over the world, he turned back to metaphysics at the end, lining up dozens of Quran verses and commentaries that predict the arrival of the Anti-Christ, the return of the messiah, or the battle of Gog and Magog. The rationalism that informs the body of his work gives way, in the Conclusion, to a mishmash of superstitions and ends with a testament "written in a time of misery: we are fleeing from one hiding-place to another, hunted down by the enemies of God, infidels, and the apostates who help them."[41] If he was taken prisoner, Suri warned, his readers were to ignore anything he might confess under torture that contradicts his teachings.

Like his main inspiration, Sayyed Qutb, Suri left incomplete the work he hoped would provide for the annihilation of unbelief and the Islamization of the world. In late 2005 he was captured by U.S. forces, and in an unknown location is undergoing the interrogations he predicted.

As of spring 2008, a debate was raging among terrorism experts inside the Washington Beltway. On one side, some analysts claimed that Al Qaeda was alive and kicking from its mountainous headquarters in Waziristan—and still *the* major threat against the West. Zawahiri's declarations of triumph continued to inundate the Internet, and these analysts took his fulminations at face value as evidence that Al Qaeda was America's worst nightmare. But to the ears of experts on the other side of the Beltway debate, Zawahiri's performances sounded more and more like delusional prophecies. These analysts argued that in fact the days of a leaderless jihad were at hand—a prospect that was all the more frightening because the enemy was now totally in hiding, embedded in discrete underground networks ranging from enclaves in Baghdad to the outskirts of London or New York. These Beltway insiders interpreted the few random assassinations and suicide bombings that had occurred in Europe or been aborted at the eleventh hour as evidence that Suri's dire predictions in his magnum opus were becoming reality, although Suri himself was in confinement and without a voice.

For all the heat generated by this debate in Washington, which had much to do with competing access to the financing of anti-terrorism intelligence in the post-Bush era, it inadvertently mimicked the clash among jihadists themselves—between advocates of the second phase, led by Zawahiri, and those of the third phase, led by Suri and his disciples. The competition between these two factions continued to rage in 2008, but ultimately they both faced the same unresolved problem: their inability to mobilize Muslim masses "under the Prophet's banner" or to translate the "call for global Islamic resistance" into mass action. This discrepancy between the cyber-hubris of jihadism and its meager results on the ground was exemplified nowhere more than in Europe, whose populations of Muslim descent were portrayed by jihadists and neocons alike as the Trojan horse of terrorism in the West. What both sides failed to appreciate was that the old continent had become the one place where the dynamic of cultural integration was creating a unique deterrent to the logic of terrorism.

CHAPTER FOUR

MISSTEPS OF MULTICULTURALISM

With the March 11, 2004, bombings on four commuter trains during Madrid's morning rush hour, Europe became a deadly battlefield of jihad as defined by the likes of Suri or Zawahiri. This spectacular operation was followed up on July 7, 2005, with the "blessed
raid" on a bus and three trains of the London Underground. The
next terrorist attempts were less successful: on July 21 a failed remake of the bombing in London two weeks earlier; in August 2006
a foiled suicide mission targeting transatlantic flights from Heath-
row to the United States; and a scheme to blow up automobiles in
the U.K., which was thwarted in London but carried out in Glasgow on June 29 and 30, 2007, by a group of young physicians, in a
conspiracy that became infamous as the "doctors' plot."

Al Qaeda did not explicitly claim responsibility for all of these
operations, especially not for those that failed. In light of the predictions Suri made in his *Call to Global Islamic Resistance,* it is
tempting to attribute these attacks instead to the third-phase jihadists in whom the engineer from Aleppo had placed all his hopes
for a "war of attrition"—individual terrorist entrepreneurs who
were recruited via the Internet or an itinerant preacher and spent

time training in an Afghan or Pakistani camp. But is it justified to interpret all incidents linked to Islam's presence in Europe as manifestations of the logic of international jihad, or could there be other, local, explanations?

In autumn 2005 when riots broke out in Clichy-sous-Bois near Paris and in other neighborhoods on the outskirts of French cities, the media dubbed them "Muslim riots." But was that accurate? And how should we interpret the assassination on November 2, 2004, of Dutch film-maker Theo Van Gogh by a young Islamist who accused him of blasphemy? How should we read the violent reactions in the Muslim world to the caricatures of the Prophet Muhammad published first in the Danish press and then reprinted throughout Europe? What do we make of the death threats against a French teacher who criticized the Prophet in spring 2006, or the outcry from offended Muslims at statements made by Pope Benedict XVI the following September? What do we see in the mesmerized crowds watching the Union Jack burn in Iran and Pakistan, after the queen of England knighted Salman Rushdie in spring 2007, opening old wounds dating back to the *Satanic Verses* affair of 1989?

The respective narrators of the war on terror and of jihad through martyrdom instantly seized on these events and claimed an exclusive right to interpret them. According to supporters of the war on terror—who issued an abundance of tracts, brochures, and editorials on this theme in the United States and Israel, and filled blogs with their predictions—Europe had become the target for attacks and violent demonstrations linked to Islamic unrest because it allowed immigrant populations to grow in its midst and yet did not, or could not, integrate them into its secular culture.[1]

As a result, these marginalized populations became infected with the virus of Islamist terrorism. In this neoconservative view, the continent has been unable to fulfill its responsibility to stand at Washington's side because it is suffering from Islam-induced necrosis. Its conciliatory elites tremble before Ahmadinejad and Bin Laden just as Daladier and Chamberlain once quaked in their boots before Hitler and Mussolini. Indeed, according to this extreme view, under the pretext of criticizing Israeli policy, these European leaders have returned to their old anti-Semitic ways, reviving an ancient anti-Jewish polemic now inspired by Islam.

An eminent British expert on Islam—and a close adviser of Vice President Dick Cheney—predicted that Europe would soon become nothing more than a demographic appendix to North Africa.[2] Other commentators went on to disparage "Old Europe" (as Donald Rumsfeld mockingly called it) for its socialist system of unemployment compensation and virtually free health care, which supposedly encouraged laziness among the children of immigrants, engendering vice, then Islamism, then jihad and terrorism.[3] In the United States, by contrast, Muslim immigrants are invested in the American dream, they work hard to better themselves and prosper, and they are proud of their civic religion under the Stars and Stripes—or so the story went.[4]

For the American polemicists who saw the world through this lens, France was the most culpable of all European countries. It was the standard-bearer of U.N. opposition to the invasion of Iraq—the "axis of weasel" because it feared incurring the displeasure of its millions of "semi-assimilated" Muslims and (not insignificantly) because it was trying to get its hands on U.S. markets in the Arab world. But sarcastic francophobes on the right were not the only ones to target France. Serious-minded left-leaning multi-culturalists in America, Britain, and northern Europe were deeply offended when France passed a law in spring 2004 that prohibited students from wearing ostentatious religious symbols—like the Islamic headscarf—in public schools. According to their interpretation, this backward law, calling to mind the Jacobinist extremism of the French Revolution, demonstrated that France was out of touch with today's world, of which "cool Britannia" with its prime minister Tony Blair, George W. Bush's closest ally, was the most dynamic emblem. As a result, on July 6, 2005, London beat out Paris in the competition for the 2012 Summer Olympics—only to be devastated the very next day by the worst terrorist attack in London's history.

If the grand narrative of the war on terror saw the proliferation of jihad as leading to Europe's decline, its mirror image—the grand narrative of jihad through martyrdom—also saw Europe as decadent, but in a different way. In this view, Europe had escaped being conquered by Muslims only because of a few accidents of history. Spain—formerly Arab Andalusia—was a Muslim territory beginning in 711 C.E., before being usurped by Christian kingdoms to the north, whose reconquest culminated in the fall of Granada in 1492. Consequently, in the grand narrative of jihad, Spain's status is comparable to that of Palestine under Israeli occupation. It is Dar al-Harb, a "land of war" where the blood of non-Muslim inhabitants may be legitimately spilled, as demonstrated by the attacks on Madrid in 2004, which killed 191 and wounded 1,755. As for the rest of Europe, it owes its "darkness of unbelief" to the unsuccessful siege of Vienna in 1683 by the Ottomans—a failure that Sunni Islamists such as Zarqawi placed at the feet of the Shiites, whose rebellion in the eastern lands of the empire weakened its western front. Had Vienna fallen, Muslim preachers would have been speaking from the pulpits of European capitals for the past three centuries, according to this view.

The new Islamist vanguard, awakened by the events of 9/11, hoped to reverse the course of history. According to their narrative, what all-out war had been unable to accomplish in the seventeenth century, post-colonial migration in the second half of the twentieth century was making a reality. God, in his divine wisdom, was supplanting the historic failures of military combat with an unstoppable demographic and religious conquest—the settling of millions of Muslim immigrants on European soil. Through targeted acts of terror, the vanguard of this growing population would eventually bring Europe's unbelievers to their knees, and the result would be the gradual Islamicization of the continent.

The proliferation of mosques and even Islamic universities in Europe are evidence of the coming triumph, in this view. Through persecution and blasphemy, frightened Christians, Jews, secularists, and other unbelievers have attempted to slow the inexorable progress of God's religion and the daily conversion of millions of Europeans, but in vain. From Salman Rushdie to the Danish caricatures, from France's anti-veiling law to Pope Benedict XVI's remarks on the Prophet, the "Zionist crusaders" have engaged in numerous hostile actions. But now they are paying the price, according to the jihadists, as they see their embassies go up in flames, their products boycotted, and their citizens taken hostage throughout the Muslim world.

From both of these perspectives—the neoconservatives' hopeless dismissal and the Islamists' hopeful conquest—indolent Old

Europe, only recently freed from the threat of annihilation by nuclear-armed missiles of the Communist bloc, is viewed as rich booty for hordes of jihadists. Despite the European Union's formidable economic clout, acquired through the inclusion of twenty-seven countries in a vibrant regional as well as global market, both sides see the E.U. as entangled by inefficient Byzantine regulations that have left it politically and militarily backward. In the jihadist narrative, Europe's destiny will be no different from that of the Byzantine Empire. Islamic Turkey's eventual presence in that bastion of European power will herald a renewed Islamic conquest—the continuance, in another form, of Mehmet the Conqueror's victorious entrance into Christian Constantinople in 1453.

Such dueling caricatures of Europe of course exaggerate the threat of jihad on the one hand or amplify its promise on the other. Nevertheless, they have convinced many people beyond the circles where they were developed. It was not necessary to be a jihad fanatic to boycott Danish products in spring 2006. A nation did not have to be nostalgic for the Crusades in order to vote against Turkey's entrance into the E.U. But the question must be asked: if Europe is infected throughout with individuals or cells whose zeal is sparked by Zawahiri's videos or Suri's writings, as commentators on both sides seem to believe, why do these terrorists take action in one country rather than another? What fine-grained differences within these societies might account for unrest and jihad in one place and its constraint in another?

Paradoxically, the United Kingdom, where social integration has been most successful and where Muslim elites have experienced the most remarkable upward social mobility and acquired the greatest visibility, has been the European nation most persistently hit by radical jihadist attacks, starting in 2005. Investigations of these operations have revealed how activists went about recruiting support in Britain's Islamic community by condemning the occupation of Iraq by Her Majesty's troops, leading to a major crisis that called into question the efficacy of "multiculturalism," an article of faith shared by Labour and Conservatives alike.

In the Netherlands, the assassination of Theo Van Gogh in 2004 occurred within a specifically Dutch version of multiculturalism—a postmodern update of the "pillarization" policies of the early twentieth century. Like the flamboyant politician Pim Fortuyn, who had been killed two years before, Van Gogh exposed the limits of a society segregated into "pillars" (*zuilen*)—different communities coexisting side by side but with little meaningful interaction, much less integration. Paradoxically, these parallel communities shared a superficial public space where there seemed to be few constraints. The sale of marijuana and the display of pornography were legal and widespread, full veiling in schools and on the street was permitted, and the public display of affection by gay couples was accepted, indeed encouraged by the honeymoon tourist industry.

Van Gogh's provocative film about Muslim women's subjugation sparked outrage within Holland's Islamic community not just because it violated a number of cultural taboos but because it called attention to the social isolation of a group that already felt marginalized by a pervasively secular society. In a gruesome attack on the film-maker, a young Muslim radical of Moroccan descent slit Van Gogh's throat and then used the knife to stab a five-page message into the victim's chest, threatening death to the film's screenwriter, Ayaan Hirsi Ali, a member of the Dutch Parliament and herself a former Muslim of Somali origin. Ali was forced into hiding for a time, was temporarily stripped of her Dutch citizenship, and went on to live in the United States under twenty-four-hour protection provided by the Dutch government. She continues to speak out on the subject of Muslim women's rights and the limits of multiculturalism.

Denmark, unlike Britain and the Netherlands, provided a very precarious political space for descendants of immigrant refugees. The historic dominance of the Lutheran Church had encouraged a strong sense of national identity, reinforced by anxiety as Denmark continued to lose territory in the twentieth century. A concept of national reciprocity, and its corollary, the welfare state, grew out of this insularity; but also—in the turbulent twenty-first century—a sense that Denmark's immigrant population, and especially its Muslim minority, was becoming a threat to the nation's political and economic stability. The caricatures of the Prophet by a group of Danish journalists emerged from this volatile social and cultural milieu and quickly went viral on the Internet. The Muslim community around the globe expressed outrage, while many proponents of free speech leaped to Denmark's defense.

France has the most numerous Muslim population in Europe by far. Nicolas Sarkozy, when he was interior minister in 2003, estimated that 5 million Muslims lived in France (compared with 1.6 to 2 million in the United Kingdom). Despite this disparity, to date no terrorist operation has taken place in France since 9/11. Yet all was not peace and quiet during several decades of Muslim immigration during the twentieth century. In the mid-1980s, attacks attributed to the Iranian secret service and linked to the civil war in Lebanon struck the country hard, and several French citizens were among the hostages detained by radical Islamist groups in Lebanon. During the next decade, the Algerian civil war spilled over onto French territory, leading to a series of attacks in 1995 and 1996 attributed to the GIA (Armed Islamist Groups).

Yet the law passed on March 15, 2004, prohibiting students from wearing ostentatious religious symbols at school aroused only meager protest from France's Muslim community. Al Jazeera, on the other hand, gave the incident extraordinary coverage, leaving Arab audiences worldwide with the impression that all Muslims from Dunkirk to Menton had taken to the streets. In a retaliatory act of terrorism, the Islamic Army of Iraq kidnapped two French journalists in Baghdad in the summer of 2004 and threatened to cut their throats unless the law was revoked. But mobilization in France against this deadly blackmail, especially among Muslim citizens, forced the kidnappers to release their hostages. The virtually unanimous condemnation of the perpetrators extended to the content of their demands, and this prevented Islamist militants in France from taking action to counter the law, for fear of being associated with the murderous terrorists in Iraq.

In autumn of the following year, a pattern of urban uprisings in France gave rise to many interpretations. Fox News Network created a special logo for its coverage of the riots: a graphic showing the Eiffel Tower supposedly in flames, with the slogan "Paris Is Burning."[5] Al Jazeera presented Muslims as victims of French discrimination and racism but refused to attribute to Islam the blatant acts of hooliganism that everyone could see on television channels around the world. Jihadists also declined to appropriate the events for their own agenda, and references to Islam were extremely rare in the forums visited by young insurgents and their Internet supporters. Zawahiri made no allusion to the situation, and attempts by French organizations loosely associated with the Muslim Brotherhood to mediate between the rioters and the state by issuing *fatwas* condemning civil disobedience came to nothing. The teenagers who were setting fire to cars did not identify themselves politically as Muslims even when they were of Muslim descent, and many with roots in sub-Saharan Africa were not members of the faith at all.

Its experience of facing terrorism in the 1980s and 1990s, and the security services' response to those threats, seems to have inoculated France against more serious infection by jihadist violence. But the absence of terrorist attacks in a country that is also home to religious rigorists and jihadists of every stripe must be understood within a deeper local context. In addition to a two-decade history of response to Islamist terrorism, this context includes a cultural fascination with the integration of individuals into modern French life and with a sense of national identity dating back to the French Revolution. Added to that is a colonial tradition based on the premise of France's "civilizing mission"—whatever ambiguities and hypocrisy adhere to such a slogan. The cultural values shared by the host society and its Muslim immigrant population have been more explicitly declared in France than in European countries boasting a multiculturalist agenda. As a result, immigrants from Muslim countries were obliged to face up to the disastrous consequences that Islamist violence would have on their own lives in French society, however innocent of participation in that violence individuals might be. All of these special circumstances of history and culture helped France's security forces adapt quickly to the challenge of jihadism after 9/11.

But the flip side of France's cultural integration is an unwillingness to address very real barriers that impede French residents of African or Middle Eastern descent from rising on the ladder of social and professional advancement. The riots in autumn 2005, unprecedented in scale relative to neighboring countries, were not an Islamist uprising but were rather a dramatic protest against the refusal of conventional French society to face the need for affirmative social, economic, and political action on behalf of immigrant populations. As many observers have pointed out, the violence was not a rejection of French secular society. On the contrary, what it strongly expressed was a demand for greater integration and acceptance.

These various manifestations of unrest and terror throughout Europe, starting in 2004, were quickly incorporated into a larger representation of the world that had been transmitted by satellite television and the Internet after September 11—a representation that was consolidated by the dramatic invasion of Iraq. In this broad view, local skirmishes transcend their specific context and become battlefields for waging a global war on terror—or, from the other perspective, they become the proving ground for jihad's eventual global triumph. But taking an international overview to the exclusion of the local perspective runs the risk of seriously distorting the history of extremist attacks, especially in Europe. Events there were part of the particular traditions and historical circumstances of the countries where they occurred, and cannot be understood outside the local milieu. To examine this proposition in more depth, we turn first to Great Britain.

Farewell to Londonistan

The As-Sahab video that glorified the 7/7 "martyrdom operations" in London reminded viewers that the events took place at a time when, according to Zawahiri, "Blair, the leader of the crusader empire, was flattering himself on his political success at the G-8 Summit [held at Balmoral], where he inaugurated Britain's presidency of the European Union, and when the crusader capital was celebrating its success as host of the Olympics, despite security measures costing millions of dollars as well as laws restricting freedoms and making Western countries into police states." Just at that point "God, the most high, sent the horsemen of Islam's wrath to strike at the heart of London" in a "blessed raid."

The suicide attacks on the British capital were preceded by several indications that underground terrorist groups in the U.K. were laying plans for a dramatic operation. A year earlier, in March 2004, the police raided a London warehouse and discovered 600 kilograms of ammonium nitrate—an agricultural fertilizer used to manufacture explosives. Thousands of people in a nightclub and a supermarket in London were to be the victims of deadly blasts. Five young British Muslims (four of Pakistani origin) were arrested and sentenced to life imprisonment in April 2007. Subsequent investigations revealed that some of the youths had attended jihad training camps in Pakistan and that their leader had been in contact with Muhammad Siddiq Khan and Shehzad Tanweer, two of the perpetrators of the 7/7 attacks the following year. These contacts had been filmed by the police, but Khan and Tanweer were considered minor jihadists and had not been disturbed.[6] The would-be martyr of a failed attack on the London Underground just two weeks after the successful explosions of July 7, 2005, was also known to the police as early as spring 2004: they had photographed him wearing a thick beard and carrying a heavy backpack on an endurance march near a jihad training camp on the border between Engalnd and Scotland in the Lake District.[7]

Previously, on April 30, 2003, shortly after Britain's participation in the invasion of Iraq, two British citizens of Pakistani origin, aged twenty-one and twenty-seven, carried out an attack in a Tel Aviv café that killed one of the perpetrators and three Israelis. On BBC radio's *Breakfast Show*, Anjem Choudhary, a spokesman for the British Islamist group Al Muhajiroun, commented: "The feeling for jihad at the current time in light of Iraq and Afghanistan and the continuing intifada in Palestine is very hot within the Muslim community," and for this reason the Tel Aviv bombing did not come as a surprise to him. From the perspective of jihadists, Israel was usurped Muslim territory where the blood of Jews could legitimately be spilled. It was no different from Kashmir, where Indian occupation made it necessary to kill Hindus. Still, by traveling to Israel on a suicide mission, the two young Britons had symbolically overturned one of the postulates of British policy on Islamism since the 1980s: that the Indian-Pakistani Muslim community in Britain was not motivated by events in the Arab Middle East.

On the strength of this axiom, London had welcomed Arabic-speaking ideologues, ranging from Abu Qatada al-Filastini and Abu Musab al-Suri to Abu Hamza al-Masri and Omar Bakri Mohammad. The security barrier between these radicals and Muslims already living in Britain, most of whom came from India and Pakistan, was assumed to be airtight, owing to linguistic, political, and cultural disparities. Britain's deliberate creation of a political sanctuary for radicals—dubbed Londonistan—offered its intelligence agents a precious source of information on developments taking place in the international Islamist movement, without causing them worry that these activists would "contaminate" the general population of Muslim immigrant workers from the subcontinent. This is how mentors of the GIA, among them Abu Qatada and Suri, came to use London as their base during the 1990s, to the great distress of residents of Paris, where the GIA's bombs were exploding. Britain agreed to extradite Rachid Ramda, an Algerian accused in France of participating in the 1995–1996 attacks, only after the London Underground explosions of 7/7. He was finally judged and sentenced in October 2007, over ten years after the events.

In his *Call to Global Islamic Resistance,* Suri nostalgically evoked the paradise that London had once represented for jihadist leaders: "When I was in Britain [1994–1997], I had an exceptional jihadist experience! For example, I was able to write for many jihadist publications that appeared in London [here he gave Libyan, Egyptian, and Algerian examples]. And London witnessed many conferences, lessons, and meetings, which were recorded and broadcast in different countries of the world where the jihadist awakening was being propagated."[8] These countries were not restricted to Arab nations: Pakistan was already one of the epicenters of global jihad, because of its proximity to Afghanistan (which at that time was under Taliban rule), the shared Pashtun (or Pathan) ethnic identity of the populations living on either side of the border, and the existence of many training camps on Pakistan's territory. Added to this was the proliferation of Pakistani jihadist organizations specializing in the assassination of Shiites and carrying out "raids" against Indian Kashmir.

The majority of the younger generation of immigrant origin, who were born in Britain or had arrived there from the Indian subcontinent as children, were reaching adulthood in the 1980s and were suddenly finding themselves confronted with a new set of cultural tensions and social dysfunctions. Because Great Britain's social structure encouraged the preservation of ethnic identities and values outside the mainstream, the religious organizations that provided a framework for Muslim social life in India and Pakistan had been transferred intact to Britain in the late 1940s when immigrants started arriving en masse from the subcontinent. But the younger generation spoke English and had only a passing familiarity with Urdu and Bengali—the languages these organizations used in communication and preaching. As late as July 2007, according to a poll carried out by the BBC on a sample of three hundred British mosques, only 6 percent of imams preached in English, 45 percent of them had been in Britain for less than five years, and 85 percent of them came from the subcontinent.[9]

Most imams were associated with the Barelwi Sufi brotherhood, whose religious framework did not equip them to deal with European modernity. Others had adopted a more scripturalist variant of Islam, such as Deobandism (from which the Taliban emerged) or the Ahl-e Hadith, which was intellectually hostile to Western culture. Still others were followers of Tabligh (Propagation of the Faith), a pietistic group founded near Delhi in 1927, which preaches total cultural separation from "infidel" (Hindu or European) society and practices a strictly codified Islam in all areas of daily life. Today, its leadership is in Raiwind, near Lahore in Pakistan, and it is probably the most important Islamic movement in the world, measured by the number of adherents. Millions of followers travel to Raiwind every year, in a pilgrimage that traces a giant web across the earth's surface.

The European center of the Tabligh group is in Dewsbury, Yorkshire, the hometown of one of the four 7/7 terrorists. It is just a few miles from Beeston, Muhammad Siddiq Khan's hometown, and from Bradford, where representatives of the local mosque council burned copies of Salman Rushdie's *Satanic Verses* in January 1989.[10] The Rushdie affair gave the first and most obvious demonstration of the way in which a closed Islamic society nested within a larger, open European society could lead to serious conflict. The young Muslims of Yorkshire had been raised with religious guidelines, constraints, norms, and values quite different from those of British society. And yet their experiences at school, their use of English, their exposure to the media, and even their friends had put them in close contact with temptations they were supposed to resist.

If this was not enough to provoke a crisis of identity, the unskilled working class to which these young Muslims belonged was in a precarious state of unemployment during the Thatcher years. It was in this context that Rushdie's novel was published, and the story it told was precisely a tale of the subtle hybridization of Britain and the subcontinent: its dysfunctions, the cultural shocks it caused, and the new civilization to which it would gradually give birth.

Rushdie's novel employed a narrative device known as magical realism, which infuses otherwise normal scenes and events with illogical, fantastic occurrences. This style of writing was unfamiliar to the young Muslims of Yorkshire, who took Rushdie's text literally and saw it as insulting and blasphemous, because it seemed to question the group's sacred values and shatter its taboos. The novel was blasted by competing Muslim imams and community leaders, who outdid one another in proffering condemnations and threats, until Khomeini issued his famous *fatwa* calling for Rushdie to be killed. For many young people, the demonstrations in which they cursed the novel were their first opportunity to publicly vent a sense of social isolation and hostility toward the dominant culture. These sentiments could not be voiced through the mediators of traditional Islam from the subcontinent. The main role of these *pirs* (brotherhood guides) was to negotiate their community's votes with British politicians before every election.

The new spokesmen for the disaffected youths of Yorkshire were English-speaking Islamist militants whose fervor had been aroused by the great jihads in Afghanistan and Pakistan. These activists of Londonistan knew how to send out faxes, use computers, and hold their own on the BBC's televised debates. Starting in the 1990s, Londonistan would become the link between global jihad and the housing projects of Yorkshire. Some young Britons with roots in the subcontinent passed directly from their confining traditional communities to identification with global jihad and anti-Western Islamist doctrine. For the most motivated among these young men, frequent trips to and from Pakistan, where they were supposed to find a wife, led to attendance at jihadist training camps or indoctrination sessions at affiliated madrasas.

In most countries of continental Europe, the Muslim population originated in states where jihad had been defeated (Algeria) or was strongly contained (Morocco and Tunisia) or had been recycled by moderate Islamist parties (Turkey). Britain was different, because the country of origin for much of its Muslim population—Pakistan—was undergoing "Talibanization" in the late

1990s. The proliferation of radical madrasas there created enclaves of unchecked fanaticism, and the ferocious competition among political and religious groups (which claimed many lives) echoed abroad. When young Pakistani militants returned to Britain, violence and instability traveled with them.

A British citizen who exemplified this turn toward violence was Omar Sheikh. But unlike so many of his comrades, he was born to a well-off British family of Pakistani descent and educated at the best schools, including the prestigious London School of Economics. After spending time in a jihadist camp in Pakistan, he kidnapped British and American tourists in Indian Kashmir in 1994. He was arrested and then exchanged for hostages in 1999 after an Indian Airlines plane was hijacked by members of Jaysh-e-Mohammed, a Pakistani Islamist organization. He went back to Pakistan and did not make headlines again until January 2002, when he kidnapped Daniel Pearl, a *Wall Street Journal* correspondent, in Pakistan. Pearl was decapitated. This gruesome murder, recorded on video, was the first in a series of hostage beheadings carried out by jihadists worldwide.[11]

Bin Laden's 1996 declaration making America and its allies legitimate targets of jihad began to transform the status of British territory in the minds of Islamists. Once a sanctuary for radicals, Britain would become a land of warfare, Dar al-Harb. The networks that had formed during the period of British tolerance would be reactivated as vectors for terrorism. From the Finsbury Park mosque in north London, Abu Hamza al-Masri preached jihad in Algeria. The Brixton mosque, south of the city, hosted former delinquents who had converted to Islam, or rediscovered it, and gave them a new identity. These places were later frequented by Zakarias Moussawi, the French-Moroccan citizen sentenced in the United States on May 3, 2006, for participating in the 9/11 plot, and by Richard Reid, the shoe bomber, a petty delinquent who had converted to Islam in prison and was handed a life sentence by an American court for trying to blow up explosives in his shoes on a Paris-to-Miami flight in December 2001. Both men had spent time in Al Qaeda camps in Afghanistan and Pakistan.

After the Taliban took Kabul in autumn 1996, Londonistan began to lose key figures, as militants like Suri left for Afghanistan. But it was Britain's participation as a U.S. ally in the war on Iraq in 2003 that opened the floodgates of Londonistan, releasing many working-class youths of Pakistani origin, as well as middle-class students, to sympathize with jihad in the Middle East, on the subcontinent, and in Britain's own backyard. By 2007 British security estimated that, out of a total of 400,000 annual trips made by Britons to Pakistan, more than 4,000 of them involved youths going for training in radical camps or madrasas.

The Iraq War was denounced by all Sunni Pakistani organizations as a crusader invasion to be resisted by any means possible, and the British branches of these organizations suddenly found themselves in radical opposition to Tony Blair's policy. The prime minister believed that Britain's multiculturalist structure was solid—it had been in place for over forty years—and that residents of Yorkshire's housing projects would accept his decision to toe the U.S. line in Iraq. He also thought that the ideologues of Londonistan valued their status as political refugees enough to remain compliant.

This did not turn out to be the case. Not only did a core of radicalized young people decide to fight "Blair the crusader" at home, but community elites stopped fulfilling their unofficial roles as guardians of the public order. This was corroborated by British security officials at the highest levels, who said they knew that community leaders possessed information they had not passed on—information that could have saved lives.[12] Some of the most politically visible spokesmen, like Sir Iqbal Sacranie, head of the Muslim Council of Britain (MCB, ideologically close to the Muslim Brotherhood), who was knighted in June 2005 on Blair's recommendation, "begged" his community to expel the black sheep from its flock, but in vain. The shock of July 2005 finally shattered Britain's multiculturalist consensus; and afterward, bewildered British authorities struggled to find alternative means of keeping the peace.

Initially, Blair sought the help of "modern" English-speaking militant Islamists in order to show good will toward the Islamic faith and to dissociate the healthy practice of religion (encouraged because it preserved the peace) from extremism (discouraged because it led to suicide attacks on British soil). A committee titled Preventing Extremism Together brought imams, activists, British and foreign academics, and government officials to 10 Downing Street to advise the prime minister and then to take their show on the road, seeking out Muslims, hearing their complaints, and offering solutions.[13] One of the most visible participants in this attempt at reconciliation was Tariq Ramadan.

The author of many books advocating the emergence of "European Muslims," Ramadan encouraged members of the faith to ally with Third Worldists and anti-imperialists in a bid to rejuvenate and dominate a left-wing movement that had been moribund since communism's demise. He presented Islam as a liberation theology. When he participated in Blair's attempts to enhance the government's legitimacy on the "Muslim street," where its popularity was at an all-time low, Ramadan drew on the social capital he had accumulated among young English-speaking Muslims, who saw him as a role model. He was supported in this endeavor by British politicians, including Ken Livingstone, former mayor of London, who was also a strong supporter of Qaradawi.[14]

After U.S. immigration denied Ramadan a visa to lecture at Notre Dame University, Oxford offered him a visiting fellowship. But despite his newly acquired academic caché, in France and Switzerland Ramadan was viewed more as a militant intellectual than as a serious scholar.[15] Still, his prestige served him well as a guest on the BBC, and his opinions as an intermediary and commentator were in high demand in times of crisis—for example, during the affair of the Danish caricatures starting in the fall of 2005 and continuing into the spring.

Unfortunately for Tariq Ramadan, his "street cred" began to suffer from his association with a prime minister whose conduct of the Iraq War incensed not only Muslims but also a majority of British citizens. In August 2006 the discovery of a plot to blow up planes over the Atlantic, though thwarted at the last minute, did not speak well for Labour's policy of relying on self-proclaimed representatives of Islam to fight terrorism. The party began to ignore the recommendations of the Preventing Extremism Together task force, and influential circles in government started to question the very foundations of multiculturalism, which was now seen as part of Britain's problem, not its solution.

The first tangible sign of this shift was the government's move to marginalize the MCB (whose leader had been knighted a year before) because its public opposition to British policy in Iraq was too radical. The second sign, which had considerable impact, was Jack Straw's spectacular comment on October 2006 when he refused to receive women wearing the *niqab* (full-face veil) in his political office. The former foreign minister, a heavyweight in the Labour Party and leader of the House of Commons at the time, triggered a national debate on the veil during an interview in *The Lancashire Evening Standard,* a newspaper published in his district. Asked later if he thought veils should be prohibited altogether, he said "Yes. It needs to be made clear that I am not talking about being prescriptive but with all the caveats, yes, I would rather."

Around that time, a veiled teacher had been dismissed from the public school where she taught, triggering protests from defenders of multiculturalism, who saw the incident as marking a dangerous move toward "French" policy—although it was unthinkable that wearing ostentatious religious symbols could be banned in a country where the Church of England was still the state religion. But the fact that one of Britain's veteran politicians had dealt a blow to multiculturalism alarmed Islamist organizations, which had prospered in the shelter of this policy.

In June 2007 Britain was shocked by another suicide mission. After two booby-trapped vehicles were discovered on June 29 in London, two members of the terrorist network suspected of planning the foiled operation rammed a 4x4 packed with explosives into the front of Glasgow Airport on the following day. The driver suffered severe burns and died, but authorities were able to track the plot to a radical group of young physicians working in British hospitals. Although the only victim of the operation was one of the perpetrators, the population was as traumatized by this "doctors' plot" as it had been after the 7/7 attacks. This was because in 2005 the suicide attackers had been members of the working class with immigrant origins—easy prey, supposedly, for extremist recruiters and jihad trainers in Pakistani or Afghan camps. Without justifying the actions of the 7/7 suicide bombers, some people saw them as victims of their deplorable social circumstances.

The suspects in the 2007 plot, by contrast, were doctors born in the U.K., the Middle East, or India who had excellent professional reputations, who enjoyed a comfortable standard of living, and whose future within the British economy was secure. They represented a segment of the English-speaking Muslim elite that British society trusted deeply enough to put its very health in their hands. With their long beards and white coats, these physicians embodied the "respect for difference" that was at the heart of the multiculturalist model. The press raised questions about "evil doctors," some of whom seemed to have fallen into jihadist ideology after settling in Britain.[16] But the real target of the public's scorn was the multiculturalist model itself. The doctors' conspiracy raised the question whether Britain could trust its English-speaking Muslim elites, on whose credibility the entire edifice of multiculturalism was built.

Three weeks earlier, on June 4, 2007, Tariq Ramadan published an editorial of 943 words in the *Guardian*. This was, in a sense, his farewell to Britain. Tony Blair had nothing left to offer him; "Bush's lapdog" was himself being pushed out of office by his own Labour Party. The academic year was coming to an end, and Ramadan felt the need to shore up his standing with his militant base, which was stung by the way the grandson of the Muslim Brotherhood's founder had allowed himself to be co-opted by Britain's "crusader monarchy." The day the article was published, Ramadan declined an invitation to a conference on "Islam and Muslims in the World" organized by Blair, because Islamist organizations like the MCB had not been included.

His *Guardian* article drove home his criticisms of British policy: "Obsession with the 'terrorist threat' rapidly colonised debate and drove the government headlong into an approach restricted to the 'fight against radicalisation and extremism,'" which Ramadan had initially supported. He continued: "Though it appeared normal to deal with the issue, the 'Muslim question' could in no way be reduced to one of security. Further, this policy was accompanied by a demeaning—and frequently paternalistic—argument on the necessity of 'integration.' Muslims, so it went, must accept those British values [liberty, tolerance, democracy, etc.] that make up the essence of 'Britishness.'"

Denying that the Muslim community in Britain had any sort of problem with integration, Ramadan observed: "The problem today is not one of 'essential values,' but of the gap between these values and everyday social and political practice. Justice is applied variably depending on whether one is black, Asian or Muslim. Equal opportunity is often a myth. Young citizens from cultural and religious 'minorities' run up against the wall of institutionalised racism. Rather than insisting that Muslims yield to a 'duty to integrate,' society must shoulder its 'duty of consistency.' It is up to British society to reconcile itself with its own self-professed values; it is up to politicians to practise what they preach."

"The illegal invasion of Iraq, blind support for the insane policies of George Bush, British silence on the oppression of the Palestinians—how could these issues not have a direct bearing on the deep discontent shared by many Muslims toward the West in general, and toward Britain in particular?" he wondered. In his own way, Ramadan was denouncing the British government's betrayal of multiculturalism. If that policy was abandoned, he suggested, he could no longer support the way Britain dealt with the "Muslim question." He was leaving, after two years of loyal service to the Crown and to Oxford.

As Ramadan's critique made clear, Britain's participation in the invasion of Iraq played a decisive role in leading some young British Muslims to take terrorist action, from the Tel Aviv bar in April 2003 to Glasgow Airport in June 2007. But Ramadan did not take into account the fact that Britain's terrorism was also made possible by a multiculturalist philosophy that encouraged groups to develop totally separate identities from other groups, and allowed those identities to prevail over shared values, morals, and ways of life. These separate identities could easily tip into hatred and attacks on people outside one's own insular community. In the tense summer of 2007, this debate—which under other circumstances might have remained academic—took a virulent political turn.

In the next issue of *Prospect*—an influential publication dealing with social questions—editor-in-chief David Goodhart published an "open letter to Tariq Ramadan" expressing the "disappointment" of a British intellectual who had "spent quite a lot of time in the past year or two defending you from the many people in the British political class who are influenced by the predominant French-American view that you are a dangerous extremist."[17] Goodhart described as "nonsense" the claim that "all this Muslim extremism in Britain is someone else's fault, probably the British government's" and asserted that "British Muslims are among the politically freest and richest in the world." For Ramadan "to assert that Britain is a kind of apartheid state where justice is 'applied variably depending on whether one is black, Asian or Muslim' is such an absurd exaggeration that it undermines your credibility when you are pointing to real grievances."

Goodhart noted the distressing fact that "between 7 and 15 per cent [of British Muslims] according to opinion polls" sympathized with the 7/7 attacks, while "a staggering 25 per cent (according to another poll) think that the action was not undertaken by Muslims at all, and was instead part of some western anti-Muslim conspiracy."[18] While recognizing that it was necessary to reform British society, Goodhart suggested that it was at least as important to change the mentalities and ideologies that had radicalized some British Muslims, making terrorism a major, recurrent problem in Britain.

David Goodhart's remarks received no reply. In 2007 Tariq Ramadan took up his new position as visiting professor in identity and citizenship at Erasmus University, Rotterdam. It was now the turn of the Netherlands, disoriented by the collapse of their own multiculturalist model in the wake of the murder of film-maker Theo Van Gogh, to call on him for help.

The Assassination of Van Gogh

On November 2, 2004, a few months after the attacks in Madrid, Muhammad Bouyeri, a young Dutch-Moroccan, assassinated Theo Van Gogh on a street in Amsterdam. Unlike the activists in the Madrid and London attacks, who had been through Afghan and Pakistani training camps or had communicated with members of Al

Qaeda, Van Gogh's assassin acted alone. He had, however, been in contact with an Islamist terrorist network based in the Hague known as the Hofstad group. Bouyeri gave the appearance of being a perfect realization of Suri's theories on global Islamic resistance, although he may not have read the Syrian ideologue's monumental work. According to Suri's analysis, attacks on well-known intellectual figures are comparatively easy to execute and are particularly spectacular. They strike fear into the hearts of unbelievers, they incite other potential militants to "resist," and they provoke anti-Islamic repression. This repression, in turn, leads to reflexive solidarity among the Muslim masses, and in this way the ideology of jihad spreads throughout the Islamic population.

In the Dutch case, however, this Islamist doctrine—a version of the political dialectic followed by European left-wing movements in the 1970s, involving a cycle of provocation followed by repression leading to increased solidarity—had ambiguous consequences for the progress of jihad. By the late twentieth century the Netherlands had become the standard-bearer of multiculturalism. The nation prided itself on a history of tolerance based on a social structure known as "pillarization" (*verzuiling*)—a system that viewed various religions as "pillars" that do not interact much with one another but together support "the dome of Dutch society." This form of social segregation or segmentation, implemented at the end of World War I, was inspired by the theories of Abraham Kuyper, a politician, theologian, and ideological agitator whose life spanned the turn of the century (1837–1920).

An evangelical Protestant, Kuyper founded an "anti-revolutionary party" in 1879 whose main article of faith was resolute opposition to "the spirit of 1789"—that is, to the social model that emerged from the French Revolution and its Enlightenment underpinnings. Kuyper denigrated this secular political philosophy for relegating religion to the private sphere and making the secular democratic state the ultimate arbiter of civil society. Kuyper's concern was to control the "dangerous classes" (the expanding industrial proletariat) by strengthening the Church, which was supposed to keep the masses away from "Godless revolutions" whose abhorrent secularism concealed evil socialism and communism.

Kuyper also understood democratic aspirations, however, and the secret of his model's success was in providing upward mobility for the Protestant and Catholic lower middle classes, which could rise through the ranks if they were willing to pursue education. His model responded to the specifically Dutch challenge of ensuring national cohesion through the rationalization of power-sharing among Protestants (a religious minority, but socially dominant), Catholics (a religious majority, but under-represented among social elites), and Jews (a presence in urban centers of the Netherlands for centuries). "Pillarization" of these three religious groups was a compromise that allowed each community to develop separately through its own places of worship, schools, charitable institutions, and even businesses and residential areas. Individuals fit their lives into a socioeconomic grid specific to their religion that defined their identity from birth to death.[19] The benefits of Dutch prosperity were rationalized and distributed among the three pillars by a minimal, neutral state represented by the monarchy and staffed by senior civil servants who were selected independently of their religious belonging.

This social structure shored up Dutch institutions until the second half of the 1960s, when a wave of protest shook it to its foundations. Mingling the thought of Marx, Mao, and Marcuse, the generation that came of age in the 1960s condemned pillarization as a stifling system that impeded individual emancipation, sexual liberation, and protest. The Dutch establishment—nothing if not pragmatic—responded with a political reorganization that allowed it to maintain its hold on power while co-opting and accommodating, through the market economy, the most acceptable demands of the younger generation. In the spirit of Protestant capitalism, "unbridled pleasure-seeking" was redirected into commercial channels. Pluralistic political parties replaced the old pillarization system, and the nation's balance of payments improved.

But during this same period the Netherlands, like every other wealthy Western European country, faced the problem of settling its burgeoning immigrant population. Huge numbers of poorly skilled laborers had been imported from Third World countries after World War II in order to rebuild Europe's devastated infrastructure. But when these nations found themselves mired in an energy crisis and economic slow-down following the Arab-Israeli war of October 1973, European governments looked for some way to send unemployed laborers back to their countries of origin. With the support of left-wing parties and human rights legislation, these immigrants managed not only to remain in Europe but also to establish families and bring relatives over. When couples had children in their host countries, these children became European citizens.

Most of the immigrants who settled in the Netherlands were originally from Turkey or Morocco. In addition to experiencing the loss of job security and the threat of deportation in the 1970s, they faced a cultural crisis unique to Dutch society. The colonial experience of both France and Britain had created a cultural relationship between former colonies and the empire's capital city that somewhat eased the stress of acculturation for its largest immigrant populations. But neither Morocco nor Turkey had been colonized by the Netherlands. Consequently, first-generation immigrants did not speak Dutch and were unfamiliar with local customs. Dutch society "managed" these outsiders by granting them the benefit (or the curse) of an updated pillarization system. Unlike the now-pluralistically-minded Protestants, Catholics, and Jews, immigrants were encouraged by Dutch society to accentuate their differences, and they were supported in this separatism by authorities in Ankara and Rabat, who discouraged expatriates from seeking naturalization. The government provided subsidies for mosques and Quran schools, and when a post-1960s decline in enthusiasm for churches and synagogues left a great many inexpensive buildings vacant, Muslim organizations expanded into them, so that these architectural landmarks would not be transformed into discotheques or replaced by supermarkets.

Like the Catholic and Protestant pillars in the first half of the twentieth century, the Muslim "pillar" was supposed to promote upward social mobility within the community as a reward for good behavior and for the pursuit of education in mosques and Islamic schools. There, students were taught in their families' original languages, under the aegis of an immigrant middle class that had succeeded in "ethnic" commerce and industry. Like the original pillarization system, its modern-day Muslim counterpart encouraged imams and leaders of Turkish or Moroccan cultural associations to serve as interlocutors for the state. Their role was to manage the needs of the community and to control it. Control was especially important, given that these populations had neither the cultural nor financial means to participate in the great equalizer of Dutch—and Western—social life, consumerism.

In 1983 the Dutch parliament passed "de-pillarization" measures that officially separated church and state, and three years later the government stopped subsidizing mosques and Muslim institutions as such. But any community-based initiative that was supposedly working toward "integration" and trying to make up for the cultural and social "delay" suffered by immigrant Muslim populations was still eligible for funding.[20] According to Dutch political logic, one acceptable definition of "integration" was a willingness to live side by side in mutual indifference, without disturbing the peace. In other words, the Muslim "pillar" was allowed—indeed encouraged—to remain standing.

For Moroccans and Turks, the outcome of all of this social reorganization was that their interaction with "native" Dutch society became even weaker than interaction between Protestants and Catholics had been at the peak of pillarization. They went back home to marry and brought their new spouses to Holland to live in a segregated community. Still, liberal measures like immigrants' right to vote and run in municipal elections allowed several hundred Muslims to be elected to municipal councils and a few to win seats in parliament. But such meager political representation painted a misleading picture of the social reality. As late as 2006, train passengers arriving at The Hague could see billboards showing the different faces of the city's population. Muslim populations were represented by a woman veiled in black, as if this was the predominant image Dutch society could conjure up of this insular community.

While Catholic and Protestant clerics under the traditional pillar system recognized the state as the arbiter of last resort in settling disputes, many imams did not identify with Dutch society and felt they had nothing in common with secular elites who happened to be culturally Muslim and who served on municipal councils or in the National Assembly. By the 1990s doubts were being raised about the naiveté of Dutch multiculturalism, and a right-wing politician, Frits Bolkestein, wondered aloud whether Islamic norms and practices were compatible with Holland's open society.[21] In January 2000 a left-wing intellectual, Paul Scheffer, wrote an article titled "Multicultural Drama" in which he expressed concern about the over-representation of young Moroccans among delinquents and the unemployed. He also worried that the community's leaders advocated cultural values at odds with those of liberal Holland. For Scheffer, failure of Muslims to integrate was largely a result of pillarization.

Islam in both its rigorist and radical variants had proved quite useful for a time in maintaining social order within a marginalized community. But by the turn of the century, the Muslim community was posing a problem in the public sphere. Some young Muslim adults who spoke Dutch and identified with Dutch culture had begun to clash with religious radicals who denounced their integrated peers as apostates, made death threats, and engaged in intimidating behavior. This growing tension between a globally permissive society and some religious radicals within the Islamic community became especially obvious when bearded young Moroccans began to harass homosexual couples in public places. The attacks of 9/11, coming in this context, sharpened antagonisms, which finally crystallized around three incidents, partially linked.

They were the rise and assassination of Pim Fortuyn, the provocations and murder of Theo Van Gogh, and the scandal and exile of Ayaan Hirsi Ali.[22]

Pim Fortuyn was a perfect example of the peculiar Dutch tradition of iconoclasm—a nonconformist produced by a conformist society to periodically expose itself to fresh ideas. The 1960s had left this former leftist with a flair for provocation, which he brandished like a saber to combat the politically correct discourse of multiculturalism put forth by the Social Democrats and Christian socialists. He made no secret of his homosexuality and was a flamboyant orator in a country where politicians tend to be austere. He dressed exquisitely, in contrast with the drab grays of his colleagues. The populist political group he created was richly endowed by real estate moguls.

Fortuyn openly professed his contempt for rigorist Islam, which the political establishment protected and favored on the assumption that its acceptance was a prerequisite for dealing with the Muslim community. His active involvement with this issue came about after bearded Maghrebis raided and sacked a gay bar Fortuyn frequented. In one of his favorite tirades, he denounced Islam as a backward religion, while boasting that he "had fun fucking young Moroccan boys"—an outrageous comment that evoked old clichés of colonial pederasty in North Africa. But beyond the stereotypes, Pim Fortuyn gave expression to an ambivalence felt in Dutch society toward its Muslim residents. Though this community mingled with non-Muslims on the streets and in the marketplace, it was doubly segregated: by Holland's de facto revival of the pillarization system for its immigrants, and by the cultural separatism preached by rigorist imams. Contrary to the situation in France, where young men and women of Maghrebi and French origin frequently lived together or married, expressing integration on a daily basis by eating, sleeping, and having children together, in the Netherlands such cohabitation was far less frequent, as it was in Britain, Germany, and most northern European countries at the time.

Fortuyn's death was as absurd as the social practices he lambasted. An esthete and lover of fur, he was struck down by a deranged animal rights activist as he was leaving a radio recording studio on May 6, 2002, a few days before the legislative elections. Citizens were stunned and angered, and the "Pim Fortuyn list" made exceptional gains in the elections. The ruling Labor Party, which symbolized the politically correct attitudes Fortuyn had condemned, collapsed. A society whose institutions were exquisitely designed to avoid violence had experienced its first political assassination in three hundred years (the last one was the murder of Cornelius and Johan de Witt in 1672, immortalized in Alexandre Dumas's work *The Black Tulip*). The result was unprecedented demonstrations and rioting that exalted the fallen rebel and defended his cause. Yet despite this initial outpouring of anguish and concern, the crime against Fortuyn was gradually written off as exceptional. He had gone too far, his assassin was unbalanced, this would not happen again. But two years later, it *did* happen again, with the murder of Theo Van Gogh.

The great-grand-nephew of the tormented master of modern painting, Theo Van Gogh was in some ways the reverse image of Pim Fortuyn. In contrast with the slim, dandified, distinguished

Fortuyn, Van Gogh was ostentatiously obese, vulgar, and obscene. He was well known for his verbal attacks on the Jewish lobby in the Netherlands, which sued him for defamation. He managed to avoid conviction by invoking the right to free expression. After 2002, in an attempt to fill the vacuum left by Fortuyn's death, Van Gogh turned his attention and animosity toward Islam. In that campaign he acquired an unlikely ally, Ayaan Hirsi Ali—a Somali woman who had sought refuge in the Netherlands to escape a forced marriage. She became an atheist and took up the fight against religious dogmatism, including the custom of genital cutting, to which she had been subjected in Somalia.

Originally a committed socialist, Ali shifted right in November 2002 and joined the Liberal Party, denouncing as shameful the compromises her former comrades had made with Islamist militants in the name of cultural authenticity and difference. She was elected to Parliament in 2003. The Liberal Party relied on her to highlight, for native bourgeois voters, the struggle their party was waging against the laxity of the Social Democrats and its consequences in the Muslim community. But Ali's attacks on religion angered certain imams and their followers and led to many death threats, forcing her to surround herself with bodyguards and travel in a bullet-proof car. She feared that her former co-religionists would kill her as an apostate, on the grounds that anyone of Muslim origin was subject to the injunctions of Islamic law, even in the Netherlands. To those who saw her provocative attacks on religion as the source of her problems, she responded that the only way to disturb the complacency consensus of a society that tolerated human rights abuses in the name of multiculturalism (and its corollary, religious separatism) was to shock public debate. But Ali's assertive attitude reinforced the hostility of many of the very people she was trying to emancipate.

In 2003 the young deputy collaborated with Theo Van Gogh on an eleven-minute film for which she wrote the screenplay. Its title was *Submission*—one of the meanings of the word "Islam," which signifies submission to God's will. The film's message was to expose the brutal treatment of women under Islamic law. In one sequence of images, young Muslim women with veiled faces wore transparent garments revealing their naked bodies, which were overlaid with projections of Quranic verses in Arabic.[23] The voice-over denounced arranged marriages and conjugal violence, as the camera zoomed in on flesh bruised by blows or lacerated by flagellation. The film began with a recitation of the first verse of the Quran and ended with a prayer to God. Hardly a cinematic masterpiece, this juxtaposition of soft porn with militant anti-Islamic language was broadcast in August 2004 by Dutch television.

Immediately, the collaborators began receiving death threats, and on November 2 Van Gogh, who chose to ignore the danger, was killed in Amsterdam in broad daylight while riding his bicycle. He begged his assailant—a twenty-seven-year-old Muslim of Moroccan origin—to let him live, but Muhammad Bouyeri slit Van Gogh's throat with a knife and then used it to pin a five-page message to his victim's chest. It was addressed to Ayaan Hirsi Ali. Written in Dutch interspersed with Arabic citations from the Quran, the text accused Ali of apostasy and submission to the Jews who dominate the world—a perennial trope of Islamist discourse.[24] The fluency of the note indicated that its author was educated, and its lyricism revealed a sort of romantic fascination with "dear Miss Ayaan Hirsi Ali" whom he nevertheless condemned to death. This kind of personal engagement with a potential victim was unusual for jihadist literature, which is usually formulated in impersonal terms.

Bouyeri survived gunfire from police, but he had expected to die and carried on his person a brief last testament written in Arabic. Titled "Bloodsoaked," it justified his actions and expressed his desire to join the martyrs in paradise. Here, too, the very personal style suggested that the author conceived and executed his crime alone. This is what he told the court that condemned him to life in prison in July 2005.

On the night of the assassination, some Dutch citizens set fire to mosques and Quran schools, in an explosion of rage toward the Muslim community. Having been largely ignored for four decades in the name of multiculturalism, Muslims suddenly found themselves condemned as criminals by association because of the actions of a lone assassin. In the midst of this panic, a government minister even called for a "war of civilizations." Clearly, some kind of action on the part of civil authorities was called for, and very soon several members of a jihadist group that had been under surveillance for some time were arrested. Some of them, including an African American student who had converted to Islam, had thrown hand grenades at police. Thirteen people, most of whom were young men of Moroccan origin, described as the Hofstad group or network, were put on trial.

A few of the accused had been in contact with Bouyeri, and others had associated with suspects in the Casablanca attacks of May 2003 and the Madrid attacks of March 2004. Still others knew jihadist veterans of battles in Afghanistan and Pakistan. As early as January 2002, the deaths of two Dutch men of Moroccan origin in

Kashmir had indicated that Islamist radicals from the Netherlands were on the move toward global jihad fronts, although their numbers were much lower than those leaving Britain.[25] A link was even uncovered between the Hofstad network and Abu Musab al-Suri, who by the time of the trial had been captured and incarcerated in an undisclosed location. Ultimately, the harshest verdicts were handed down to those who had attacked the police or who possessed a weapon.[26] The trial, which ended in March 2006, did not succeed in linking Van Gogh's murder to an organized conspiracy.

Bouyeri's action was consistent with Suri's call for cells or individuals to act autonomously and to select high-visibility, accessible targets from civil society. As Suri anticipated, such actions precipitated anti-Muslim repression, which in turn raised up new volunteers for armed jihad and global Islamic resistance. Holland's self-satisfied multiculturalism was quickly replaced by general anxiety over the million or so people of Muslim origin in the country— around eight percent of the Dutch population. Decades of deliberate cultural ignorance were replaced practically overnight by a logic of confrontation, expressed in the electoral success of parties that made the struggle against Islamization their campaign platform. In Amsterdam, Rotterdam, and The Hague, middle-class residents had moved from downtown areas to the suburbs, and were replaced by greater numbers of impoverished immigrants. The Dutch press predicted that the country's three main cities would be predominantly Muslim within ten years. In November 2005, Frits Bolkestein, a former European commissioner, announced that he opposed universal direct suffrage in mayoral elections, for fear that Amsterdam would elect its first Muslim magistrate.[27] National identity was now at stake in this panic, and multiculturalism, once valued, had given way to fears of balkanization.

In a bid to reassure worried citizens and to capture volatile votes, the government chose to impose restrictive measures on immigration and to reinforce police controls. Ayaan Hirsi Ali herself was the most spectacular victim of these measures. A documentary broadcast in spring 2006 revealed that the deputy had lied about her family name and her birth date when she requested political asylum in the Netherlands in 1992.[28] For this offense, her colleague in the Liberal Party, Rita Verdonk, serving as minister of interior, announced that Ali would be stripped of her Dutch citizenship—as if the sacrifice of Ali would reestablish the social order that her provocative questions had disturbed. By trying to throw a provocative individual out of the country, the authorities hoped that the underlying causes of unrest would disappear—along with the more fundamental question of why the dysfunctions of the Dutch social system could be addressed only through provocation, as the activists of the 1960s had already shown. The international scandal triggered by the Dutch government's treatment of Ali led it to reverse its decision and give back her passport. In the meantime, however, she had left Holland for Washington, where in late 2006 she became a fellow of the American Enterprise Institute, one of the most influential neoconservative think tanks.

Dutch television channels, deprived of Ali's smiling face, replaced her with the charismatic Tariq Ramadan. The grandson of the Muslim Brotherhood's founder had just begun a two-year term at Erasmus University, named after a great humanist thinker of the sixteenth century who opposed the clerics' monopoly on thought, stood for emancipation of the critical mind, and helped to usher in the European Renaissance. Just as the British establishment had called on Ramadan to help repair its social fabric after the July 7, 2005, attacks—a mission that he ultimately called into question in harsh terms—the Dutch establishment called on him in 2007 to perform the same service in Holland after the ostracism of Ayaan Hirsi Ali. Ramadan held the chair in identity and citizenship, where his duties included teaching alongside well-known Dutch academics, contributing to public debate, and deploying his vision of Islam in Europe—all of this supported by the institutional weight of both the university and local political authorities.

The figures who supported Ramadan were not only the expected multiculturalism networks but also Rita Verdonk, the minister who had initially stripped Ali of her citizenship. As the most visible interlocutor between the Dutch political sphere and the Muslim community, Ramadan became the de facto head of an Islamic "pillar." The disturbing questions about social tolerance of human rights abuses that Ali had raised were pushed aside in an attempt to cobble together traditional pillarization under the aegis of the "jurisprudence of minorities." This framework encouraged Muslims living in the West to follow *sharia* except when it conflicted with the laws of their host countries. It relied on a concept, *wasatiyya*, that could be traced back to the Muslim Brotherhood— "centrism" between radical jihadism and secularism. Sheikh Qaradawi was its main proponent, and Tariq Ramadan was quickly becoming its best-known spokesman.

This concept of "minority Islamic law" aimed at bringing Muslim populations in the West together in a community regulated by religious teachings. It advocated reaching necessary compromises with European societies, until such time as the whole of Europe becomes Islamic, as Qaradawi fully expected it one day would and as the Byzantine Empire had been before it. Ramadan's project meshed quite well with the multiculturalists' vision in the Netherlands and Britain as far as means were concerned—though ends were quite another matter. Both Ramadan and the multiculturalists believed that populations of Muslim origin should be structured along community lines, which would maintain public order and social peace, in a double framework of *sharia* and secular law. It remains to be seen whether this ambiguity will thrust Dutch society back to the very same state that produced Muhammad Bouyeri.

From Multiculturalism to the War on Terror

By 2005, Holland's postmodern version of pillarization, which the Netherlands had hoped would both satisfy and silence its Muslim population, had led to the same impasse as the culture of dissociation through which Britain had hoped to keep Yorkshire youths out of Londonistan. These two multiculturalist approaches had created separate communities, one "native" and the other Muslim. The native community complacently ignored the Muslim community as long as the peace was not disturbed. Meanwhile, the Muslim community fell under the guidance of rigorist religious leaders for whom cultural integration with the host society was anathema—not least because it would mark the end of their own influence.

Once the failure of multiculturalism had been declared, the refusal to think about the need for integration and to apply policies that favored a community of interests above the expression of difference pushed the pendulum of dominant political discourse in the Netherlands and Britain toward the neoconservative grand narrative. Making terrorism the framework through which to interpret international relations and social upheaval in Europe, and making Islam the underlying cause of terror and threats to Western hegemony throughout the world, led to increased hostility toward Islamic civilization in public opinion. In the minds of many non-Muslim Europeans, Islam was reduced to the forms of extremism that had taken over its public expression—through spectacular martyrdom operations in Madrid and London, and through a high-profile murder and death threat in Amsterdam.

This was the troubled European context in which Danish caricatures of the Prophet Muhammad were published in September 2005.

CHAPTER FIVE

THE PROPAGANDA BATTLE IN EUROPE

With hindsight, most observers agree on the facts of the Danish caricature case. It all started when the author of a book about the Prophet, written for young adults, could not find an illustrator.[1] After the assassination of Theo Van Gogh, he wondered if the European literary community was imposing self-censorship in its conflict with "Islamist obscurantism." He shared this view with the chief editor of the cultural pages of the daily newspaper *Jyllands-Posten,* who tested the hypothesis by asking forty syndicated Danish cartoonists for drawings representing the Prophet. Twelve cartoonists responded, and their work was published in the newspaper's cultural section on September 30, 2005.

Some of the cartoons were rather neutral, while others presented the Prophet as inspiring the terrorism that had been making headlines during the previous four years. The most widely circulated drawing showed the Prophet wearing a turban shaped like a bomb on the verge of exploding. The caption accompanying it was the Muslim profession of faith: "There is no god but God and Muhammad is His messenger." Another showed him calling to the perpetrators of suicide attacks: "Stop! We've run out of virgins!" Like the lacerated female bodies onto which verses from the Quran were projected in Van Gogh's film *Submission,* these cartoons were an attempt to provoke viewers into thinking about the relation between violence, terrorism, and the foundational principles of Islam. But in the Muslim world at large the cartoons were perceived as a major offense.

The Danish caricature scandal took on global dimensions in a matter of months, as heads of Muslim states allied with Islamists in a public-relations campaign against Islamophobia. Even while waging their own battles against Islamist radicalism, these Muslim leaders had to accommodate the outrage of radicals in order to neutralize their message, which they were quickly spinning into the larger narrative of jihad through martyrdom. But when Iran's President Ahmadinejad emerged as the main beneficiary of the affair, Sunni states and movements dissociated themselves from the imbroglio. On the other side, the narrators of the war on terror seized the uproar as an opportunity to annex advocates of free expression to their cause. From George Bush to *Charlie Hebdo*—a left-leaning satirical French weekly—a motley coalition opposing "Islamist fanaticism" took shape around the unifying issue of free speech.

As a form of satiric representation, caricature assumes a degree of cultural complicity between artist and audience. But in the Danish case, the political cartoons came up against the complex system of taboos that apply to representations of the Prophet. Images that were intended for one kind of sympathetic consumer were projected, via the Internet, onto a world stage whose audience did not share the underlying assumptions of the satirist. And not surprisingly, various political entrepreneurs were quick to magnify this semantic misunderstanding according to their own interests.

But the words grew especially venomous because of deeper strains within Danish society—between rigorist imams, on one hand, who managed to express the disquiet felt by part of the Muslim population and, on the other hand, a political establishment that was forced to make concessions to the ruling right-wing Danish People's Party. Many representatives of the government took advantage of the scandal to reiterate their rejection of a "multiethnic society," which they saw as a major threat to national identity and to the prosperity of a country with only 5.4 million inhabitants, of whom approximately 450,000 (8.4 percent) were immigrants or descendents of immigrants, and 200,000 of these immigrants were Muslims.[2]

In the Kingdom of Denmark

Unlike the Dutch pillarization system, which arose from the need for coexistence between Protestants, Catholics, and Jews, Denmark's social structure reflected the near-absolute dominance of the Protestant Lutheran Church. Religious homogeneity encouraged a deep-seated feeling of national identity that persisted over the course of the twentieth century despite growing secularization. Danish nationalism was further reinforced by territorial losses that had reduced the nation-state to the Jutland peninsula and a clutch of islands separating the Baltic from the North Sea. As recently as 1978, the kingdom of Denmark, which had once reigned over Iceland, Scandinavia, Germany, and England, was pressured into granting home rule to Greenland. Anxiety about the country's territorial losses was counterbalanced by a very strong sense of social solidarity, which in turn generated the ideology of the welfare state. In providing a broad social safety net for its residents, Denmark joined the company of the Netherlands and other northern European countries.

In the decades following World War II, the Danish government, led by a Social Democratic party until 2001, had made the importation of cheap labor easy, especially workers from Turkey and Pakistan. Later on, a generous policy of political asylum attracted many refugees fleeing the crisis in the Middle East. Palestinians, Lebanese, Iraqis, Iranians, Egyptians, Somalis, and Afghans were among the immigrants who settled in Denmark. In the mid-1990s, Talaat Fouad Qasem—one of the main leaders in exile of Egyptian Gamaa al-Islamiyya and a close associate of Ayman al-Zawahiri—worked out of Copenhagen, where he was in touch with some of the imams who would organize opposition to the caricatures of the Prophet ten years later. The blind Egyptian cleric Omar Abdel-Rahman, leader of the Gamaa who was later handed a life sentence in the United States for master-minding the first attack on the World Trade Center in 1993, made Denmark his European platform. During that decade, an influx of refugees, many of whom depended on the state welfare system for their survival, quickly saturated government-subsidized housing projects and formed ghettoes on the outskirts of big cities.[3]

A growing number of "native" Danes began to express anger that their taxes were being swallowed up by a population with a high rate of unemployment, low productivity, and questionable political activities. Unlike the Netherlands or Britain, where the logic of multiculturalism created a separate space for minority groups, Denmark preached assimilation, but it was very difficult to blend so many different kinds of newcomers into a small, mono-ethnic host society with no secular tradition of integration. In the decade before 9/11, growing social unease in one of the richest, if smallest, countries in Europe led the ruling Social Democrats to restrict the right of asylum, make the reunion of immigrant families more difficult, and limit the amount of social assistance available to noncitizens. These measures earned the Danish government criticism from several think tanks in the European Union, while articles in the European press described Denmark as xeno-phobic.[4]

Some Social Democrats focused particularly on the presence of Muslims, who were accused of subscribing to values that perpetuated "otherness" and prevented assimilation. Disagreements flared, and the Danish police responded by cracking down on young people belonging to ethnic minorities. This repression made public life more difficult for Muslim elites who were playing by institutional rules—such as deputies and leaders of associations—and much easier for Islamist imams who claimed that Muslim youths were being discriminated against because of their religious beliefs. The parliamentary elections of November 20, 2001, held in an atmosphere of crisis caused by the 9/11 attacks, brought a right-wing coalition to power. It strengthened legislation against foreigners and gave the police new anti-terrorist powers. The Danish People's Party, an extreme right-wing group, made considerable gains. Its parliamentarians—thirteen percent of the total—voted to strengthen the law further, making it the most restrictive in Europe with respect to naturalization and family reunion.

The March 2004 attacks in Madrid, and especially the assassination of Theo Van Gogh in nearby Holland the following November, struck an even deeper chord of fear and distrust in the Danish population. A number of Danes began to think of Muslims as religious fanatics who abused political asylum, engaged in nefarious activities such as drug trafficking, and sometimes conspired to commit heinous crimes. Young Muslims, many of whom already felt marginalized, stigmatized, and harassed by police, were described as "cancerous tumors" by a right-wing party leader who was keen to prevent "metastases."[5]

In this poisonous atmosphere, a small group of imams managed to trigger a global scandal on the basis of a dozen cartoons of the Prophet Muhammad published on September 30, 2005, in a respected center-right daily, the *Jyllands-Posten,* the most widely read newspaper in Denmark. Fairly mediocre as political satire, the Danish caricatures, in keeping with the genre, used exaggeration to emphasize a question that puzzled the Western public: could the assassination of civilians—innocent bystanders who were in a sense hostages to a political conflict beyond their control—be attributed to the doctrines of Islam?

According to Zawahiri, Suri, and company, such a question was wrongheaded from the start, because there *are* no innocent civilians. Islam recognizes only combatants and noncombatants. But every Western taxpayer, including foreign residents, is a de facto Zionist-crusader combatant from the moment they give money to the government. And each eligible voter is an accessory to the crimes committed by his country's army during the invasion and occupation of Afghanistan, Palestine, Kashmir, Iraq, and so on. All financial or diplomatic relations with the United States, Israel, or

India constitute an alliance or form of connivance. The few "legal innocents" (such as children) killed in attacks on Western territory are collateral damage for which jihadists take no responsibility.

Extremists like Zawahiri based their arguments on a literal, noncontextual interpretation of selected Quranic verses as well as a wide range of prophetic sayings, some of which are considered "weak" (or unauthentic) by the majority of commentators. But many moderate, modern Muslims interpreted these same sacred texts as allegories, and contextualized them in order to reject their wholesale application to the present-day world. They denounced those who use the Prophet or the Quran to legitimize killing innocent people, claiming that they do not represent Islam. However, these contemporary-minded Muslims also took into account their community's deep resentment against Israeli policies in Palestine, and U.S. and British policies in Iraq. They recognized widespread support for the spirit and actions of the resistance. Moderate Muslims became accustomed to taking up positions near the center of the political spectrum, making sure that their critique of jihadists did not come across as an apology for the West and its misdeeds.

The narrow space these moderates carved out was gradually taken over by preachers like Sheikh Qaradawi, who, on the basis of verses from the Quran, justified martyrdom operations in Israel and Iraq as "legitimate resistance" but condemned the 9/11 attacks. Other more radical preachers, imams, and jurists to whom the Internet granted a global audience extended Qaradawi's premise to attacks on civilians in the United States and Europe, and also to attacks against Muslims accused of apostasy or heresy, whether they lived in Muslim or non-Muslim countries.

Much of the non-Muslim European public was troubled by the

multiple responses of Islamic voices on the issue of terrorism, and this frustration is what the Danish cartoons targeted. But many moderate Muslims in Europe, along with other non-Muslims in the West, saw the situation differently. For them, satirizing the Prophet reduced Islam to the image that extremists display of it. The satirists cast themselves as dangerous Islamophobes, because they gave the impression that Europe and the West insulted the Prophet and blasphemed the sacred texts. There was no better rec-ipe for pushing the Muslim masses into the arms of the radicals.

The Danish caricatures put Muslim leaders of states allied with the West in a particularly delicate position, while providing an op-portunity for extremists to stir up more trouble. To prevent their Islamist opposition from taking over the protest movement and transforming it into anti-regime uprisings, the leaders of West-leaning Muslim nations had to join the protest in order to con-tain it. This strategy was successful in the Sunni world. Neither Al Qaeda nor its sympathizers were able to mobilize activists by de-crying the cartoons. In his video-taped declarations at the time, Zawahiri gave the affair hardly any attention. Iran, on the other hand, saw an advantage in channeling the anger of the Muslim masses against the West at a time when tensions were rising over questions of nuclear energy. In response to the Danish caricatures, Ahmadinejad organized a competition for the best cartoon on the Holocaust, thereby proclaiming himself the hero and champion of a humiliated and offended Muslim community.[6] This strategy echoed that of Khomeini in issuing a *fatwa* calling for the execu-tion of Salman Rushdie on February 15, 1989, for the publication of the *Satanic Verses*.

Prior to publication of the cartoons, the *Jyllands-Posten* had translated and published a few radical sermons preached in a mosque in a poor quarter of the city of Aarhus. The newspaper revealed that the imam who gave the sermon, a Sunni Lebanese from Tripoli, Raid Hlayhel, had sought and received asylum in Denmark, and Danish taxpayers were paying for his gravely ill child to receive medical treatment. Nonetheless, every Friday this imam lambasted the West and Denmark in particular for their unbelief and their policies toward Muslims.

With animosity running high on both sides, an ad hoc Committee for the Defense of the Prophet Muhammad denounced the publication of the cartoons as a deliberate insult to Islam and organized a demonstration of several thousand people. The protest was led by three imams: Hlayhel, the Lebanese from Aarhus, who identified himself as "a graduate of the Islamic University of Medina," an institution where Muslim Brothers are influential; another imam of Lebanese origin, naturalized in Denmark a few months before; and the main figure serving on this committee, Ahmed Abu Laban. A Palestinian born two years before the creation of Israel, Abu Laban was brought up in Egypt, where he studied for a degree in chemical engineering and sympathized with the Muslim Brotherhood. He worked as an engineer while pursuing political and religious activities, then moved to the United Arab Emirates. But his proselytizing aroused suspicion in both of his adoptive countries, and he was no longer welcome in either. In 1984, thanks to help from a Dane who had converted to Islam, he arrived in Denmark as a refugee fleeing oppression by Middle Eastern states and became part of an Islamist circle that had made Copenhagen a modest appendix to Londonistan. In the years before the Internet came into wide use, the Gamaa Islamiyya periodical *Al-Mujahidun* had

Abu Laban's mosque as its address, and the exiled Egyptian group's emir, Omar Abdel-Rahman, was hosted there.

During the turbulent 1990s, Islamist refugees living off social welfare were under suspicion from the press and some politicians. Still, the Danish administration continued to welcome Abu Laban. In 2004 he was the keynote speaker at a public conference on the struggle against Islamist extremism organized by Danish intelligence, where the affable sixty-year-old was perceived as a bulwark against fundamentalism, the necessary mediator between the police and sensitive groups. On the front lines against the *Jyllands-Posten* in the cartoon scandal, he took the initiative of contacting the Egyptian ambassador in Copenhagen. The ambassador, in turn—representing the concerns of her colleagues in the Muslim world—requested an interview with the prime minister to protest the publication of the cartoons. But she was turned away by the authorities, who claimed that the government had no right to interfere in the press's freedom of expression.

When indignation about the cartoons began to boil up in the Middle East and Pakistan, the ambassador arranged for a group of imams from Denmark to visit Cairo. Abu Laban was still banned from entering Egypt, so the delegation was headed by his colleague, Hlayhel. He put together a forty-three-page paper in Arabic, photocopied in color and titled "To the Rescue of the Prophet Muhammad, May God's Blessings Be upon Him." The paper began with a brief presentation about Denmark—a country the author assumed most of his readers did not know—which included the fact that the cross appears on the national flag, and the claim that Muslims are regularly persecuted there. Hlayhel then reproduced the condemned cartoons, along with others from a different newspaper and a few images from the Internet. The most offensive image showed a man with a snout and pig's ears and was titled "This is the real picture of Muhammad." The caricature had been taken from a pig-calling competition held in a French village and had nothing to do with Islam or its prophet. As tensions mounted, the official religious authorities in Egypt and the Arab League took over the campaign to express Muslim indignation worldwide.

In late 2005 and early 2006, legislative elections were held in Egypt. The Muslim Brothers were expected to win in the districts where the government allowed them to run, and the ruling party, whom the Brothers accused of unbelief, was determined to take advantage of this opportunity to present itself as the strongest defender of Islam. But no one was able to control the chain reaction that had been set off throughout the Muslim world. Demonstrations were organized by Islamist movements and broadcast by Al Jazeera. Blogs, Internet forums, and the Arab press sent a message, in unison, that the offense to Islam was recognized and shared by all, governments and Islamists alike, and that major issues were at stake that the public could not afford to ignore. Even Günter Grass, the German novelist and Nobel laureate, testified that the Danish cartoons were the work of extreme right-wing Islamophobes.[7] Red flags bearing white crosses went up in flames.

Passions burned hottest in Palestine. Hamas's victory in the parliamentary elections on January 25, 2006, had enflamed opposition to Hamas in Israel, the United States, and the European Union (which provided a large portion of the Palestinian Authority's budget): they had refused to confer legitimacy on a party that neither rejected violence nor recognized Israel—even though it had won election in a democratic poll. That led to a high state of tension, and resentment against Denmark, an E.U. member state, was an adequate outlet.

On Friday, February 3, the day of collective prayers and the weekly sermon, preachers in Palestine mobilized the faithful against the offense to the Prophet; the headquarters of the European delegation in Gaza were attacked and demonstrations and marches were held elsewhere—all broadcast by Al Jazeera. Muslims and others asked Europe and the West how they dared to question the legitimacy of a democratically elected majority in the Palestinian parliament while using the pretext of another democratic value, freedom of speech, to insult the most sacred figure in all of Islam? In the minds of these critics, the West was cherry-picking its democratic values according to its own political and economic advantage.

In contrast with the Rushdie novel—a difficult text, the denunciation of which had depended on second-hand interpretations—the cartoons' message was immediate and accessible on the Internet. The caricatures easily reached, and shocked, millions of Muslims around the world. Speaking from Qatar, Sheikh Qaradawi declared February 3 a Day of Rage for the "billion and a half Muslims in the world," announcing: "We are not a community of jack-asses, which anyone may mount as he pleases, but a community of lions who . . . take revenge for affronts to their sacred values." Qaradawi expressed indignation at the "double standards" applied to freedom of the press in the West, noting that it was admissible to insult the Prophet of Islam but not to express doubts that the Holocaust had happened, as the condemnation of Roger Garaudy in the French courts had made clear.

Qaradawi reminded his international audience that King Faysal of Saudi Arabia justified the oil embargo in October 1973 by explaining that he was defending Arab honor and could live without Western goods. The sheikh called on Muslims to defend the honor of Islam once again, by purchasing Asian instead of Western products. A campaign to boycott Danish goods was launched, despite the long tradition of *halal* certification borne by meat and milk exports from Denmark. Websites took up the banner of the Arab boycott of Israeli goods and specialized in identifying Danish products, from Lurpak butter to Lego, while supermarkets took out full-page newspaper advertisements to inform consumers that they did not sell Danish goods.

The Arabic-language site www.no4denmark.com organized a competition to defend the Prophet. The winner would receive 100,000 Saudi riyals. "The Danish prime minister calls demonstrators extremists! Bush calls on Muslims to be silent! The drama of oppression and insults to Muslims in Europe continues! We must express our freedom of opinion just as they express theirs," was the banner above the slogan that won the competitions: "I boycott therefore I am." A website for the "popular boycott network," which denounced "slandering the prophet" (*sabb al-nabi*, an expression that was widely used at the time of the Rushdie affair), took advantage of the crisis to remind visitors that Coca Cola and Pepsi "give the Zionists $4.6 billion a year," while another demanded that "the queen of Denmark apologize to the Prophet and Muslims" and that the Danish government "promise the incident will not be repeated."

After his trip to Cairo, Raid Hlayhel went to his homeland of Lebanon, where he brought the Shiite pro-Syrian foreign minister on board. Then he traveled to Damascus. At that time, the international community, as well as a U.N. special investigator, was look-ing into the assassination of Lebanese Prime Minister Rafiq Hariri, and the Syrian government was under suspicion. After the assassi-nation, the Hariri family—as the influential leaders of the Leba-nese Sunni community—took the reins of the Fourteenth March Movement, which opposed the Syrian occupation of Lebanon. But back in Damascus, the ruling Alawite minority had been listening carefully to the Sunni imam of Aarhus, and they recognized the advantage of representing themselves as the Prophet's most ardent defenders in Lebanon.

This put the Hariri family and their followers in a difficult posi-tion, because of their close relations with European (and especially French) individuals and institutions. By then, Parisian newspapers had also published the twelve cartoons. The low-circulation tab-loid daily *France Soir* put them on its front page on February 1. The newspaper's owner, a French-Egyptian Copt named Raymond Lakah, promptly fired the editor-in-chief and published a com-muniqué in which he stated that he rejected such blasphemy. But when the satirical weekly *Charlie Hebdo* did the same in a special edition on February 8, it sold half a million copies, prompting the French Council on the Muslim faith to take the paper to court. Meanwhile, a government spokesman called for a responsible exer-cise of freedom of expression, since President Chirac was making a state visit to Saudi Arabia the following month. But the French government's prudence, and the refusal by most British news-papers—still smarting from the memory of the Rushdie affair in 1989—to publish the cartoons (a decision followed by most U.S. newspapers) had no effect on the actions of Syria and its ally, Iran.

A huge demonstration was organized in Damascus, a city where uncontrolled crowds were not normally allowed to congregate and move around. The demonstrators burned the Danish embassy on Saturday, February 4, the day after Sheikh Qaradawi's Day of Rage. Next, the crowd attacked the French embassy, either because *France Soir* had published the cartoons or because Syria was generally hostile to the Chirac government, which was very critical of Syrian policy in Lebanon. In Beirut, another demonstration organized by Sunni Islamist groups on February 5 attacked the Danish diplomatic chancery, in the Christian neighborhood of Ashrafiyyeh— the first violation of Christian territory by a non-Christian mob since the end of the war. The Lebanese government attributed this threatening signal to "Syrian elements," although it had proof of participation by Lebanese Sunni Islamists. In Tehran the following day, "spontaneous" demonstrations were limited to stones lobbed against the walls of the Danish embassy, while a few protestors scaled its gates—perhaps a reminder of the hostage-taking operation carried out against the U.S. embassy in November 1979.

By this point most Arab leaders were worried that the protest over the cartoons had reached unmanageable proportions, and they were searching for a way out. The Saudi foreign ministry convinced the Danish prime minister to express his regrets on the Al Arabiyya television channel. And then President Ahmadinejad announced that Iran was organizing a competition for the best cartoon on the Holocaust. This surprise move accomplished two important goals for Iran. By posing as a champion of a popular Arab and Islamic cause, the Shiite president gained a political advantage against Sunni leaders, who had come across as lukewarm. And at a time when Tehran was being condemned by the international community for resuming uranium enrichment activities at its nuclear power plants, Ahmadinejad turned the spotlight of world opinion back on the misdeeds of the West. He seemed to be suggesting that Europe hardly had the right to make grand speeches in the name of great moral principles at a time when it was insulting the Prophet and causing the entire Muslim community to suffer.

From that point on, the cartoon affair, like the Rushdie affair before it, became a pawn in the struggle between Sunnis and Shiites for global dominance within Islam. By early 2006 many in the Sunni world were convinced that the Shiite majority in Iraq wanted to join its co-religionists in Iran, Lebanon, and Syria in creating a Shiite axis that would take control of the Gulf and its oil wealth.

With the aim of firing off a final salvo that would put an end to the Dutch cartoon affair, various Sunni Islamic associations organized an International Conference in Defense of the Prophet Muhammad on March 22 and 23, 2006. It took place at the initiative of several parties, particularly two websites: Islam Online, headed by Qaradawi, and Al-Islam Al-Yawm (Islam Today), headed by Sheikh Salman al-Awda, a former Islamist dissident co-opted by the Saudi leadership. Qaradawi, with links to the Muslim Brotherhood, and Awda, with strong non-jihadist salafist credentials, were the two principal spokesmen of moderate Islamism.

The conference was held in Bahrain, an island nation in the middle of the Gulf. With its Shiite-majority population and a reigning family of Sunnis, Bahrain provided an appropriate setting for Qaradawi to announce the creation of an International Organization for the Defense of the Prophet. This organization's aim was to implement a "civilized" mode of protest against attacks on the Prophet's person or his teachings. It would not encourage demonstrations but would carry out an economic boycott and foster a renewal of preaching activities aimed at guiding Europeans out of error and toward Islam. On that occasion, a Moroccan visitor to the Islam Online website asked whether anger or demonstrations were the best response to attacks on the Prophet; she was told that neither of these reactions was advantageous to the propagation of Islam. Only "correct preaching [would] offer salvation from unbelief and error." The tumult surrounding the caricatures simply demonstrated that "the world today, especially in Europe and America, has abandoned religions that deviated from the right path, and needs a religion that will save it from modern error. There is none but Islam."[8]

Imams from Denmark traveled to the conference in Bahrain, but the organizers did not highlight their presence. In Copenhagen, a French-Algerian anti-Islamist journalist had posed as a radical sympathizer and had filmed them with a hidden camera.[9] In his documentary, which was broadcast on European television while the imams were at the conference, they rejoiced at having made Denmark bend to their will. They expressed their hope for the death of a secular Muslim parliamentarian and evoked a suicide attack. Ultimately, the imams were forced to publish embarrassed denials. In any case, the time for war on the West was past. It was now time to mitigate the Shiite offensive, which had taken over mobilization in defense of the Prophet and was using it to further its peculiar agenda against Sunni interests in the region.

And with that, the fire finally went out. Abu Laban returned to Denmark, where he continued to enjoy political asylum. He spent the following year presenting himself as a man of good faith who wished only to repair Denmark's reputation; tragically, he died of cancer in February 2007. As for Hlayhel, he went back to his native Lebanon, to a suburb of Tripoli on the fringes of the Palestinian camp of Nahr al-Bared, where he continued to preach against the pro-Western leaders of the Sunni community who ruled the country from Beirut. And in Copenhagen, the small mermaid that guards the entryway to the harbor was covered in an Islamic veil for a few hours on May 20, 2007—maybe an ironic reminder of a local affair that ignited a global firestorm.

Rome and Constantinople

On September 12, 2006, Pope Benedict XVI delivered an important lecture at the University of Regensburg in Bavaria, entitled "Faith, Reason and the University: Memories and Reflections."[10] The event occurred five years and a day after the attacks on New York and Washington, and 323 years to the day after Christians triumphed over the Ottoman army that was besieging Vienna. This event put an end to jihad expansion in Europe and signaled the start of the Ottoman Empire's inexorable decline.

In a delivery reminiscent of his years as a young professor of theology at Regensburg, where he had been known as Joseph Ratzinger, the pope spoke as an intellectual accustomed to the probing give and take of academic discourse. His lecture displayed the sharp and uncompromising mind that had served him well as prefect of the Congregation for the Doctrine of the Faith under his predecessor, John Paul II. The theme of the lecture was the importance of reason in faith, and the necessity for theology to open itself up to reason as the framework for cultural dialogue. Abandoning the diplomatic caution normally exhibited by the

Supreme Pontiff (which he had become only the previous year), Benedict—in the course of making his argument—quoted a polemic against the Prophet Muhammad written by the "erudite Byzantine emperor Manuel II Paleologus" in the fourteenth century.

Having barely recovered from the injuries of the Danish cartoons, and having endured a summer war between Israel and Hezbollah, along with nuclear threats from Ahmadinejad, the Muslim world found itself reeling once again from an insult to the Prophet. "The pope's statements are more of an offense to Islam than the cartoons were, for they emanate from a leader who represents millions of people, and not from a simple journalist," declared one of the figures of the Egyptian Muslim Brotherhood, Abdel-Moneim Abul-Futuh. He predicted an "extreme reaction," which would not come from the region's governments in their attempt to pressure Europe but would be "spontaneous and popular."[11]

And indeed, on September 15, after prayers, demonstrators set fire to churches in Gaza, the West Bank, and Iraq—focal points in the conflict with Israel and the United States. This motivated a number of eastern Christians to leave the cradle of Christianity and join their co-religionists elsewhere. Two days later, an Italian nun was killed in Somalia, and effigies of the pope were burned in public squares in Iran. The Mujahedin Council of Iraq, created by Zarqawi, called on Muslims to "break the cross and spill the wine" and repeated the Prophet's prediction that God would help Muslims "conquer Rome" after vanquishing Constantinople.[12]

Hostile declarations and demonstrations spread from the Maghreb to Indonesia. Morocco recalled its ambassador to the

Holy See, and the Egyptian government summoned the apostolic nuncio. Middle Eastern governments asked the Vatican to explain the pope's remarks, and in response the Holy See issued effusive apologies and explanations, denying that the pope had any intention of offending Muslims. Benedict himself made soothing statements to the ambassadors of all the Muslim countries who gathered at his summer residence in Castelgandolfo on September 25.

Nevertheless, Zawahiri called the pope a liar in a declaration posted on the Internet the following day.[13] Al Qaeda's ideologue saw the "pope's insults to the Prophet" as the most recent in a long series of humiliations inflicted on Islam in Europe, from the Rushdie affair to the offensive cartoons and the prohibition on headscarves in France. On October 15, thirty-eight *ulema* from twenty-five different countries signed a letter to the pope, in which they refuted his allegations regarding Islam "in a spirit of exchange and openness." These *ulema* were part of a moderate Islamist trend generally co-opted by the leaders of their respective countries, whose task would be to calm the waters.

In late November, the man who had spoken out against Turkey's entry into the European Union when he was merely Cardinal Ratzinger made a high-tension trip to Istanbul, finally responding to an old invitation extended by the Orthodox patriarch. He was received by the "moderate Islamist" prime minister Tayyip Erdogan with a minimum of protocol. Some radical Islamists organized hostile demonstrations, which Zawahiri extolled. In ancient Constantinople, as the Ottoman armies under Bayazid laid siege to the city between 1394 and 1402, the Emperor Manuel had written the sentences that could still incense the Muslim world six centuries later. In modern Istanbul, the successor to Saint Peter visited the Blue Mosque and reflected, turned toward Mecca.

Any public declaration made by the pope becomes a political fact the moment it is made, whatever its author's subjective intention may have been. The Holy Father's words are weightier than anything Cardinal Ratzinger might have said, and this includes quoting a sentence penned by a Byzantine emperor at the turn of the fifteenth century. Benedict's lecture has been discussed at length by partisans of every persuasion. Yet whether they rejoiced that a pope had finally stood up to Islam, deplored his radicalism and lack of prudence, or condemned him for having insulted the Prophet, most of these polemicists were unfamiliar with the content and context of his words.

"Show me just what Muhammad brought that was new, and there you will find things only evil and inhuman, such as his command to spread by the sword the faith he preached."[14] This is the sentence written by Manuel Paleologus that Pope Benedict XVI quoted. Although the pope briefly described the context in which the statement had been formulated and noted that the statement was "abrupt," it came from the pope's mouth, and that is what triggered the scandal. In the annotated version of the speech posted online by the Vatican on October 6, 2006, the pope, after mentioning the source of the excerpt, explained in a note: "In the Muslim world, this quotation has unfortunately been taken as an expression of my personal position, thus arousing understandable indignation. I hope that the reader of my text can see immediately that this sentence does not express my personal view of the Quran, for which I have the respect due to the holy book of a great religion.

In quoting the text of the Emperor Manuel II, I intended solely to draw out the essential relationship between faith and reason. On this point I am in agreement with Manuel II, but without endorsing his polemic."[15]

Manuel uttered his sentence in the course of a closely regulated debate with a Persian teacher originally from Baghdad who had arrived in Ancyre (now Ankara), Anatolia, shortly before. Though Manuel was the heir to the formerly prestigious throne of Byzantium—he would succeed his father as emperor in February 1391—he was in reality no more than a vassal of Bayazid, forced to accompany the Ottoman sultan on his military campaigns and on the hunting parties he organized in his winter quarters. The Constantinople that Manuel would eventually rule preserved only the memory of empire: its territory was reduced to the city and a few European possessions.

In the winter of 1390 or 1391, Ancyre was under the yoke of a Muslim power which allowed theological controversy to flourish among men of good company and all faiths. A true renaissance in philosophical thought was moving among some of the best minds in the Byzantine Empire. These men attempted to shake the millenarian city's intellectual and religious sclerosis, but in vain, and too late: soon, it would pass under Ottoman domination. Manuel was close to this last thrust of Greek spirit, of which the Platonic philosopher Gemisthus Plethon and his disciple, later Cardinal Bessarion, were the most remarkable representatives, seeking the path to salvation through the ancient city's revival and a closer relation with Roman Christianity. Manuel's mode of argument, in debate with his Muslim adversary, appealed first to reason, which emerged from Greek philosophy and which he placed in the service of revealed faith. Through reason, he attempted to convince the Persian that his beliefs were superior.

In countering Manuel's arguments, his interlocutor also presented arguments that were grounded more in logic than in religious authority. The erudite Persian did not reply directly to Manuel's question about the propagation of Islam by the sword. Rather, he compared all of Islamic law (*sharia*) to Christian law, pointing out the absurdity of such practices as celibacy and virginity, which would lead to the disappearance of the human race, and forgiveness of one's enemies, which would allow them to fight another day. The Persian deduced that Islam's rational legislation was preferable, because it provided a golden mean between the extremes of the Jewish legal system ("eye for eye, tooth for tooth") and the Christian legal system ("whosoever shall smite thee on thy right cheek, turn to him the other also").

The pope did not mention this fine point about the golden mean when he quoted Manuel's side of the debate. The point he wished to make—following Manuel's argument—was this: "Not to act in accordance with reason is contrary to God's nature." Jihad, because it relies on physical combat to compel men to adopt Islam, is irrational. Faith is a matter for the soul, and therefore is in the realm of conviction, not of violence. "To act in accordance with reason," according to the pope's speech, was characteristic of Christianity alone. This was the only religion that merged Greek philosophical inquiry with Biblical faith. "This convergence, with the subsequent addition of the Roman heritage, created Europe and remains the foundation of what can rightly be called Europe."

After asserting that the basis of all reason was Greek philosophy and then placing Islam beyond the realm of reason, the pope expressed his view that the Church has faced three stages of "dehellenization" which threaten its rational foundation: Protestant reform in the sixteenth century, which sought to return to Scripture as the sole authority, abandoning the role of reason in interpreting the Word; liberal theology in the nineteenth and twentieth centuries, which reduced questions of doctrine and ethics to the subjective judgments of believers, without the learned guidance of the established Church; and cultural pluralism, which, today, seeks to allow each culture to adapt the Scriptures to its own contemporary circumstances. For the pope, Greek rationalism is the very root of Christianity for the simple reason that the New Testament was originally written in Greek. No one can claim to follow the teachings of Christ, or to put faith in him, without making a journey through Hellenic reason. That Christian faith cannot be dissociated from reason is what the beginning of the Gospel according to John illustrates: "In the beginning was *logos*," the Word, which the pope translated as "reason."

Today, the pope sadly observed, "it is widely held that only positivistic reason and the forms of philosophy based on it are universally valid. Yet the world's profoundly religious cultures see this exclusion of the divine from the universality of reason as an attack on their most profound convictions." Secular philosophy cannot lead society to the kind of dialogue it so desperately requires, because the message of positivism and secularism cannot be heard by "the world's profoundly religious cultures." The Catholic Church is the only institution that can carry on a living dialogue between reason and faith.

This lesson falls squarely within the doctrine of the faith that

Cardinal Ratzinger vigorously defended before his elevation to pope. Critiques of Protestantism, positivism, and globalization run throughout his work and have earned him the enthusiastic support of devout Catholics who wish to see the Church's identity reaffirmed in a world marked by the relativism of values, just as they have met with the disapproval of believers for whom love of one's fellow humans seems more important than the defense of religious institutions—even if that means diluting these institutions. The lecture at Regensburg strongly reiterated the pope's defense of the Catholic Church and stated the fundamental philosophical position from which he intended to lead the debate with Islam.

The fact that the pope made this speech just one day after the fifth anniversary of the 9/11 attacks and exactly on the 323rd anniversary of the Ottoman defeat at Vienna was not a coincidence. He called upon the figure of Manuel II to speak the words about faith and reason that, for diplomatic reasons, the pope could not utter himself. All of the evidence suggests that the sentence the pope quoted did indeed express his own view of Islam, the Vatican's justifications and denials notwithstanding.

In any case, Muslim critics took it literally. Manuel described Christianity at a time when it had been defeated by jihad. He was a vassal when the dialogue took place, and by the time the transcript was written down Constantinople was under siege. The jihad that the emperor condemned, and which later destroyed Byzantium, served as a historical metaphor in the 2006 speech at Regensburg— a foreshadowing of the jihad that would lead to attacks on Spain and Britain in the third millennium. Indeed, this is what Zawahiri and company gloated about. The pope's message was that contemporary Europe had to take up that impetus of resistance once again. By introducing the reference to the Prophet into his speech through the theme of jihad and violence, the pope was of course addressing a topic that concerned many Europeans in 2006—be they Catholics, Christians, nonbelievers, or even Muslims—who feared they might one day be victims of a "martyrdom operation" in a metro, train, or airport.

Pope Benedict XVI also indulged in a small lesson in islamology, using as his source the words of two Christian Arabists.[16] According to the pope, Manuel knew of the verse in the Quran that stipulates: "There is no compulsion in religion" (II, 256). But he also knew that this verse, which dates from the earliest period of revelation, was abrogated by other verses (revealed at a later date) which commanded Muslims not only to fight Jews and Christians until they paid tribute and submitted (IX, 5) but also to kill "associators" (*mushrikin*; IX, 29), a term that designated pagans and polytheists who worshipped other gods in addition to the God of the monotheists. But for contemporary radical Islamists and their predecessors throughout history, Christians fall into the category of polytheists because they "associate" the Holy Spirit and Jesus to God as part of the Holy Trinity.

A reply to the pope was signed and published on October 15, 2006, by thirty-eight moderate Islamist theologians and a few members of mystical brotherhoods—scholars who were generally close to their respective governments, and some of whom engaged in preaching in European countries.[17] Neither Sheikh Qaradawi nor any of his many centrist disciples were on the list. None of the signatories were former Saudi dissidents associated with Salman al-Awda's website Al-Islam Al-Yawm, and there were no high-ranking members of the Muslim Brotherhood. And of course the names of jihadists and religious rigorists who opposed any dialogue with "Benedict the Charlatan" (*dajjal,* a term that also signifies "the Antichrist") were absent.

Those who signed the reply represented a trend within contemporary Islamic institutions that aims to preserve a nonconfrontational line with the Christian Church, on the assumption that Muslims will derive more benefits than disadvantages from an interfaith dialogue. These men have allied with the pope in his fight against atheism, and the very first lines of their reply pay homage to Benedict's efforts to oppose "the hegemony of positivism and materialism on the lives of individuals." In other words, the *ulema* wished to make clear that their protest flowed from *inside* a shared alliance with Christian clerics in opposing secularism. And like the Persian man of letters who responded to Manuel's statements, they built their arguments on deductive logic, not on authoritative quotations taken from sacred texts, as other Muslim theologians might have done.

The scholars who signed this declaration began by contesting the pope's claim that the verse "There is no compulsion in religion" was revealed early on and then abrogated at a later date. They cited other, later verses with a similar meaning, arguing that this verse constituted Islamic doctrine on the topic. This position could not have been taken by jihadists, nor even by centrist ideologues or the Muslim Brothers. They had all read classical texts by the theologian Ibn Kathir (1300–1373), a slightly older contemporary of Manuel Paleologus, who is cited abundantly in all their texts and declarations and featured in most curricula in madrasas and Islamic universities of the Sunni world. In his exegesis of the Quran, Ibn

Kathir writes that the verse "no compulsion in religion" is abrogated by the verse "on war," which calls on all nations to enter Islam: "Fight those who believe not in God nor the Last Day, nor hold that forbidden which has been forbidden by God and His Messenger, nor acknowledge the religion of Truth, [even if they are] of the People of the Book, until they pay the *jizya* [tribute] with willing submission, and feel themselves subdued" (IX, 29).[18]

The line of reasoning followed by the clerics who signed the letter to the pope, and who contradicted Ibn Kathir, although they did not say so, was their own point of view. This is indeed one of the main difficulties of interfaith dialogue: who is qualified to interpret sacred texts and speak in the name of Islam? The signatories registered their opinion that the "specialists" the pope referred to in his interpretation of Islam were not the slightest bit qualified to speak for the faith. These orientalist academics had misunderstood Islamic doctrine, and only the *ulema* themselves were qualified exegetes.

The thirty-eight clerics reminded their readers that Christianity, whose founder declared "I did not come to bring peace, but a sword," was hardly exempt from violence. Indeed, the history of Christianity abounds in atrocities, from the Crusades to colonization. Islamic law, by contrast, spares noncombatants from violence (though in practice this category was often reduced by contemporary jihadists to a bare minimum that does not include civilians in Israel, Iraq, India, Europe, or the United States). The text ended with homage to Pope John Paul II, who had never allowed himself to comment on Islam. But the clerics acknowledged and accepted the regrets expressed by the Vatican and by Pope Benedict XVI, whom they courteously invited to abandon his intellectual ambitions—a holdover from his days as Professor Ratzinger—in favor of tending his flock.

Putting aside the calculated or involuntary misunderstandings, the polemics, and the outrageous statements issued worldwide, the pope's speech seems to have expressed his considered position that the Catholic Church, the quintessence of European culture and the exclusive outcome of an encounter between Greek reason and Biblical faith, was the only institution that could provide intellectual resistance to the expansion of violence hiding under the guise of jihad. And in that sense, the pope's words constituted a theological appropriation of the grand narrative of the war on terror.

Even though Benedict XVI reminded the Muslim theologians of their responsibilities and earned himself a response whose vivacity falls short of addressing questions of violence and terrorism, we remain here in the narrow framework of theology. Muslims in general, and those who had settled in Europe in particular, were still prisoners, through such reasoning, of the dogmatic aspects of their religion—as "moderate," Islamist, or jihadist *ulema* continued to argue for the right to authentic interpretation. Christian and Muslim clerics, on the other hand, found common ground for agreement on one important point: their rejection of the secular experience. And yet it is toward that experience we now turn, in order to observe how France—the European country that made secularism into a principle of the national pact—integrated into its culture the largest population of Muslim origin in Western Europe, while bombs were exploding in London and Madrid. That cultural integration, as we will see, imposed a shared set of values and laws that took precedence over contradictory divine injunctions.

The Paradox of the French Banlieues

On August 19, 2007, as Britain was beginning to recover from the shock of the doctors' plot in late June, the *Financial Times* published a poll on attitudes toward Muslims among citizens of the United States and five European countries (the United Kingdom, France, Italy, Spain, and Germany).[19] Almost 40 percent of Britons polled felt that the presence of Muslims constituted a threat to national security, while only 20 percent of French respondents felt that way and 70 percent believed the contrary. Almost 40 percent of Britons (and the same proportion of Germans and Americans) stated they would object to their child's marrying a Muslim, in contrast to only 18 percent of French respondents.

In Britain, 46 percent of those polled said they felt Muslims had excessive political power, as against 10 percent in France. Over half of British respondents expected a terrorist attack to occur in the following year, compared with 15 percent in France and 30 percent in both Spain and the United States. Unsurprisingly, the French (at 70 percent) were most in favor of banning religious symbols and clothing from schools and workplaces, but around 50 percent of British respondents now shared this opinion—an astonishing change of attitude in a country where multiculturalism had reigned supreme. The British were closely followed in this opinion by Germans and Spaniards. Only the Italians and Americans expressed a contrary majority view.

Finally, 80 percent of French respondents saw no problem in being simultaneously a Muslim and a citizen of France, while less than 60 percent of Britons were sanguine about British citizenship for Muslims—the lowest score in the five countries polled. London's *Financial Times,* ordinarily less than indulgent with France, noted with surprise that "France emerged as the country most at ease with its Muslim population. The French were most likely to say they had Muslim friends, to accept if their child wanted to marry a Muslim, and to say Muslims in their country had received unjustified criticism and prejudice. This surprising result came less than two years after riots in the French *banlieues* [urban outskirts] and only three years after the French government banned head-scarves and other religious symbols from public schools."[20]

A year earlier, on June 22, 2006, the Pew Research Center's Global Attitudes Project had published a study titled "The Great Divide: How Westerners and Muslims View Each Other—Europe's Muslims More Moderate."[21] Of all the countries polled, France—just six months after the riots—had the highest proportion (74 percent) of respondents who saw no contradiction between being a pious Muslim and living in a modern society. The numbers for the other three E.U. countries polled were considerably lower: Germany at 26 percent, Britain at 35 percent, and Spain at 36 percent. Among all the Muslim populations polled worldwide, French Muslims (at 48 percent) were the most likely to believe that Arabs had carried out the 9/11 attacks. Among British Muslims, 56 percent exonerated Arabs completely, while another 17 percent attributed responsibility to some Arabs and not solely to Israel's Mossad or other obscure forces.

In France, 65 percent of the population had a good opinion of Muslims in 2006, as did 63 percent of Britons (though this proportion would drop significantly a year later) and 54 percent of Americans. When Muslims were asked if they had a favorable opinion of Christians, 91 percent of French Muslims answered in the affirmative, compared with 71 percent of British Muslims, 27 percent of Pakistanis, and 17 percent of Turks. Even more remarkably, 71 percent of French Muslims had a positive opinion of Jews, compared with 32 percent in Britain (and 1 percent in Jordan, to take one Middle Eastern example).

Finally, when Muslims polled were given a list of six negative traits that are sometimes associated with Westerners (selfishness, arrogance, violence, greed, amorality, fanaticism) and were asked to assign percentages to each one, British Muslims ranked Westerners quite high on that negative scale (between 67 and 44 percent). French Muslims, by contrast, ranked their non-Muslim compatriots far lower, negative opinions ranging from 51 to 26 percent. French Muslims also gave Westerners a better report card with regard to positive traits (respect for women, generosity, tolerance, honesty, piety) than their British co-religionists (a range of 77 to 51 percent, as against a range of 56 to 42 percent). The exception was piety, which only 26 percent of French Muslims associated with other French citizens. But in France, where not many people practice religion and faith is not generally considered a social virtue, this was a realistic assessment, not a stereotype.

These figures, gathered one year apart by two polling organizations that could not be accused of pro-French bias, surprised many observers in Britain and the United States. Evening news programs in these two countries had interpreted the riots in France's *banlieues* in autumn 2005 from the perspective of the grand narrative of the war on terror. Fox News' coverage was especially egregious. Entitled "Paris Is Burning" (an allusion to the famous novel by Dominique Lapierre and Larry Collins, *Is Paris Burning?*), it included a graphic of the Eiffel Tower ringed in flames, while commentator Bill O'Reilly, in his typical inflammatory style, explained to viewers that France was "under bitter siege by Muslims." And yet the weak French government was so cowed that President Chirac "won't even use the military to protect lives and property." Reminding his viewers that Chirac and the French media had worked to undermine the war on terror, he warned them that "we're living in a very dangerous world where fanatics and terrorists abound. France had buried its head in the sand, and now has a disaster on its hands."[22]

On CNN, anchors announced that young people were "making bombs" in *banlieues* all over France—supposedly the new battlefields in the war on terror. The map that the network used to follow the evolving story featured little exploding icons in the cities where the riots were breaking out, though the accuracy of these statements could be measured by the mistakes on the map, which placed the southwest city of Toulouse in the southeast Alps region, moved the central city of Lyon to the Pyrenees border area with Spain, and mixed up the two distant cities of Cannes and Montpellier.[23]

Hundreds of Internet postings and printed articles emanating from the United States interpreted the riots as a sort of divine punishment that had struck France under Chirac in a manner appropriate to its sins. On November 7 one of the main websites supporting the war on terror, DEBKA*file,* provided a special report titled "France's Ramadan Uprising—a Ticking Bomb for Europe." "Mostly Muslim gangs of youths [began] surging out of the immigrant suburbs to invade town centers; they fired their first gunshots at policemen; the number of torched cars peaked to 1,400;

and disturbing new slogans were hurled, depicting Paris as 'Baghdad-on-the-Seine' and their campaign as the start of Europe's Ramadan Intifada. A single slogan made a mockery of President Jacques Chirac's efforts of the last three years to distance France from President George W. Bush's Iraq war."[24] Claiming to have proof that the riots were caused by organized Islamist networks, the site reported that Al Qaeda had recruited between 35,000 and 45,000 combatants in France, who received indoctrination through local and regional leaders, organized themselves into military units, and gathered regularly to train in handling weapons and explosives.

Another website, Jihad Watch, claimed that Arabs in France had long been waging a "low-intensity Intifada" against synagogues, kosher shops, and Jewish schools. It stated that the French political class had played down these attacks and kept them out of the media, in an attempt to prevent them from spreading to less specific targets.[25] But now it was clear that the attempt had failed. In *America Alone: The End of the World as We Know It*, columnist Mark Steyn noted: "France has been here before, of course. Seven-thirty-two. Not 7:32 Paris time, which is when the nightly Citroen-torching begins in the 'burbs, but 732 AD—as in one and a third millennia ago," when the Battle of Poitiers allowed Charles Martel to stop the advancing Muslim armies under the command of General Abdel-Rahman and thus to halt the first attempt of Muslims to conquer Europe. Today, thirteen centuries later, Muslims have advanced far beyond Poitou: there are tens of millions of them in Europe. Immigrants and their children constitute today's Muslim armies, according to Steyn. Europe has lost the modern-day version of the Battle of Poitiers because its cowardly rulers have allowed believers of Islam to settle in Europe and overrun the continent—so the narrative went.

On ogrish.com, two youths of African origin, their faces masked by rags that vaguely resemble Palestinian *keffiyehs,* exclaim in accents strongly tinged by the *banlieues,* against a background of burning cars: "Allah-oo Akbar, cousin! Hey, where are we? In Je-ru-sa-lem? Two kids died, two of our li'l brothers, and now they're shooting at a mosque, too much!"[26] The 37-second clip, which follows a staccato audio-visual pattern alternating between anti-riot squads and howling rioters (subtitled "Sarkozy, you fascist!"), was seen around the world. "Shooting at a mosque" referred to a tear-gas grenade fired near a former warehouse that had been transformed into a prayer room in Clichy-sous-Bois, where Muslims had gathered for the additional prayers said at night during Ramadan. Nothing suggests that police were aiming at this informal mosque. But when a photograph of a bearded imam wearing a robe and a knitted skullcap, standing in front of an industrial wasteland and wiping away his tears, appeared on the front page of the *Herald Tribune,* this coverage by a respected newspaper lent credence to the idea of a confrontation between the West and Islam.[27]

Two years and several sociological studies later, more nuanced analysis has invalidated these widespread claims that the revolt in the banlieues could be dubbed "Muslim riots"—let alone that they represented acts of terrorism and were therefore a legitimate episode in the grand narrative of the war on terror. The basic facts in the case are well established. On October 27, 2005, two boys aged fifteen and seventeen, of Mauritanian and Tunisian origin, died by electrocution in Clichy-sous-Bois, a working-class suburb on the edge of Paris, when they ran into a power station while trying to evade a police patrol. They had been playing sports and were hurrying home to break the fast of Ramadan with their families. There were eleven children in the family of the first boy, six in the other. Their fathers were both garbage collectors working for the Paris municipal authorities. A third teenager, who survived the 20,000-volt shock and told the story, was a Turkish Kurd, the son of an unemployed bricklayer.

In a tense climate caused by the politicization of immigration and delinquency preceding the designation of right-wing candidates for the spring 2007 presidential election, which Nicolas Sarkozy won, the death of the two boys became a symbol that brought into focus the difficulties encountered by the French system of integration. Car-torchings began almost immediately. Hundreds of cars were set on fire each night for three weeks, providing a Halloween-like spectacle of black and orange that the media could not resist. Flames shooting skyward from abandoned vehicles lit the evening landscape from late October to mid-November, as groups of adolescents in the background, wearing hoodies reminiscent of the ghettoes made glamorous by Hollywood, passed before housing projects and industrial zones. The number of cars torched *in one night* reached 1,408 on November 6.

Images on YouTube and other websites spoke an audio-visual language that related these events to suicide attacks and car bombings from Baghdad to London. And yet, with the exception of the two teenagers who were electrocuted accidentally, only two people—a journalist and a retiree—were killed by hooligans, and no one was killed by police. It was rather the "sacrifice of cars" that gave speechless expression to the frustrations of a population with no other access to political discourse. As in the practice of animal sacrifice, the rioters channeled their violence into four-wheeled sacrificial victims, perhaps as a way to keep it from spreading to humans.

But more than animal sacrifice, the riots became a form of self-sacrifice which the practitioners forced the larger society to witness. Cars—essential to daily life in the banlieues, many of which are not well connected by public transportation networks—were torched even though they belonged to residents of the projects. Nurseries, kindergartens, gymnasiums, and other public facilities used by the local community went up in flames. One interpretation of this inward-turning self-destruction is that the rioters were so spatially isolated that it did not occur to them to venture beyond their neighborhoods onto unknown turf.

The 2005 riots in France barely witnessed thefts or hold-ups. The fires seemed to have just one purpose: to draw attention to individuals who would otherwise have remained socially invisible, and to send the message that integration had failed, despite the promises made by France's "civil religion," secularism. The rioters were not asking for the creation of autonomous spaces, ruled over by imams and dotted with *halal* butcher establishments; they did not wish to create Islamistans on the outskirts of France's cities. In a message burned onto television and computer screens throughout France, the rioters seemed to be saying, "We're here! Notice us! Let us in!"

Detailed analysis of the neighborhoods where the riots and fires broke out, and comparisons with neighborhoods where these events did not occur, showed that they mainly took place in "sensitive urban zones" that were home to adolescent males from sub-

Saharan Africa, who had many siblings but often no functioning family unit, largely because fathers were absent.[28] The social groups they formed were not strongly religious, and Muslims coexisted with Catholics, evangelical Christians, and animists. North Africans, who make up the vast majority of the Muslim population in France, were underrepresented among the rioters, compared with sub-Saharan African teenagers. The latter were largely uninterested in Islam or its clerics, and Islamists (including radical ones) were no better able to control the riots or channel their energy into mobilization than were politicians belonging to the radical left. The movement did not produce a single durable slogan that would have explained its orientation. Nor did it rally significant support from other social groups, including older immigrants. The eruption was "proto-political," and the young people who led it acted alone.[29]

On November 6, when the tear-gas grenade fell near the informal mosque in Clichy-sous-Bois, the Union of Islamic Organizations in France (UOIF, an offshoot of the Muslim Brotherhood and the main element in the French Council on the Muslim Faith) condemned the police's "irresponsible act . . . committed at prayer time, as well as the excessive statements made by some politicians, who exacerbated the climate and encouraged certain young people to intensify . . . their anger."[30] The union called on "all the young Muslims involved in these events to calm their anger, meditate, and follow the opinion issued today by Dar Al-Fatwa," the body that issues *fatwas* applying in France in the name of the UOIF. The union also requested that judgment be passed and sentences issued for those who "dared to disturb the faithful in their peaceful prayers during the holy month of Ramadan." And finally, the union

observed that "these events seem to have exposed the grave deficiencies in the French model of integration, which has clearly sunk
tens of thousands of young people from the difficult neighborhoods into desperation and misery."

The *fatwa* was titled "On the Difficulties Concerning France."
Quoting the Quran (V, 64), "God loves not those who do mischief,"
the introduction stipulated that "the right to express one's distress
or unease does not cancel out the rights of innocents, who saw
their cars and businesses go up in flames." Then came the text of
the *fatwa* itself: "It is absolutely forbidden for any Muslim who
seeks divine satisfaction and grace to participate in any way in any
action that strikes blindly at private or public property, or that can
threaten someone's life. Contributing to these actions is unlawful."

The organization sought to come across as the perfect mediator
between the government and the rioters, who were presumed to be
mostly Muslim. At the same time, its leaders wished to protect the
cars and shops owned by many Muslims in the *banlieues,* whose
support the organization was cultivating. Boasting that it could restore peace by invoking Islamic injunctions that might have more
power than discredited civil laws, the organization expected that
the unnerved authorities, in return, would grant it a wider political
berth. While observing the "grave deficiencies" of the integration
model in France, the organization was implicitly championing a
French Muslim community that could administer its own urban
space and control its social subgroups, while the union guaranteed
social peace. In this unspoken bargain with the state, the community would receive, in return, concessions on public services such
as education, on the influence of Muslim associations, and so on.

This position was in line with the Muslim Brotherhood's global strategy in Europe, which notable figures in the movement, like Sheikh Qaradawi, frequently mentioned. Its initial stages were implemented during the second half of the 1990s, when Islamic vigilantes were set up to hunt down drug dealers in crowded housing projects. The long-term impact of that effort was limited, however. More recently, after French authorities prohibited veiling in schools, the UOIF encouraged Muslim girls to wear headscarves on the first day of school in September 2004. The union hoped to provoke a legal battle that would go all the way to European tribunals, where, it calculated, the weight of Anglo-Saxon law would invalidate France's ruling. This strategy came to naught when two French journalists were kidnapped in Iraq and threatened with beheading if the veiling law was not repealed. The French Muslim community condemned the actions of the kidnappers and refused to be associated with them around this issue.

The anti-riot *fatwa* of November 2005 turned out to be equally unsuccessful at mobilizing the French Muslim community around a set of demands. The language used in the communiqué and *fatwa* was ineffective for several different reasons. The French seemed to be clumsily translated from Arabic; it was grammatically incorrect and misused legal terminology. The text indicated that the organization's "mufti" was not fully aware of the disconnect between his reading of events and the perceptions of the young people he was addressing. As for the Quranic verse mentioned in the *fatwa*, it consisted of an attack on Jews, whom it accuses of "rebellion and blasphemy." The quote was taken from the phrase that ends the verse: "Every time they kindle the fire of war, God extinguishes it; but they . . . strive to do mischief on earth. And God loves not those who do mischief." The relation between adolescents, most of them of African origin, setting fire to cars in the outer cities, and the "mischief" of Jews was unclear at best. The incomprehension and misunderstanding between the Islamic discourse used by the Muslim Brotherhood and the street language of the rioters could not have been greater.

All of the media hand-wringing may have actually persuaded UOIF leaders that radical Islamism was indeed the hidden hand behind the car-torching in the *banlieues*. Or perhaps they were just paying lip service to the grand narrative of terrorism, hoping to turn it to their own advantage. Whatever they were thinking, they seized the opportunity to claim they could end the riots by invoking God's law and enacting the Brotherhood's peaceful social agenda. If their operation was successful, they expected to reap political rewards from mainstream power brokers.

But what they did not take into account was the fact that the vast majority of Muslim citizens and residents were just as bewildered by the violence, and distant from it, as their non-Muslim compatriots. The young rioters, for their part, were as indifferent to the UOIF's strategy as they were to Al Qaeda's rhetoric and the absurd babblings of Fox News and company. The riots gradually burned themselves out with no help from the Brotherhood— though resolutions could be heard in the top echelons of society to "do *something*" to improve the integration of young Africans into French culture.

The Battle for Europe

Europe was thus dragged, kicking and struggling, into the middle of a propaganda war with very real and tragic consequences. The opponents—American neoconservatives promoting the grand narrative of a war on terror, and factions in the Middle East promoting a grand narrative of jihad through martyrdom—sought to use the old continent as their echo chamber. The suicide attacks in Britain, the assassination of Theo Van Gogh, the Danish cartoons, Pope Benedict XVI's lecture at Regensburg, and the riots in the French *banlieues* were seized upon as opportunities for these two competing ideologies to sharpen their rhetoric and gain some kind of strategic advantage. But beyond the facile arguments and simplistic reasoning encouraged by front-page headlines and breaking news stories, what we find on careful examination is that the historical and social context within each country played a crucial role in determining which interpretation of events would be amplified in recruiting and mobilizing supporters.

Britain and the Netherlands had taken multiculturalism to its most extreme expression, neglecting the urgent need for a common national identity that immigrants of Muslim origin and their settled descendants could share with the "native" population. This neglect produced fragile enclaves incapable of resisting radicalization by Islamist militants. The logic of violent jihad, assassinations, and suicide attacks found favorable terrain there. As a result of the disruptive violence of just a few hundred individuals, two nations began to question some of the basic assumptions of their social structure.

Similarly, the Danish cartoon affair and the statements of Pope Benedict XVI in Regensburg were emblematic of the approach of Denmark's political system and the Vatican toward questions of full Muslim participation in contemporary European culture, which is still denied to a certain extent. Here, too, the problem of how to integrate the concerned populations as citizens arose, as did the question of which kinds of government policies to implement. But both incidents also illustrated the dangerous excesses of the transnational Islamist movement, which interfered between Europe and its Muslim population in an attempt to prove that the community had been victimized by the host society. The Islamists were assisted in this cause by pan-Arab television channels, websites, and even powers-that-be. Only when contradictions internal to the Middle East transformed these events into fodder for conflict between Sunnis and Shiites, or between states and radical movements, were the main actors willing to reduce tensions in Europe, lest they threaten other interests.

Finally, riots in the *banlieues* of Paris and other cities revealed, paradoxically, the resistance of the French social fabric to terrorist corrosion. In this case, it was primarily the narrators of the war on terror who tried to annex events to their cause, with breathless headlines and close-up shots of "Paris burning." But in fact, the French riots had next to nothing to do with terror or jihad. What the burning cars demonstrated night after night was the shortcomings of the French system of integration, which had failed to offer certain marginalized populations full participation in a vast culture reaching across the Mediterranean to Africa. But by so forcefully expressing their sense of frustration, isolation, and exclusion, these rioting youths also inadvertently pointed out the promise of a society that rejects ideologies of separatism and embraces the ideology of inclusion, however often it fails to realize that dream fully.

CHAPTER SIX

THE CHALLENGE OF CIVILIZATION

The war between George W. Bush and Osama Bin Laden defeated both of its protagonists. The sorcerer's apprentices in the White House and Tora Bora had relied on the magic of their grand narratives of terror and martyrdom to reorder the world, but as sectarian clashes multiplied from Palestine to Iraq, Israel to Afghanistan, Lebanon to Pakistan, Bush and Bin Laden found themselves powerless to control the flow of events. Neither democracy nor jihad have prevailed in the Middle East. And with Iran's recent entry into the nuclear arena—raising fears in both Washington and the Arabian peninsula—the long-term crises in the Levant and the Gulf, far from being solved through military pressure or terrorist blackmail, now endanger not only world peace but also the global balance of economic power, through skyrocketing fuel prices. By casting doubt on development models based on abundant, cheap energy, these trends threaten to destabilize not just Western nations but poor countries as well.

The U.S. administration has emerged from this trial weakened and challenged on all fronts. The simplistic notion of a "new American century" that underpinned neoconservative ideology during George W. Bush's two terms in office was no match for the resilient "complicated Orient." But Al Qaeda and its affiliates were equally unsuccessful at mobilizing the Islamic world against the West. Zawahiri and Bin Laden were unable to galvanize the Muslim community in the Middle East and Europe, despite the grand hopes they had pinned on the spectacle of September 11, 2001. They were forced to fall back on a virtual *umma*, online and on satellite television. Their failure lies in the gap between the digital universe, where a mind-numbing stream of jihad declarations and communiqués poured forth, and the daily reality of suicide attacks that mired Iraq, Afghanistan, and Pakistan in misery, led the second intifada in Palestine to a dead-end, and wreaked havoc in Europe.

On December 16, 2007, during his fourth conversation with a "journalist" from As-Sahab, Zawahiri devoted almost 100 minutes to convincing Internet viewers that jihad would triumph.[1] But in fact, each of his statements served to mask jihad's failure. Defense of the stillborn Islamic State of Iraq gave way to attacks on Sunnis who collaborated with the United States and other "merchants of religion." But his fiercest expressions of hatred were directed at the Shiites of Hezbollah and Iran whom Zawahiri accused of having "stabbed Islam in the back." Al Qaeda's top leadership had become so isolated from players on the ground that Zawahiri was forced to open a question-and-answer session on the Internet in a bid to widen recruitment.

Al Qaeda's grand narrative of global jihad through martyrdom was also being shredded from within by militants who, in retrospect, considered 9/11 to be a political catastrophe. In November 2007 "Dr. Fadel," one of the top leaders of Egyptian Jihad, condemned Zawahiri from his prison cell, holding him personally responsible for the movement's setbacks. Zawahiri counter-attacked in a 190-page response, *Al Tabria* (*Exoneration*), which he posted online. The title itself testified eloquently to the battle for legitimacy that was raging inside the jihadist movement. By 2003, after the invasion of Iraq, anti-Western and anti-American resentment in the Sunni world was being channeled into organizations affiliated with the Muslim Brothers, the jihadists' despised rivals. As for Shiites, Ahmadinejad's Iran—which the Sunni jihadists abhorred even more—had taken command of the battle against the West, thanks to its nuclear saber-rattling and the precious oil reserves that backed it up, marginalizing Al Qaeda even further.

The consummate failure of the two grand narratives that were imposed on the world in 2001—the war on terror and jihad through martyrdom—makes a new, realistic geopolitics necessary: a sober, far-sighted vision that takes into account the regional tensions and diverse social components of the Middle East and the Gulf, and leaves aside the ideological intoxications of military conquest and suicidal terrorism.

Transformation of the United States' Role

By the last year of President George W. Bush's second term, it was clear that his presidency would leave a disastrous legacy in the Middle East, one whose consequences would reach far beyond the failure to rid the world of terrorists. In hindsight, the war in Iraq resembled an invasion from colonial times or the cold war era, rather than the surgical, postmodern military operation its original planners had envisioned. Instead of a mission similar to the liberation of Kuwait in 1991, what the Bush administration got was a costly occupation that faced bloody resistance from its inception.

Through its experiment in Iraq, the world's only military superpower rediscovered a principle it had encountered before, in Vietnam: that force is just one aspect of global influence, and not necessarily the most important one. Furthermore, when the use of force proves ineffective against an adversary who uses unconventional methods of combat—including suicide attacks—its deterrent capacity in the next crisis is weakened, and the credibility of the administration is undermined. At the beginning of the twenty-first century, no other nation can deploy as many aircraft carriers or troops as the United States. But these are ill-adapted to the demands of occupation, as the dramatic abuses at Abu Ghraib prison demonstrated. When political instability and insurrection drag on for years, the problem of replacing exhausted troops and support personnel becomes critical, and more difficult.

As long as Washington's management of Gulf security guaranteed reasonably priced petroleum, Chinese industrialists could flood the planet with low-cost consumer goods and invest their profits in U.S. Treasury bonds, which kept the dollar afloat and allowed the United States to live on credit. But with American troops bogged down in Iraq, long-term deliveries of Gulf oil and gas became uncertain, and prices on futures markets rose steeply. Asian consumption kept demand high despite the rising cost, while speculators invested in barrels of crude as a sort of reserve currency. As a result, the value of the dollar plummeted.

These financial vicissitudes made American corporations easy prey for international operators. The sovereign wealth funds of oil-exporting countries (the pool of state-controlled financial reserves set aside for investments in foreign assets) were used to buy or invest in U.S. banks and other businesses, raising eminently political concerns in the land of free enterprise. The attempt by Dubai Ports World (the Emirates corporation that runs the port of Dubai) to purchase management contracts for a number of major American ports gave senators chills in 2005 and 2006. Citing the security risks such an operation would entail, they blocked it by a virtually unanimous vote.

During the heyday of Reaganomics and continuing into the Clinton years, when market regulation was relaxed and the global economy was booming, U.S. territory was thought to be insulated from terrorist aggression by the immense oceans that lie to the east and west. The Canadian and Mexican borders also seemed secure, though there were signs that the Canadian border was more permeable than believed. In December 1999 an Islamist Algerian terrorist, Ahmed Ressam, was arrested as he was crossing from Canada into the United States. He had undergone training at a jihadist camp in Afghanistan and planned to drive a vehicle loaded with explosives to the Los Angeles International Airport, where his attack would be timed to coincide with the millennium celebrations. Other radical Islamists had obtained political asylum and settled in Canada. Similarly, the Mexican border, with its steady stream of clandestine labor immigrants, was suspected of letting through Muslim terrorists as well.

The trauma of September 11, 2001, made the United States particularly sensitive about its borders, and Americans became more amenable to political interventions that would limit free-market movement. For some, capital investments from Muslim countries were viewed as potential threats to national security and for a time were restricted. Although vigilance continues to prevail in financial activities linked to the border (as in the Dubai Ports case), elsewhere in the United States the sovereign wealth funds of the Gulf states, pumped up by petrodollars, have bought interests in major American institutions, including U.S. banks endangered by the subprime crisis of 2007.

As the economy of the Gulf surges, debate has raged in the United States and the West between those who see sovereign wealth funds as the salvation of Western capitalism, which desperately needs liquidity and investment capabilities, and those who see these funds as Trojan horses, insidiously hostile to the West. Managers of sovereign wealth funds are keen to explain to anyone who will listen that their sole objective is capitalist profit, that their participation in Western business is minor, and that they have no political agenda—certainly not one of allowing Muslim states to control strategic sectors of American production or the banking system.

These worries were fueled by statements made by Bin Laden— or his digital doppelganger—in 2007 to commemorate 9/11. On a note disconnected from the usual rhetoric of jihadism, he developed a lengthy and surprising argument on the subprime crisis and the impoverishment of the middle classes in the United States. His solution was mass conversion to Islam. This argument, coming soon after Zarqawi's death and the disappointing debut of the Islamic State of Iraq, sought to increase Al Qaeda's attractiveness by striking new alliances with anti-imperialist or left-wing movements, whatever their cause, at a time when Iran seemed to be the main beneficiary of the American debacle in Iraq. The jarring tone of Bin Laden's statements opened Al Qaeda up to ridicule in some quarters, but they showed that the jihadists were trying to engage with the global economic crisis and subvert it for their own benefit.

Whatever the reality of his financial threat—which was more propaganda than action plan—Bin Laden was extensively quoted in the media, and the magnitude of the reaction reflected a feeling, by now widespread in the United States, that the country had been deeply injured by the cost of the war in Iraq and the financial crisis it had precipitated. The world's greatest power could no longer undertake the kind of unilateral action that had been George W. Bush's trademark. The administration's wavering attitude toward an attack on Iran illustrated this transformation perfectly. Throughout 2007, in response to Ahmadinejad's combative declarations, belligerent statements emanating from the highest echelons of power in the United States and Israel suggested that a preventive strike on Iran's nuclear sites was in the offing. But the ideologues who were gathered behind Dick Cheney faced organized opposition from the Department of Defense and the State Department. Planners at the Pentagon knew that U.S. armed forces would find it almost impossible to engineer an attack on Iran while managing the occupation of Iraq, where the Shiite populations of Basra, Najaf, and Baghdad would likely rise up against any such strike.

In spring 2007 when I was visiting Tehran, observers told me that a U.S. strike on Iran was unlikely, since the administration knew that this action would be followed immediately by an Iranian attack on a neighboring oil-rich emirate, triggering a global economic and energy crisis. The *National Intelligence Estimate* published in November 2007 confirmed this view. It showed that a strike on Iran would not only have unmanageable consequences on the ground in Iraq, but if Iran was pushed too far it might retaliate by bombing the Strait of Hormuz, through which oil and methane shipments pass, or it might strike one of its oil-producing neighbors. Such measures would cause the price of a barrel of crude to hit peaks no market could bear, and the global economy would suffer tremendously. The United States could not risk such disastrous consequences.

Furthermore, according to the NIE, Iran had put an end to its military nuclear program in 2003 after the leadership analyzed its costs and benefits in the context of international negotiations. Tehran would not be able to resume a weapons-production program before 2009 at the earliest. These revelations, based on high-level military and civilian intelligence, convinced the U.S. executive branch to abandon the option of a strike against Iran.

The report had significance at two levels. First, it showed that—a year before the end of Bush's term—the political authority of the White House was already weak in relation to high-level administrators, who read between the lines and concluded that the United States no longer had the means to carry out unilateral military action. And second, the authors of the NIE report emphasized that—regardless of Ahmadinejad's posturing—the Iranian leadership was open to a new foreign policy based on a realistic assessment of the costs and benefits of their actions.

In other words, the clerical establishment of the Islamic Republic might eventually participate in complex and conditional negotiations—a possibility that should not be closed off by unilateral action, according to the NIE. An approach based on force alone—

an option whose limitations had been exposed by the invasion of Iraq—presented more risks than anticipated benefits. A multilateral approach that would lead to the beginning of negotiations was the only sensible alternative. The fact that such negotiations would have uncertain outcomes gave rise to intense debate among the principal candidates in the 2008 U.S. presidential primaries. Senator Barack Obama and Senator John McCain both insisted that any talks with Iran would be conditional and would constitute neither appeasement nor capitulation.

President Bush's successor will have to bury the grand narrative of the war on terror and accept the reality of many power centers in the world today. With its military capacity stretched thin and its economic and financial superiority challenged by new competitors, the United States is being forced to align its own goals with those of its allies and deal with a new set of actors who are leading the world toward multipolarity. As Fareed Zakaria, editor and columnist of *Newsweek,* noted in 2008, a "post-American world" is taking shape before our eyes.[2] To thrive in this new environment, Washington will need to abandon the hubris of the Bush administration and return to the path of multilateralism. The United States simply can no longer afford to be the lone horseman of the West.

Zakaria wonders about "the rise of the rest," and chief among them, of course, are China and India, whose current strength lies in their demographic dynamism combined with an economic and entrepreneurial boom. There are two other poles, however, at either end of a vast, shared geographical space within which the Middle East is situated: Europe and the Gulf. These entities do not spring to mind as readily as the Indian subcontinent and the Far East, if only because European demographic growth is stagnant or aging, while the Gulf's still-small population (except in Saudi Arabia) is strongly marked by migrant labor. These frailties, however, are compensated by two strong points.

First, in an uncertain global economy, the European Union, with its twenty-seven member states, represents a zone of considerable economic power and stability, as evidenced by the strength of the euro, which has risen consistently while the war on terror has continued. As for the Gulf, its vast oil fields will make it the main exporter of petroleum for decades to come, increasingly so as other oil-producing nations, including the United States, consume their more limited reserves. The liquidity pumped into its sovereign wealth funds has transformed the states of the Gulf Cooperation Council into the planet's bankers.

In a multipolar world consisting of Asia and the United States to the east and west, what role can Europe and the Gulf play in integrating the Middle East into an extended regional economic union that will help mitigate the recurrent crises of the Levant and the Gulf? And what future relationship can this new region have with the United States, in the aftermath of the war on terror and the shattered dream of "a new American century"?

Europe's Place

Europe is now one of the strongest regions of the world, comparable to Asia or the Americas. As the immediate neighbor of the Middle East and North Africa, it is also an echo chamber for tribulations in the Levant and the Gulf, and these urgent concerns have become a factor in both the domestic and foreign policy of European nations.

During President Bush's two terms in office, Europe's voice was barely heard. Because the attack of September 11 occurred on U.S. territory, it naturally fell to the United States to take the initiative in reacting, but from the beginning Europe mobilized at the side of its ally. Later, when the United States decided to invade Iraq, Europe was called upon once again to align its policy with that of Washington. This alignment entailed accepting the neoconservatives' "new American century" project to reshape the Middle East and spread democracy throughout the region. In this grand scenario, "Old Europe" seemed to be little more than a continental Euro-Disney, where tourists from the United States and Asia could visit the chateaux of the Loire Valley or the Grand Canal in Venice while carefully skirting those parts of the urban jungle populated by Muslim jihadists.

Europe's response to the United States' invitation to join the Iraq invasion was fractured. France and Germany refused to comply and were mocked in Washington. Britain, on the other hand, went along with American policy, reviving the "special relationship" between the two countries made famous by Winston Churchill at the end of World War II. Partially as a result of its participation in the "coalition of the willing," Britain became a soft target of terrorism. When riots broke out in French *banlieues* in the autumn of 2005, hawkers of the grand narrative on terror claimed that France too was the victim of an intifada because of its cowardice in rejecting the Iraqi adventure. There was in fact no link between the fictitious cause and its imaginary effect, yet Europe undeniably had become a locus of global jihad—as the attacks in London, the murder of Theo Van Gogh in Amsterdam, and the global outcry following the publication of the Danish cartoons made plain.

In the Netherlands and Britain, where it was believed that social peace could be reinforced by religious networks—not all of which proved reliable—these disruptive events have triggered an existential debate within the Muslim population. The authorities, too, have been forced to question a multiculturalist dogma that seems to have eased the way, in some cases, for extremists. But of course Muslims who have recently become European citizens and are appearing in growing numbers on the political scene cannot be reduced to Al Qaeda militants, and they are not necessarily represented by the Muslim Brothers and their allies—who claim to be the key negotiators between the Muslim "community" (the borders of which they defined) and political authorities. In spite of recurrent riots in underprivileged neighborhoods, and social barriers ranging from academic failure to job discrimination, a slow but irrepressible movement of cultural integration and upward social mobility is taking place in Europe's population of Muslim origin.

The nations of the "old continent" are providing diverse terrain for live experimentation in possible ways of coexisting in the postmodern world—a world that is experiencing real difficulties but also developing hybrids that show new fertility and adaptability. Children of "mixed" couples who trace some of their roots to North Africa or the Middle East are growing up at a time when the first immigrant elites are assuming high-ranking positions in government administration and business or top-tier ministerial offices. Others have become artists or sports champions who inspire

THE CHALLENGE OF CIVILIZATION

Europeans of all backgrounds. No matter what contradictions may result, the outcome will be the triumph of a shared identity and destiny over Islamist irredentism and exaltation of difference, and over European xenophobia.

Such hybrids appear to the south and east of the Mediterranean as well. The French language in North Africa and part of the Middle East, and English in most of the Middle East and the Gulf, are key vectors of participation in this globalized world. Exchanges through travel, ideas, information, and entertainment broadcast by the media pass not only to and from America but through Europe just as much as inside the Arab and Muslim world. These exchanges shape an informal, every-day cultural identity that cannot be reduced to radical hostility toward the West, as proclaimed by the jihadists, or hatred against Muslims and Islam, as formulated by European chauvinists. Rather, this identity is constructed through an ever-changing process of fascination and rejection, where friendship and enmity mingle in the register of intimacy. Despite discourses that demonize the Other—plumbing the depths of abomination in the form of Zarqawi's beheadings, or painting an offending caricature in the Danish case—there exists between Europe and its "Near East," as the traditional European designation of the region indicates, an alternative to the failed narratives of jihad and the war on terror.

That alternative is the economic integration of the Middle East and Europe, creating a fertile space where entrepreneurial classes can grow and democratic processes can take root, especially to the south and east of the Mediterranean. Turkey already provides one example of integration between Europe and the Middle East. Regardless of the vicissitudes of politics, economic ties with the European Union have strengthened civil society, pluralism, and democracy in Turkey and have managed to transform the Islamist opposition into a ruling party that respects Ataturk's legacy of secular republicanism while erasing Ataturkism's authoritarian and militaristic dimensions.

But much of the Mediterranean basin around which many of humanity's greatest civilizations were built today lies fallow. The European Union turns mostly toward the Atlantic, to entrepreneurial opportunities in the West, while the nations of the Gulf are attracted by the flow of currency from the Far East, where the dire need for oil makes China and other developing nations generous with their payments. Between these two giants, the Mediterranean today remains economically neglected. But this ancient hub has a potential asset that both Europe and the Gulf lack: a wealth of human resources, which can be used for good but also for ill. With education and jobs, these populations will take a great part in the advancement of civilization. But if neglected they run the risk of embracing a neomedieval nightmare that blends misery with jihadist rage. Europe and the Gulf can look after their own best interests by embracing the rational option: favoring a renaissance in the Mediterranean that boosts the economic potential of its population. This option does not mean a union restricted to the countries that border this ancient hub of trade. The economic complementarity of these countries is too limited to make such a union work. What is needed, rather, is a much larger economic alliance, with the Mediterranean at its center but radiating out to Europe and the Gulf as well.

Each of the complementary regions has its own drawback. Europe is growing old and lacks the entrepreneurial dynamism and investment capital that would allow it to hold its own in the new century. The Gulf is underpopulated and needs to build academic and scientific institutions as well as a sophisticated industrial and economic policy in order to consolidate its vast wealth. North Africa and the Levant need jobs and education for a large population that otherwise would have no option except mass emigration. An economic renaissance centered on the Mediterranean would bring together, in one dynamic region, Europe's industrial and technological wealth and its academic and scientific expertise; the Gulf's petroleum assets and financial clout; and the human resources and rich cultures of the Levant and North Africa.

But any regional consolidation of the economic interests of Europe, the Mediterranean, and the Gulf must come up with a way to address the persistent structural conflicts that Washington's military engineering failed to resolve.

Two Crises in the Middle East

The main systems of conflict around which the Middle East revolves are found in the Levant and the Gulf. The crisis in the Levant is rooted in Israeli-Palestinian enmity and reaches into neighboring Lebanon and Syria. While this conflict is the focus of much anxiety throughout the world, the crisis in the Gulf is far more complex and dangerous for world peace, because it grows out of the rivalry between Iran and the Arab countries for supremacy over a body of water through which much of the planet's energy resources flow. Disagreement extends even to the Gulf's name: "Persian" according to the Iranians (and most scholars) and "Arabian" according to the Arabs. Underlying this antagonism is an age-old conflict between Sunnis and Shiites for hegemony over the meaning of Islam—although Shiism is not restricted to the Farsi sphere, having deep roots in the Arab culture of Iraq and Lebanon.

By exercising influence over Hezbollah in Lebanon, Tehran has become a central player in both of these conflicts. With Iran's help, Hezbollah was not only able to defend itself against Israel's attacks (and even claim "divine victory") during the summer of 2006 but—after the end of Emile Lahoud's term in December 2007—was also able to block any candidate to the Lebanese presidency it considered unacceptable. The compromise that was finally reached in May 2008 incorporated a number of Hezbollah's preconditions.

The Annapolis talks convened by President Bush in late November 2007 in an attempt to find a peaceful solution to the Israeli-Palestinian conflict followed almost two terms during which the White House did no more than rubber-stamp Sharon's and Olmert's policies. In reality, these talks brought Palestinian and Israeli leaders together only in order to create a front against the Iranian axis. Indeed, what these talks demonstrated was that the United States' attempt to guarantee that the road to a negotiated peace in Jerusalem would run through Baghdad had failed. The breakdown of the war on terror paradoxically redirected that road through Damascus, southern Beirut, Gaza, and Tehran.

Ahmadinejad's threats to bomb his neighbors or the Strait of Hormuz if the United States continues to put pressure on Iran to dismantle its nuclear-enrichment program has created a "balance of terror" in the Gulf region. But this situation is not without danger for Ahmadinejad himself. By holding Iran hostage to this rationale, he deprives his country of full access to the wealth represented, on both sides of the Gulf, by a combination of energy resources and investment potential. By escalating the spiral of threatened violence and general chaos, he strengthens the hand of both neoconservatives in Washington and neo-Khomeinists in Tehran.

Set against this race to mutual destruction is another possibility: the integration of Iran within an economic union that would link it with its Arab neighbors across the Gulf, and, along a network of pipelines, with Europe. Such integration depends on the constraints that economic prosperity imposes on all its beneficiaries. Exporting natural gas to Europe requires durable agreements and stable relations between producers and consumers all along the way—much more so than does oil, which can take flexible routes and may have many alternative destinations. Natural gas pipelines preclude rash threats of cataclysm, which menace first and foremost the interests of those who make the threats.

Paradoxically, another crucial factor in the future peace and prosperity of the Gulf region is nuclear energy. To prepare themselves for coming decades when production plateaus are reached or global warming forces nations to scale back on their use of fossil fuels, the Gulf states must start investing in nuclear energy. A string of civilian nuclear power installations along either side of the Gulf will deter any armed adventure. Radioactive fallout from bombing Bandar Abbas in Iran or Dammam in Saudi Arabia would be indifferent to nation or faith and would devastate Persians and Arabs, Sunnis and Shiites alike. When an economic region becomes sufficiently integrated in this way, hostile actions by any individual nation become self-destructive.

As a party with vested interests in the region, Europe could pro-

vide nuclear power installations as well as maintenance and security. The confidence bred by economic prosperity would deter terrorism in the long run, and in turn such confidence would allow
the region's leaders to see nuclear energy not as a specter of global
annihilation but as the key to sustainable development, and a com-
plement to oil resources, the abuse of which will have a hazardous
impact on the environment.

A New Space in a Multipolar World

The embryonic region I have just described is no utopia. After the
fiasco of the war on terror and armed jihad, joint economic development involving Europe and the Gulf around a Mediterranean
hub is the only viable alternative for future peace and prosperity in
the Middle East. Purely political solutions, without economic in-
centives, are bankrupt from the start. The failure to resolve the
Palestinian-Israeli crisis provides an excellent illustration of this
point. The Oslo peace process in the 1990s came to a halt in the
violence of the second intifada because the small regional entity
made up of Israel, Palestine, and perhaps Jordan and Egypt had no
economic viability in the eyes of major international investors. The
Oslo process was just a political exercise, instigated by governments alone, isolated from the world of banking and transnational
corporations. For this reason, it was doomed to fail. The frustration and despair experienced by jobless Palestinians were as great
as their original expectations had been. And a few years later some
found an exit strategy proportionate to their disappointment in
the form of suicide attacks.

The Levant and the Gulf today appear linked only to the extent that one conflict has contaminated the other—Iranian interference in Lebanon, so-called martyrdom operations seeping from Palestine to Iraq, and so on. But other peaceful manifestations of the link between these two regions are just as important, albeit not as visible, as the violent ones. Enterprising young Lebanese and Palestinians have managed to escape unemployment in Beirut, Ramallah, or Gaza and become businessmen, bankers, traders, or political advisers in Qatar, Dubai, and Abu Dhabi. Peace will enable them to find opportunities for their native countries in the networks they have built in the Arabian peninsula. There, they rub shoulders with other expatriates: young Europeans, growing numbers of whom are second- or third-generation Muslim immigrants, who are investing their knowledge and international relationships in the Gulf. Banks are exploring the possibility of financing future nuclear development with current oil and gas revenues.

The warp and weft of peace and prosperity will rest on a framework of commitments from the Gulf to the North Sea. This entails not only the movement of capital, goods, and services but also massive investment in the education of younger generations and a shared management of culture. The first prerequisite is the circulation of languages and expertise, but also of tomorrow's elites in a cultural space where each individual can find familiar markers. In antiquity, the empire of Alexander the Great owed its fecundity to the coexistence of Greek, Levantine, and Persian civilizations in a single space. The Susa weddings were the physical expression of a universal culture born of mixture and hybridization which transcended the borders that normally impede travelers, goods, and ideas. The early Islamic empire also blended the traditionally incompatible and hostile cultures of the Byzantine Mediterranean and Sassanid Persia, to create a new era characterized by exceptional development in science and technology. Fifteen centuries later, this region is not the center of civilization anymore, but it remains the planet's nerve center, capable of sending painful shocks around the world as long it remains isolated by conflict and poorly integrated into the global economic system.

The European Union's experience has shown that a vast economic, legal, and cultural space may be formed not through conquest or warfare but through the reciprocal adhesion of its members. However, the obstacles being raised to Turkey's entrance into the EU make clear that a simple extension of the European Union to include countries of the Mediterranean and the Gulf is not a realistic option for the foreseeable future. On the other hand, academic and cultural exchanges are well under way, while capital from the Gulf states is financing development in many sectors of the Maghreb, opening up fruitful opportunities for the export of European industry and technology to the region. This creation of local jobs may slow down migration to Europe while decreasing social instability in North Africa.

If Europe and the Gulf do not find the political will to bring about this economic renaissance, the Mediterranean will face many dangers—this is the principal lesson to be drawn from years of warfare between jihadists and the military forces of the United States. Europe and the Gulf states have no other viable option but to accept the challenge of building a hybrid civilization together, stretching from the North Sea to the Gulf, via the Mediterranean hub. If they fail to do so, they run the risk of declining together, joining other forgotten worlds in the museums of tomorrow.

The lesson for the United States in the Middle East is also clear.

After the failures of the Bush presidency, American influence can no longer manifest itself through armed force first and foremost but through the search for alliances with local actors. In Iraq, the triumphalist beginnings of the U.S. invasion have already given way to subtle compromises with both Sunnis and Shiites who were demonized or considered extremist at one time or another. These alliances were designed to allow for a calm withdrawal of American troops in the "post-Bush" period and to avoid chaos in the region. Such policies will succeed only if the responsibility for security and stability are shared with other nations that have a financial stake in Iraq's recovery. These actors are, first and foremost, the European Union and the Gulf Cooperation Council.

The United States' unipolar policy led to the weakening of the United States as the key broker in the region. As a result, new brokers are now emerging. Turkey, under the aegis of the moderate Islamist A.K. Party, has become involved in Arab affairs—a move the West had blocked since World War I and the fall of the Ottoman Empire. Turkish leaders not only mediated on behalf of Hamas Islamists after their victory in the Palestinian legislative elections in January 2006, they also hosted Syrian-Israeli talks in the spring of 2008. These events took place outside the realm of the Bush administration. Even Israel, a faithful U.S. ally, prepared itself for a multipolar future by entering into negotiations that would allow it to distance itself from the purely unilateral logic that prevailed when Ariel Sharon was prime minister. Although Israel's strategy of offering Syria a few guarantees in order to detach President Assad from Tehran and to loosen the pro-Iranian axis in the Levant is clear for all to see, the fact remains that such initiatives, whether Turkish or Israeli, show striking autonomy in comparison with the alignment expected of them during the war on terror.

How to manage this emerging multipolarity in the Middle East in concert with all parties concerned—including the European Union and the Gulf states—is the principal challenge that faces George W. Bush's successor. To transcend terror and martyrdom, and to ensure the decisive marginalization of jihadist radicalism, the United States has no choice but to abandon ideology and go back to politics.

NOTES

BIBLIOGRAPHY

ACKNOWLEDGMENTS

INDEX

NOTES

1. From the War on Terror to the Fiasco in Iraq

1. On Saudi Islamism, see Stephane Lacroix's seminal dissertation, "Les Champs de la discorde: Une sociologie politique de l'islamisme en Arabie Saoudite, 1954–2000" ("The Fields of Discord: A Political Sociology of Islamism in Saudi Arabia, 1954–2000"), Institut d'Etudes Politiques, December 2007.

2. *Le Monde*, May 2, 2007.

3. Official list of all Guantánamo detainees, Department of Defense, May 15, 2006.

4. Philip D. Zelikow, "Legal Policy in the Twilight War," March 10, 2006, http://www.state.gov/s/c/rls/rm/65947.htm.

5. Declaration made on June 27, 2005, cited in the *National Journal*, February 4, 2006.

6. An initial study, carried out by the law firm of Denbeaux & Denbeaux, presented most of the detainees as having been seized haphazardly and as having no significant intelligence value. See *Report on Guantanamo Detainees: A Profile of 517 Detainees through Department of Defense Data*, law.shu.edu/aaafinal.pdf, *Second Report on the Guantanamo Detainees: Inter and Intra-Departmental Disagreements About Who Is Our Enemy*, law.shu.edu/news/second_report_guantanamo_3_20_final.pdf, and *The Guantanamo Detainees during Detention; Data from Department of Defense Records*, law.shu.edu/news/guantanamo_third_report_7_11_06.pdf. The Department of Defense commissioned West Point Academy's Combating Terrorism Center to carry out another study, which, contrary to the previously cited ones, argued that the vast majority of the detainees

did indeed pose a threat, and criticized the Denbeaux report. See L. T. C. Joseph Felter and Jarret Brachman, *CTC Report: An Assessment of 516 Combatant Status Review Tribunal (CSRT) Unclassified Summaries,* July 25, 2007, www.ctc.usma.edu/csrt/CTC-CSRT-Report-072407.pdf.

7. Tom Malinovsky, of Human Rights Watch, argues that the sociological profiles of detainees in Guantánamo resemble a sample of "hundreds of thousands of angry young Muslims" rather than a terrorist cell as such. *Los Angeles Times,* March 16, 2006. Writing as Anonymous, Michael Scheuer published *Through Our Enemies' Eyes: Osama Bin Laden, Radical Islam and the Future of America* (New York: Potomac Books, 2003) and *Imperial Hubris: Why the West Is Losing the War on Terror* (New York: Potomac Books, 2007).

8. See the texts in Mark Danner, *Torture and Truth: America, Abu Ghraib, and the War on Terror* (New York: New York Review Books, 2004), pp. 108–214.

9. See the testimonies of Shafiq Rasul, Asif Iqbal, and Rhuhel Ahmed, "Composite Statement: Detention in Afghanistan and Guantanamo Bay," put online by the Center for Constitutional Rights, July 26, 2004 (their story was retold in Michael Winterbottom's 2006 film, *The Road to Guantánamo*). Mourad Benchellali, a French citizen, has published *Voyage vers l'enfer (A Trip to Hell)* (Paris, 2006). See also his article in *Le Monde,* June 17, 2006: "Les bonbons de Guantánamo" ("The Bonbons of Guantánamo"). See also *By the Numbers: Findings of the Detainee Abuse and Accountability Project,* Human Rights Watch, April 26, 2006, http://hrw.org/reports/2006/ct0406.

10. Giorgio Agamben, *Means without End (Notes on Politics),* trans. Vincenzo Binetti and Cesare Casarino (Minneapolis: University of Minnesota Press, 2000). See also *An Architektur,* "Zones extraterritoriales et camps: Espaces juridico-politiques dans la 'guerre au terrorisme'" ("Extraterritorial Zones and Camps: Legal and Political Spaces in the 'War on Terrorism'"), February 2003, http://eipcp.net/transversal/0603/anarchitektur/fr. See also Scott Michaelsen and Scott Cutler Shershow, "The Guantanamo 'Black Hole': The Law of War and the Sovereign Exception," *Middle East Report,* online, January 11, 2004.

11. John H. Yoo, "Kerry Fails the Guantanamo Test," *Wall Street Journal,* November 2, 2004. In August 2002, Boalt Law School professor John Yoo, then deputy assistant attorney general, presented a legal argument in which he claimed that the interrogation methods used at Guantánamo could not be classified as torture. See Danner, *Torture and Truth,* pp. 108–114.

12. *Times* online, June 14, 2006.

13. The material for the first articles, published in the *New Yorker* by the investigative journalist Seymour Hersh, also appeared in his book, *Chain of Command: The Road from 9/11 to Abu Ghraib* (New York: HarperCollins, 2004).

14. Mary Ann Tétrault, "The Sexual Politics of Abu Ghraib: Hegemony, Spectacle, and the Global War on Terror," *NWSA Journal,* vol. 18, no. 3, 2006, pp. 33–50.

15. The full reports by Taguba and Schlesinger are in Danner, *Torture and Truth,* pp. 271–400.

16. Fouad Ajami, *The Foreigner's Gift: The Americans, the Arabs, and the Iraqis in Iraq* (New York: Free Press, 2006), pp. 248, 250.

17. I would like to thank Loulouwa Al-Rashid, who is researching her doctoral dissertation on contemporary Iraq at the Institut d'Etudes Politiques under my supervision, for having allowed me to develop these thoughts on the basis of my reading of her fieldwork and her remarkable analyses.

18. In a *fatwa* published in the daily newspaper *Al-Hayat* on September 2, 2004, Sheikh Qaradawi opined that "combating American civilians [was] a duty for Muslims [*wajib ala al-muslimin*], since they are in Iraq to help the soldiers and occupation forces." This *fatwa* was confirmed on November 19 but later invalidated before Western diplomats in Qatar. In reality, the notion of "civilian" is not a restrictive one. For Sheikh Qaradawi, the only distinction that counts separates combatants (including anyone who helps them) from noncombatants. I would like to thank Nabil Mouline, a Ph.D. candidate at the Institut d'Etudes Politiques, for having brought these *fatwas* to my attention.

19. See *Al-Bay'a li Tanzim Al-Qaeda bi Qiyadat Al-Sheikh Osama Ben Laden,* 3 Ramadan 1425 ("Allegiance to Al-Qaeda Organization, under the Leadership of Sheikh Osama Bin Laden, October 17, 2004"),

in the compilation of Zarqawi's declarations, titled *Al-Kitab Al-Jami' li Khutab wa Kalimat Al-Sheikh Al-Mu'tazz bi Dinihi Abu Musab Al-Zarqawi. Al-Arshif Al-Jami' li Kalimat wa Khitabat Asad Al-Islam Al-Sheikh Abu Musab Al-Zarqawi Rahamahu Allah Kama Nushirat wa bil-Tartib Al-Zamani,* 14 Jumada I 1425 ("Compendium of the Speeches and Declarations of Sheikh Abu Musab Al-Zarqawi, a Defender of His Religion: The Complete Archive of the Words and Speeches of the Lion of Islam, Sheikh Abu Musab Al-Zarqawi, May God Have Mercy Upon Him, as Published in Chronological Order"), June 10, 2006, 1st ed., Shabakat Al-Buraq Al-Islamiyya, p. 172, http://press-release.blogspot.com.

20. See the letter from Zawahiri to Zarqawi, signed Abu Mohamed and dated Saturday, July 9, 2005, at http://www.fas.org/irp/news/2005/10/letter_in_arabic.pdf.

21. The figures are from the BBC: "Iraq Violence: Facts and Figures," October 26, 2006, http://news.bbc.co.uk/2/hi/middle_east/5052138.stm.

22. See Mohammed M. Hafez, *Suicide Bombers in Iraq: The Strategy and Ideology of Martyrdom* (Washington: United States Institute of Peace Press, 2007).

23. See Christoph Reuter, *My Life Is a Weapon: A Modern History of Suicide Bombing* (Princeton: Princeton University Press, 2004), for an excellent introduction to the phenomenon.

24. Declarations made by Iranian President Mahmud Ahmadinejad on July 25, 2005, during his second television appearance after he was elected. See MEMRI *Special Dispatch Series,* no. 945, for excerpts. The Iranian president has celebrated martyrdom a great many times since then.

25. On the Sadr family, it is beneficial to read Hamid Nasser, *Les Processus du courant sadriste de pere en fils (Processes of the Sadrist Trend, from Father to Son),* master's thesis, Institut d'Etudes Politiques, as well as the report by the International Crisis Group, "Iraq's Muqtada Al-Sadr: Spoiler or Stabilizer?," *Middle East Report,* no. 55, July 11, 2005.

26. Jean-Pierre Filiu has explored the political fortunes of Shiite apocalyptic literature in the contemporary context: see *L'Apocalypse dans l'Islam* (Paris: Fayard, 2008).

2. Martyrdom Operations among Shiites and Sunnis

1. On the evolution of relations between Damascus and Hezbollah, read Emile Al-Hokayem, "Hizballah and Syria: Outgrowing the Proxy Relationship," *Washington Quarterly*, vol. 30, no. 2, spring 2007, pp. 35–52.

2. In an interview with Hezbollah's associate secretary-general, Sheikh Naim Qassem, held in the southern quarter of Beirut, which the party controls, Sheikh Qassem told me that Hezbollah, allied with Iran, was the only effective opponent to Americanization of the Middle East. He added that the party was determined to prevent the election of a Lebanese president hand-picked by Washington without Hezbollah's approval. The United States' defeat in Iraq, he insisted, could not be compensated by political success in Lebanon.

3. Joseph Alagha proposes this classification in *The Shifts in Hizbullah's Ideology: Religious Ideology, Political Ideology, and Political Program* (Amsterdam: Amsterdam University Press—ISIM Dissertations, 2006), pp. 108–109.

4. Naim Qassem, *Hizbullah: The Story from Within* (London: Saqi Books, 2005), pp. 55–57, 45, 44.

5. Qassem, *Hizbullah*, pp. 47, 48.

6. Nasra Hassan, "An Arsenal of Believers," *New Yorker*, November 19, 2001.

7. Shaul Mishal and Avraham Sela, *The Palestinian Hamas: Vision, Violence, and Coexistence* (New York: Columbia University Press, 2000), esp. pp. 49–82.

8. Opinion polls in the 1990s showed rates of approval for "martyrdom operations" ranging between 21.1 and 32.7 percent, while disapproval ranged between 54.5 and 70.1 percent, according to the data presented by Mohammed M. Hafez, *Manufacturing Human Bombs: The Making of Palestinian Suicide Bombers* (Washington, DC: United States Institute of Peace Press, 2006), p. 20. Identical tendencies appear in the figures presented by Mia Bloom, *Dying to Kill: The Allure of Suicide Terror* (New York: Columbia University Press, 2005), p. 193.

9. For this document and relevant commentary, see Khaled Hroub,

Hamas: Political Thought and Practice (Washington: Institute for Palestine Studies, 2000), pp. 306–312, 246.

10. See a discussion of these opinions in David Bryan Cook, "Radical Islam and Martyrdom Operations: What Should the United States Do?" (Rice University, March 2005), http://www.rice.edu/energy/publications/docs/DavidCook_martyrdom.pdf.

11. On these statements, see the Kuwaiti publication *Al-Mujtama* (the mouthpiece of the local Muslim Brotherhood), March 19, 1996.

12. *Al-Hayat*, August 4, 1997.

13. Fatwa published in the Jordanian weekly *Al-Sabil* (the mouthpiece of the Muslim Brotherhood), no. 121, March 12, 1996.

14. *The Holy Qur'an*, VIII, 60. Abdullah Yusuf Ali's rendition uses "terror" for the Arabic *turhibuna*, to which Sheikh Qaradawi referred. The Quranic term has several meanings, but the context in which Qaradawi used it gave a positive connotation and a religious basis to the implementation of terror against God's enemies. These are identified in the preceding verse as "the unbelievers"—infidels or *kuffar*. The definition of this term does not include Jews (who are People of the Book), but a scholar or the author of a jihadist *fatwa* may designate Israelis, by extension, as "enemies of God."

15. This interpretation of Al Jazeera's discourse owes a great deal to the original, profound reflections of Claire Talon, who is researching a doctoral dissertation on the Qatari television channel at the Institut d'Etudes Politiques. I wish to thank her here.

16. The translated, annotated text appears in Gilles Kepel and Jean-Pierre Milelli, eds., *Al Qaeda in Its Own Words*, trans. Pascale Ghazaleh (Cambridge: The Belknap Press of Harvard University Press, 2008).

17. Lawrence Wright, *The Looming Tower: Al-Qaeda and the Road to 9/11* (New York: Knopf, 2006).

18. According to Mohammed M. Hafez, p. 20, the rate of approval for suicide attacks rose to 66.2 percent in December 2000 and stayed at similar or higher levels until October 2003, when it peaked at 74.5 percent. Similar tendencies were observed by Mia Bloom, p. 193.

19. Communiqué of April 24, 2002, trans. in David B. Cook, *Understanding Jihad* (Berkeley: University of California Press, 2005), p. 177.

20. Cited in Barbara Victor, *Army of Roses: Inside the World of Palestinian Suicide Bombers* (New York: Rodale Books, 2003), p. 41.

21. René Girard, *Violence and the Sacred*, trans. Patrick Gregory (Baltimore: The Johns Hopkins University Press, 1979).

22. Between September 11, 2001, and February 2005, according to Mohammed M. Hafez.

3. The Third Phase of Jihad

1. Abu Musab Al-Suri, *Dawa Al-Muqawama Al-Islamiyya Al-Alamiyya (Call to Global Islamic Resistance)*. The DCIA Counterterrorism Center, Office of Terrorism Analysis, translated part of the work into English under the title *The Call for Islamic Resistance: Abu Mus'ab Al-Suri, Umar Abd Al-Hakim* in October 2006. See also internal debates regarding the strategies and goals of the global jihadist movement in the study "Cracks in the Foundation: Leadership Schisms in al-Qa'ida from 1989–2006," by the Combating Terrorism Center at West Point, September 2007, http://ctc.usma.edu/aq/aq3.asp. The best material on Suri's life is to be found in Brynjar Lia, *Architect of Global Jihad: The Life of Al Qaeda Strategist Abu Mus'ab Al-Suri* (London: Hurst, 2007).

2. See *Al-Bay'a li Tanzim Al-Qaeda . . .* in *Archives*, p. 172, http://press-release.blogspot.com/.

3. See the video titled *Shahid Al-Umma wa Amir Al-Istishhad (Martyr of the Community and Prince of Martyrs)*, As-Sahab, broadcast on June 23, 2006, by Al Jazeera and available at http://www.youtube.com.

4. See the video titled *Al-Idwan Al-Sahyuni 'ala Ghazza wa Lubnan (The Zionist Attack on Gaza and Lebanon)*, broadcast by As-Sahab on July 27, 2006.

5. See *Al-Ilm lil-Amal: Ghazwat Manhattan (Knowledge for Action: The Raid on Manhattan)*, September 2006, parts 1 and 2, As-Sahab.

6. See *Arba'at Sanawat ba'd Ghazawat New York wa Washington (Four Years after the Raids on New York and Washington)*, September 2005, As-Sahab. Al Jazeera broadcast excerpts from this interview with Zawahiri on the fourth anniversary of the September 11 attacks. Starting on December 7, 2005, the entire video of this interview was available on jihadist websites.

7. See *Wasaya Fursan (Testament of Knights)*, August 2005, As-Sahab.

8. See *Majles Shura Al-Mujahidin fil-Iraq: Al-Hay'a Al-Ilamiyya. Bushra lil-Muslimin fi Kulli Makan: Al-Ilan an Qiyam Dawlat Al-Iraq Al-Islamiyya. Kalimat Al-Mutahaddith Al-Rasmi lil-Dawla, Wizarat Al-Ilam (Consultative Council for the Mujahedin in Iraq: Media Corps. Good News for Muslims Everywhere: Declaration of the Establishment of the Islamic State of Iraq. Speech by the Official State Spokesman, Ministry of Information).*

9. In a video broadcast on Al Jazeera on December 8, 2005, Zawahiri called on the community to mobilize in aid of the Muslim victims of the earthquake that had occurred in Pakistan.

10. On January 6, 2006, Al Jazeera broadcast a video in which Zawahiri called on President Bush to "admit defeat" in Iraq, and accused the Arab League of having acted for Washington's benefit by hosting a reconciliation conference on Iraq.

11. On January 31, 2006, Al Jazeera's news program included a clip from a video by As-Sahab, in which Zawahiri launched a violent diatribe against President Bush, announcing his imminent defeat in Afghanistan and Iraq, warned Pakistani President Musharraf that he would be punished for collaborating with the United States, and presented his condolences to the Pakistani people, calling on them to join Mullah Omar and the Taliban. This video was shot after U.S. forces bombed an Afghan village, hoping to hit Zawahiri. Available on http://www.memritv.org/clip/en/1015.htm.

12. In a video broadcast by Al Jazeera on March 5, 2006, Zawahiri called on Muslims to fight "on four fronts" against the west, and especially the United States, to defend the dignity of the Prophet Muhammad, who had been insulted by the cartoons.

13. Ayman Al-Zawahiri, *Min Tora Bora ila Al-Iraq (From Tora Bora to Iraq)*, March 2006.

14. A video produced by As-Sahab was posted on jihadist websites, for example, alhesbah.org, on April 12, 2006.

15. *Ritha Shahid Al-Umma wa Amir Al-Istishhadiyyin Abi Musab Al-Zarqawi Rahamahu Allah (Elegy for the Martyr . . . Abu Musab Al-Zarqawi, God's Mercy Be Upon Him)*, June 30, 2006, in Archive, p. 320, http://www.e-prism.org.

16. As-Sahab posted a video on July 7, 2006. It is available, in three parts.

17. See the video *Da'wa lil-Islam (Invitation to Islam)*, September 2006, As-Sahab, posted on alhesbah.org on September 2, 2006.

18. See the recording by As-Sahab, posted on September 29, 2006.

19. *Qadaya Sakhina ma' Al-Sheikh Ayman Al-Zawahiri (Hot Topics with Sheikh Ayman Al-Zawahiri)*, September 2006, As-Sahab.

20. *Abu Musab Abdel-Wudud, Amir Al-Jama'a Al-Salafiyya lil-Da'wa wal-Qital: Bayan wa Bushra bi Indimam wa Mubaya'at Al-Jama'a Al-Salafiyya lil-Da'wa wal-Qital lil-Sheikh Abi Abd Allah Osama Ben Laden (Abu Musab Abdel-Wudud, Emir of the Salafi Group for Preaching and Fighting: Announcing that the Group Has Joined Sheikh Abu Abdallah Osama Ben Laden)*, September 13, 2006, and also *Bayan min Al-Thabitin ala Al-Ahd fil-Jama'a Al-Islamiyya Al-Misriyya, Wihdat Al-Saff (Communiqué from the Steadfast Members of the Egyptian Jamaa Islamiyya/Unity in the Ranks)*, April 2006, As-Sahab.

21. *Haqa'iq Al-Sira' Bayn Al-Islam wal-Kufr (The Truth about the Struggle between Islam and Unbelief)*, November 2006, As-Sahab, posted on November 11, 2006.

22. *Al-Mu'adala Al-Sahiha (The Correct Equation)*, As-Sahab.

23. *Durus wa Ibar wa Ahdath Izam min Sanat 1427 (Lessons about the Great Events of 2006)*, As-Sahab, 2007, posted on February 15, 2007.

24. *Liqa ma' Al-Sheikh Ayman Al-Zawahiri (Interview with Sheikh Ayman Al-Zawahiri)*, As-Sahab, posted on May 5, 2007.

25. *Ritha' Qa'id Al-Istishhadiyyin Al-Mullah Dadallah Rahamahu Allah (Elegy for the Leader of Martyrs, Mullah Dadallah, God's Mercy Be Upon Him)*, As-Sahab, http://www.youtube.com.

26. On June 25, 2007, an image with voice-over was posted on alhesbah.org, titled *Arba'una 'Aman 'ala Suqut Al-Quds (Forty Years After the Fall of Jerusalem)*, As-Sahab.

27. *Nasihat Mushfiq (Advice from One Who Is Concerned)*, As-Sahab, July 2007.

28. *Al-Hall (The Solution)*, September 7, 2007, As-Sahab, http://www.dailymotion.com/video/x2xe4o_2007-ben-laden-reapparait-en-video_news and *Wasaya Shuhada Ghazwatayy New York wa Wash-*

ington (Testaments of the Martyrs of the Raids on New York and Washington), As-Sahab, September 2007.

29. http://www.youtube.com.

30. *Ilhaq bil-Qafila (Join the Caravan)*, January 4, 2004, in *Archives*, p. 32, http://press-release.blogspot.com/.

31. *Min Abi Musab Al-Zarqawi ila Al-Sheikh Osama Ben Laden (From Abu Musab Al-Zarqawi to Sheikh Osama Ben Laden)*, *Archives*, p. 58.

32. *Al-Bay'a li Tanzim Al-Qaeda bi Qiyadat Al-Sheikh Osama Ben Laden (Allegiance to Al-Qaeda Organization, Under the Leadership of Sheikh Osama Ben Laden)*, October 17, 2004, *Archives*, p. 172.

33. *Silsilat Muhadarat La Yadurruhum Man Khazalahum*, series of talks held on September 19, September 30, October 7, and October 14, 2005.

34. Abu Mohamed Al-Maqdisi, *Al-Zarqawi: Munasara wa Munasaha, Amal wa Alam (Zarqawi: Assistance and Reprimands, Hopes and Pain)*, July 2004, www.tawhed.ws.

35. *Kalima fi Sharit Nahr Alan Armstrong (A Word on the Beheading of Alan [sic] Armstrong)*, October 10, 2004, *Archives*, p. 168.

36. *Hadha Balagh lil-Nas (This is a Declaration to the People)*, April 24, 2006, *Archives*, p. 511.

37. The declaration of the Islamic State of Iraq, made by Sawt Al-Khalifa in October 2006, can be viewed on www.cvc-online .blogspot.com.

38. Communiqués claiming responsibility for military operations carried out by the Islamic Army of Iraq were posted by Al-Boraq and can be viewed on *Muntada Bayanat Al-Jaysh Al-Islami fil-Iraq* ("Forum for Communiqués of the Islamic Army in Iraq"), Shabakat Al-Boraq Al-Islamiyya, http://www.alboraq.info/archive/index. php/f-5.html.

39. Abu Musab Al-Suri, *Dawa*, p. 27.

40. http://ekhlaas.biz/forum/showthread.php?t=112263.

41. Abu Musab Al-Suri, *Dawa*, p. 37.

4. Missteps of Multiculturalism

1. See among other works: Lorenzo Vidino, *Al-Qaeda in Europe: The New Battleground of International Jihad* (Amherst, NY: Prometheus Books, 2005); Bat Ye'Or, *Eurabia, the Euro-Arab Axis* (Washington:

Fairleigh Dickinson University Press, 2005); Bruce Bawer, *While Europe Slept: How Radical Islam Is Destroying the West from Within* (New York: Random House, 2006); and Mark Steyn, *America Alone: The End of the World as We Know It* (New York: Regnery Publishing, 2008).

2. Interviewed by the German daily *Die Welt* on July 28, 2004, on the question of Europe's future, Professor Bernard Lewis replied: "Europe will become part of the Arab West, the Maghreb, by the end of this century at the latest. Migration and demography are working towards this. Europeans marry late and have few or no children. But immigration remains strong: Turks in Germany, Arabs in France, and Pakistanis in Britain marry young and have many children. According to current trends, Europe will have Muslim majorities in the population by the end of the 21st century at the latest."

3. On January 23, 2003, Donald Rumsfeld declared that France and Germany represented "old Europe" and claimed the continent's center of gravity was shifting to the east. "Outrage at 'Old Europe' Remarks," BBC News, January 23, 2003.

4. "Islam in America," *Newsweek*, July 30, 2007, pp. 24–33.

5. http://usmedia.over-blog.com/article-1159693.html.

6. Mike Ingram, "Britain: Outstanding Questions on July 7 Bombings Warrant Independent Inquiry," August 6, 2005, http://www.wsws .org/articles/2005/aug2005/lond-a06.shtml. See also the *Independent*, the *Sunday Times*, and the *Washington Post* of July 18, 2005, as well as *AFX News*, July 21, 2005.

7. Mokhtar Said Ibrahim, a 27-year-old of Ethiopian origin, had tried to blow up a bomb on bus #26 in east London. A Luton court condemned him to five years in prison in February 1996; despite his record, he received British nationality in September 2004. He was arrested on July 29, 2005, in London. *Times*, January 16, 2007.

8. Abu Musab Al-Suri, *Dawa*, p. 723.

9. Inquiry published on July 22, 2007, on the BBC website http://news .bbc.co.uk/1/hi/uk/6275574.stm.

10. Kepel, *Allah in the West* (Stanford: Stanford University Press, 1997). Lisa Appignanesi and Sara Maitland, *The Rushdie File* (Syracuse, NY: Syracuse University Press, 1990).

11. Among others, see Bernard-Henry Lévy, *Qui a tué Daniel Pearl?* (Paris: Grasset, 2003); Mariane Pearl and Sarah Crichton, *A Mighty*

Heart: The Brave Life and Death of My Husband, Danny Pearl (New York: Scribner, 2007).

12. Raymond Whitaker and Paul Lashmar, "On 7/7 Anniversary, Jeep Passenger Appears in Court Over Bomb Attacks," *Independent*, July 9, 2007.

13. British Home Office, "Preventing Extremism Together," *Working Group Reports*, August–September 2005.

14. "Ken Livingstone Cover Story," *Prospect*, no. 133, April 2007. Discussion among Ken Livingstone, Simon Parker, David Goodhart, and Tony Travers.

15. Gilles Kepel, *The War for Muslim Minds: Islam and the West*, trans. Pascale Ghazaleh (Cambridge: The Belknap Press of Harvard University Press, 2006).

16. The British tabloids offered profiles of the physicians involved in the failed attacks of London and Glasgow. On August 12, 2007, the *Sun* published a front-page picture of Mohamed Asha, the instigator of the attacks, under the headline: "Dr. Evil." On August 27, 2007, the *Daily Mail* described the group as the "Doctors Terror Gang."

17. David Goodhart, "Open Letter to Tariq Ramadan," *Prospect*, no. 135, June 2007.

18. The Pew Research Center, Pew Global Attitudes Project, "The Great Divide: How Westerners and Muslims View Each Other—Europe's Muslims More Moderate," http://pewglobal.org/reports/display .php?ReportID=253.

19. Christophe de Voogd, *Histoire des Pays-Bas des origines à nos jours* ("History of the Netherlands, from the Origins until Today") (Paris: Fayard, 2004), p. 213.

20. Marie-Claire Cecilia, "Netherlands: The Pillars Are Shaken," *Le Monde diplomatique*, March 2005, http://mondediplo.com/2005/ 03 /04netherlands.

21. Frits Bolkestein, "Moslem in de Polder" ("Muslims in the Netherlands"), *Foreign Policy*, no. 112, autumn 1998, pp. 138–141, and Paul Scheffer, "Het multiculturele drama" ("The Multicultural Drama"), *NRC-Handelsbald*, January 2000, as well as Marie-Claire Cecilia, "L'Islam aux Pays-Bas: un modèle d'intégration en question" ("Islam in the Netherlands: Challenges to an Integration Model"), 2004, www.islamlaicite.org/article285.html.

22. On Pim Fortuyn, see Peter Ven Der Veer, "Pim Fortuyn, Theo van

Gogh, and the Politics of Tolerance in the Netherlands," in *Public Culture Journal*, vol. 18, no. 1, http://www.publicculture.org/articles/ volume_18_number_1/pim_fortuyn_theo_van_gogh_and_th. On the assassination of Theo Van Gogh, see Ian Buruma, *Murder in Amsterdam: The Death of Theo van Gogh and the Limits of Tolerance* (London: Penguin Books, 2006), p. 278. Ayaan Hirsi Ali has published several works, including *Infidel* (New York: Free Press, 2007) and *The Caged Virgin: An Emancipation Proclamation for Women and Islam* (New York: Free Press, 2006).

23. Various interpretations of these verses (IV, 34), differing in intensity, have been proposed. See for example Pickthall: "Men are in charge of women, because Allah has made the one of them to excel the other, and because they spend of their property [for the support of women]. So good women are . . . obedient, guarding in secret that which Allah has guarded. As for those from whom you fear rebellion, admonish them and banish them to beds apart, and scourge them. Then if they obey you, seek not a way against them. Lo! Allah is ever High Exalted, Great." In Arberry's version: "Men are the managers of the affairs of women for that God has preferred in bounty one of them over another, and for that they have expended of their property. Righteous women are therefore obedient, guarding the secret for God's guarding. And those you fear may be rebellious admonish; banish them to their couches, and beat them. If they then obey you, look not for any way against them; God is All high, All great." In Ali's rendering: "Men are the protectors and maintainers of women, because Allah has given the one more [strength] than the other, and because they support them from their means. Therefore the righteous women are devoutly obedient, and guard in [the husband's] absence what Allah would have them guard. As to those women on whose part you fear disloyalty and ill conduct, admonish them [first], [next], refuse to share their beds, [and last] beat them [lightly]; but if they return to obedience, seek not against them means [of annoyance] for Allah is Most High, Great [above you all]." For interesting general remarks on differences between various English renditions, see http://www .theabodeofpeace.com/korans.html. See Muhammad M. Pickthall, *The Koran* (New York: Alfred Knopf, 1930); A. J. Arberry, *The Koran Interpreted: A Translation* (London: George Allen & Unwin, 1955);

and A. Y. Ali, *The Meaning of the Holy Quran* (Beltsville, MD: Amana Publications, 1989; 1st ed. 1934).

24. The text is available on the website of the Dutch ministry of justice: http://www.om.nl/dossier/moord_op_theo_van_gogh/.

25. Report by AIVD (Dutch intelligence and security apparatus), "Recruitment for the Jihad in the Netherlands, from Incident to Trend."

26. Dossier on the Bouyeri trial available on the Dutch ministry of justice website (see note 24, above).

27. Announcement made on Dutch television on November 27, 2005. See *Septentrion*, vol. 35, no. 1, first trimester of 2006, p. 82.

28. On May 11, 2006, the Dutch national television station, NPS, broadcast a documentary titled *Holy Ayaan*, in which Ali was accused of having lied about her name, her date of birth, her status, and even her forced marriage. The video is at www.zembla.vara.nl/dossiers.1963.0.html.

5. The Propaganda Battle in Europe

1. Kaare Bluitgen, *Koranen og profeten Muhammeds liv (The Quran and the Life of the Prophet Muhammad).*

2. Open Society Institute, "Muslims in the EU—Cities Report," EU Monitoring and Advocacy Program, Denmark, Preliminary Research Report and Literature Survey, 2007, p. 5, http://www.eumap.org/topics/minority/reports/eumuslims/background_reports/download/denmark/denmark.pdf.

3. Open Society Institute, "Muslims in the EU," p. 20.

4. "L'extrême droite danoise alimente une xénophobie bien-pensante" ("The Danish extreme right is fueling self-righteous xenophobia"), *Le Monde*, February 9, 2006.

5. "Pia Kjaersgaard, leader of the far-right party, has managed to make xenophobic opinions banal—such as the one, expressed recently, comparing Muslims to a 'cancerous tumor.'" *Le Monde*, "L'extrême droite."

6. A competition for the best Holocaust cartoon was organized in February 2006 in Tehran at the initiative of *Hamsharhi*, an Iranian daily newspaper. The competition provided the opportunity for an exhibition organized by Iran Caricature, a local association, and based on the selection of 200 drawings out of a total of 1,100 sent from

over 60 countries. The contest ended on September 14, 2006. On September 2, a jury of five cartoonists had chosen the best three, whose authors received cash prizes ranging from $5,000 to $12,000.

7. See Khaled Chamt's article of February 11, 2006, on the Al Jazeera website.

8. Dialogue with Dr. Abdel-Sattar Fath Allah Said, "Practical Advice for Defending the Prophet," islamonline.net, February 6, 2006,   http://www.islamonline.net/LiveFatwa/Arabic/Browse.asp?hGuestID=pc58id.

9. Mohamed Sifaoui, *L'affaire des caricatures (The Affair of the Cartoons)* (Paris: Editions Privé, 2006).

10. http://www.vatican.va/holy_father/benedict_xvi/speeches/2006/september/documents/hf_ben-xvi_spe_20060912_university-regensburg_en.html.

11. "Les propos de Benoît XVI font craindre une crise plus violente que celle des caricatures" ("Benedict XVI's Statements Arouse Fears of a More Violent Crisis Than the One Caused by the Cartoons"), *Le Monde*, September 15, 2006.

12. See www.alarabiya.net, September 18, 2006.

13. See video on http://www.youtube.com.

14. Theodore Khoury (introduction, critical edition, translation, and notes), *Manuel II Paléologue, Entretiens avec un musulman, 7eme controverse (Manuel II Paleologus, Conversations with a Muslim, 7th Controversy)* (Paris: Editions du cerf, 1966).

15. http://www.vatican.va/holy_father/benedict_xvi/speeches/2006/september/documents/hf_ben-xvi_spe_20060912_university-regensburg_en.html.

16. The scholars in question are Theodore Khoury, a Catholic theologian, born in Lebanon in 1930, who has rendered the Quran in German; and Roger Arnaldez (1911–2006), a French scholar of Islam. Both worked for Muslim-Christian dialogue.

17. "Open Letter to His Holiness Pope Benedict XVI," http://www.islamicamagazine.com/letter/.

18. See Abdelwahab Meddeb's remarks in Jean Bollack et al., *La Conférence de Ratisbonne: enjeux et controverses (The Regensburg Conference: Wagers and Controversies)* (Paris: Bayard, 2007), p. 91.

19. Daniel Dombey and Simon Kuper, "Britons 'More Suspicious' of Muslims," *Financial Times*, August 19, 2007, http://www.ft.com/

cms/s/0/114ea332-4e8a-11dc-85e7-0000779fd2ac.html.

20. Ibid.

21. http://pewglobal.org/reports/display.php?ReportID=253.

22. *The O'Reilly Factor,* November 7, 2005, Fox News Network. See also Larry Collins and Dominique Lapierre, *Is Paris Burning? How Paris Miraculously Escaped Adolf Hitler's Sentence of Death in August 1944* (New York: Simon and Schuster, 1965).

23. The map of France that CNN used was later posted with commentary numerous times on the Internet. See for example http://www.freerepublic.com/focus/f-news/1522115/posts.

24. http://www.debka.com/article.php?aid=1107.

25. See for instance http://www.frontpagemagazine.com/Articles/Read.aspx?GUID=66855023-B05A-499E-B81E-8A7310270F45.

26. See www.liveleak.com.

27. The *Herald Tribune,* November 4, 2005. See coverage on www.jihad-watch.org/.

28. Hughes Lagranges and Marco Oberti, *Emeutes urbaines et protestations: une singularité française* (*Urban Riots and Protests: A French Particularity*) (Paris: Sciences-Po, 2006).

29. Gérard Mauger, *L'Emeute de novembre 2005; une révolte proto-politique (The November 2005 Uprising: A Proto-political Rebellion)* (Paris: Editions du Croquant, 2006).

30. www.uoif-online.com.

6. The Challenge of Civilization

1. Video recording entitled "Qira't al Ahdath/A Review of Events, December 2007, 97 mn and 35 sec, accessed on http://lauramansfield.com/Sm.rm. Dr. Fadel, or Sayed Imam al-Sharif, attacked Zawahiri in a book entitled *Guidebook for Jihad Work in Egypt and the World,* posted on the web in November 2007, and gave a long interview, behind the bars of his Egyptian prison, to the Cairo correspondent of *Al Hayat* daily, published from December 8, onwards. The story and background of the Fadel/Zawahiri dispute was told by Lawrence Wright, "The Rebellion Within: An Al Qaeda Mastermind Questions Terrorism," *The New Yorker,* June 2, 2008.

2. Fareed Zakaria, *The Post-American World* (New York: Norton, 2008).

BIBLIOGRAPHY

1. From the War on Terror to the Fiasco in Iraq

Agamben, Giorgio. *Means without End: Notes on Politics.* Trans. Vincenzo Binetti and Cesare Casarino. Minneapolis: University of Minnesota Press, 2000.

Ajami, Fouad. *The Foreigner's Gift: The Americans, the Arabs and the Iraqis in Iraq.* New York: Free Press, 2006.

Allawi, Ali A. *The Occupation of Iraq: Winning the War, Losing the Peace.* New Haven: Yale University Press, 2007.

Bremer, L. Paul, III. *My Year in Iraq: The Struggle to Build a Future of Hope.* New York: Simon & Schuster, 2005.

Campbell, Kurt, and Michael E. O'Hanlon. *Hard Power: The New Politics of National Security.* New York: Basic Books, 2006.

Chandrasekaran, Rajiv. *Imperial Life in the Emerald City: Inside Iraq's Green Zone.* New York: Knopf, 2006.

Courbage, Youssef, and Emmanuel Todd. *Le Rendez-vous des civilisations.* Paris: Seuil, 2007.

Daanlder, Ivo H., and James M. Lindsay. *America Unbound: The Bush Revolution in Foreign Policy.* Washington, D.C.: Brookings Institution Press, 2003.

Danner, Marc. *Torture and Truth: America, Abu Ghraib and the War on Terror.* London: Granta, 2004.

Diamond, Larry. *Squandered Victory: The American Occupation and the Bungled Effort to Bring Democracy to Iraq.* New York: Henry Holt, 2005.

Droz-Vincent, Philippe. *Les Vertiges de la puissance: "Le moment américain" au Moyen-Orient.* Paris: Découverte, 2007.

Faath, Sigrid, ed. *Anti-Americanism in the Islamic World.* London: Hurst, 2006.

Filiu, Jean-Pierre. *L'Apocalypse dan l'Islam.* Paris: Fayard, 2008.

Goldsmith, Jack. *The Terror Presidency: Law and Judgment inside the Bush Administration.* New York: Norton, 2007.

Gordon, Michael R., and General Bernard E. Trainor. *Cobra II: The Inside Story of the Invasion and Occupation of Iraq.* New York: Pantheon, 2006.

Gordon, Philip. *Winning the Right War: The Path to Security for Iraq and the World.* New York: Times Books, 2007.

Greenberg, Karen J., ed. *The Torture Debate in America.* New York: Cambridge University Press, 2006.

Greenberg, Karen J., and Joshua L. Dratel. *The Torture Papers: The Road to Abu Ghraib.* New York: Cambridge University Press, 2005.

Hafez, Mohammed M. *Suicide Bombings in Iraq: The Strategy and Ideology of Martyrdom.* Washington, D.C.: United States Institute of Peace Press, 2007.

Hashim, Ahmed S. *Insurgency and Counter-insurgency in Iraq.* London: Hurst, 2006.

Herring, Eric, and Glen Rangwala. *Iraq in Fragments: The Occupation and Its Legacy.* New York: Cornell University Press, 2006.

Hersh, Seymour. *Chain of Command.* New York: Harper Collins, 2004.

Jabar, Faleh A. *The Shi'ite Movement in Iraq.* London: Saqi, 2003.

Kagan, Robert. *Dangerous Nation: America's Place in the World from Its Earliest Days to the Dawn of the Twentieth Century.* New York: Knopf, 2006.

Lafourcade, Fanny. *Le Chaos irakien: dix clefs pour comprendre.* Paris: Découverte, 2007.

Lia, Brynjar. *Globalisation and the Future of Terrorism: Patterns and Predictions.* London: Routledge, 2005.

Margulies, Joseph. *Guantanamo and the Abuse of Presidential Power.* New York: Simon & Schuster, 2006.

Mearsheimer, John J., and Stephen M. Walt. *The Israel Lobby and U.S. Foreign Policy.* New York: Farrar, Straus and Giroux, 2007.

Mueller, John. *Overblown: How Politicians and the Terrorism Industry Inflate National Security Threats, and Why We Believe Them.* New York: Free Press, 2006.

Packer, George. *The Assassins' Gate: America in Iraq.* New York: Farrar, Straus and Giroux, 2005.

Pollack, Kenneth M. *The Persian Puzzle: The Conflict between Iran and America.* New York: Random House, 2005.

Preble, Christopher. *Exiting Iraq: Why the U.S. Must End the Military Occupation and Renew the War against Al Qaeda.* Washington, D.C.: CATO Institute, 2004.

Richardson, Louise. *What Terrorists Want: Understanding the Enemy, Containing the Threat.* New York: Random House, 2006.

Ricks, Thomas. *Fiasco: The American Military Adventure in Iraq.* New York: Penguin, 2006.

Simpson, Alan K. *The Iraq Study Group Report.* Washington, D.C.: United States Institute for Peace, 2006.

Smith, Julianne, and Thomas Sanderson, eds. *Five Years after 9/11: An Assessment of America's War on Terror.* Washington, D.C.: CSIS Press, 2006.

Woodward, Bob. *State of Denial: Bush at War, Part III.* New York: Simon & Schuster, 2006.

Yoo, John. *War by Other Means: An Insider's Account of the War on Terror.* New York: Atlantic Monthly Press, 2006.

2. Martyrdom Operations among Shiites and Sunnis

Alagha, Joseph. *The Shifts in Hizbullah's Ideology: Religious Ideology, Political Ideology and Political Program.* Amsterdam: Amsterdam University Press, 2006.

Al-Bostani, Abbas Ahmad, trans. *L'Imam al-Husayn et le jour de Âchourâ.* Paris: Bibliothèque Ahl-Elbeit, 1984.

Aliq, Nasser Hassan. *Falsafat al istishhad: Allah wa-l watan fi khitab al muqawama al islamiyya.* Beirut: Dar al-Mawassim, 2004.

Ansari, Ali M. *Iran, Islam and Democracy: The Politics of Managing Change.* 2nd ed. London: Chatham House, 2006.

Asad, Talal. *On Suicide Bombing.* New York: Columbia University Press, 2007.

Baudelot, Christian, and Roger Establet. *Suicide: l'envers de notre monde.* Paris: Seuil, 2006.

Bloom, Mia. *Dying to Kill: The Allure of Suicide Bombing.* New York: Columbia University Press, 2005.

Chehab, Zaki. *Inside Hamas: The Untold Story of the Militant Islamic Movement.* New York: Nation Books, 2007.

Cook, David. *Martyrdom in Islam.* New York: Cambridge University Press, 2007.

Coville, Thierry. *Iran: la révolution invisible.* Paris: Découverte, 2007.

Dabashi, Hamid. *Iran: A People Interrupted.* New York: New Press, 2007.

Dassetto, Felice, and Brigitte Maréchal. "Le suicide offensif en Islam." *Maghreb Machrek* 186 (Winter 2005–2006).

Delpech, Thérèse. *Iran and the Bomb: The Abdication of International Responsibility.* Trans. Ros Schwartz. New York: Columbia University Press, 2007.

——— *Le grand perturbateur: réflexions sur la question iranienne.* Paris: Grasset, 2007.

Emirates Centre for Strategic Studies and Research. *Iran's Nuclear Program: Realities and Repercussions.* Abu Dhabi: ECSSR, 2006.

Firestone, Reuven. *Jihad: The Origin of Holy War in Islam.* New York: Oxford University Press, 1999.

Gambetta, Diego, ed. *Making Sense of Suicide Missions.* London: Oxford University Press, 2005.

Girard, René. *Violence and the Sacred.* Trans. Patrick Gregory. Baltimore: Johns Hopkins University Press, 1977.

Hafez, Mohammed M. *Manufacturing Human Bombs: The Making of Palestinian Suicide Bombers.* Washington, D.C.: United States Institute of Peace Press, 2006.

Hroub, Khaled. *Hamas: Political Thought and Practice.* Washington, D.C.: Institute for Palestine Studies, 2000.

Jafarzadeh, Alireza. *The Iran Threat: President Ahmadinejad and the Coming Nuclear Crisis.* New York: Palgrave, 2007.

Jorisch, Avi. *Beacon of Hatred: Inside Hizballah's Al-Manar Television.* Washington, D.C.: Washington Institute for Near East Policy, 2004.

Kepel, Gilles. *Jihad: The Trail of Political Islam.* Trans. Anthony F. Roberts. Cambridge: Harvard University Press, 2002.

Khosrokhavar, Farhad. *Suicide Bombers: Allah's New Martyrs*. Trans. David Macey. London: Pluto, 2005.

Khosrokhavar, Farhad. *Quand Al-Qaida parle: témoignages derrière les barreaux*. Paris: Grasset, 2006.

Melman, Yossi, and Meir Javedanfar. *The Nuclear Sphinx of Tehran: Mahmoud Ahmedinejad and the State of Iran*. New York: Carroll and Graf, 2007.

Mishal, Shaul, and Avraham Sela. *The Palestinian Hamas: Vision, Violence and Coexistence*. New York: Columbia University Press, 2000.

Mohammad-Arif, Aminah, and Jean Schmitz, eds. *Figures d'Islam après le 11 Septembre: disciples et martyrs, réfugiés et migrants*. Paris: Karthala, 2006.

Nakash, Yitzhak. *Reaching for Power: The Shia in the Modern Arab World*. Princeton: Princeton University Press, 2006.

Nasr, Vali. *The Shia Revival: How Conflicts within Islam Will Shape the Future*. New York: Norton, 2005.

Noe, Nichols. *Voice of Hezbollah: The Statements of Sayyed Hassan Nasrallah*. London: Verso, 2007.

Norton, Augustus Richard. *Hezbollah*. Princeton: Princeton University Press, 2007.

Oliver, Anne Marie, and Paul F. Steinberg. *The Road to Martyrs' Square: A Journey into the World of the Suicide Bomber*. New York: Oxford University Press, 2005.

Pape, Robert A. *Dying to Win: The Strategic Logic of Suicide Terrorism*. New York: Random House, 2005.

Qassem, Naim. *Al Mehdi al Mukhaless*. Beirut: Dar al-Hadi, 2007.

——— *Hezb allah: al minhaj, al tajriba, al mustaqbal*. Beirut: Dar al-Hadi, 2004

——— *Hizbullah: The Story from Within*. Trans. Dalia Khalil. London: Saqi, 2005.

Reuter, Christoph. *My Life Is a Weapon: A Modern History of Suicide Bombing*. Princeton: Princeton University Press, 2004.

Saad-Ghorayeb, Amal. *Hizbu'llah: Politics and Religion*. London: Pluto, 2002.

Sageman, Marc. *Understanding Terror Networks*. Philadelphia: University of Pennsylvania Press, 2004.

Sayyed Ahmed, Rifʿat. *Hassan Nasrallah: thaʾir min al janoub.* Damascus: Dar al-kitab al-arabi, 2006.

Takeyh, Ray. *Hidden Iran: Paradox and Power in the Islamic Republic.* New York: Times Books, 2006.

Tamimi, Azzam. *Hamas: Unwritten Chapters.* London: Hurst, 2007.

Tilley, Virginia. *The One-State Solution: A Breakthrough for Peace in the Israeli-Palestinian Deadlock.* Ann Arbor: University of Michigan Press, 2005.

Victor, Barbara. *Army of Roses: Inside the World of Palestinian Women Suicide Bombers.* New York: Rodale Books, 2003.

Wright, Lawrence. *The Looming Tower: Al Qaida and the Road to 9/11.* New York: Knopf, 2006.

3. The Third Phase of Jihad

Atwan, Abdel Bari. *The Secret History of al-Qaʿida.* London: Saqi, 2006.

Bonney, Richard. *Jihad: From Qurʾan to bin Laden.* London: Palgrave, 2004.

Brisard, Jean-Charles, and Damien Martinez. *Zarqawi: The New Face of Al-Qaeda.* New York: Other Press, 2005.

Cook, David. *Understanding Jihad.* Berkeley: University of California Press, 2005.

Gerges, Fawaz A. *The Far Enemy: Why Jihad Went Global.* New York: Cambridge University Press, 2005.

Hoffman, Bruce. *Inside Terrorism.* Rev. ed. New York: Columbia University Press, 2006.

Hussein, Fuʾad. *Al Zarqawi: al jil al thalith li al qaʿida.* Beirut: Dar al-Khiyal, 2005.

Ibrahim, Raymond. *The Al Qaeda Reader.* New York: Broadway Books, 2007.

Kepel, Gilles, and Jean-Pierre Milelli, eds. *Al Qaeda in Its Own Words.* Trans. Pascale Ghazaleh. Cambridge: Harvard University Press, 2008.

Lawrence, Bruce, James Howarth, and Osama bin Laden. *Messages to the World: The Statements of Osama bin Laden.* London: Verso, 2005.

Lia, Brynjar. *Architect of Global Jihad: The Life of Al Qaeda Strategist Abu Musʿab al-Suri.* London: Hurst, 2007.

Napoleoni, Loretta. *Insurgent Iraq: Al Zarqawi and the New Generation.* New York: Seven Stories Press, 2005.

Sageman, Mark. *Leaderless Jihad: Terror Networks in the Twenty-first Century.* Philadelphia: University of Pennsylvania Press, 2008.

4. Missteps of Multiculturalism

Bawer, Bruce. *While Europe Slept: How Radical Islam Is Destroying the West from Within.* New York: Random House, 2006.

Buruma, Ian. *Murder in Amsterdam: The Death of Theo van Gogh and the Limits of Tolerance.* London: Atlantic Books, 2006.

Kagan, Robert. *Of Paradise and Power: America and Europe in the New World Order.* New York: Knopf, 2003.

Kepel, Gilles. *Allah in the West: Islamic Movements in America and Europe.* Trans. Susan Milner. Syracuse: Syracuse University Press, 1990.

Kepel, Gilles. *The War for Muslim Minds: Islam and the West.* Trans. Pascale Ghazaleh. Cambridge: Harvard University Press, 2004.

Mosaddeq Ahmed, Nafeez. *The London Bombings.* London: Duckworth, 2006.

Vidino, Lorenzo. *Al-Qaeda in Europe: The New Battleground of International Jihad.* New York: Prometheus Books, 2005.

Voogd, Christophe de. *Histoire des Pays-Bas des origines à nos jours.* Paris: Fayard, 2004.

Ye'or, Bat. *Eurabia, the Euro-Arab Axis.* Washington, D.C.: Fairleigh Dickinson University Press, 2006.

5. The Propaganda Battle in Europe

Bollack, Jean, Christian Jambet, and Abdelwahab Meddeb. *La Conférence de Ratisbonne: enjeux et controverses.* Paris: Bayard, 2007.

Brouard, Sylvain, and Vincent Tiberj. *Français comme les autres? Enquête sur les citoyens d'origine maghrébine, africaine et turque.* Paris: Les Presses de Sciences-Po, 2005.

Castel, Robert. *La Discrimination négative: citoyens ou indigènes?* Paris: Seuil, 2007.

Favret-Saada, Jeanne. *Comment produire une crise mondiale avec douze petits dessins.* Paris: Les Prairies Ordinaires, 2007.

Giro, Mario. *Gli occhi di un bambino ebreo: storia di Merzoug, terrorista pentito.* Milan: Guerini e associati, 2005.

Khoury, Théodore, ed. *Manuel II Paléologue: Entretiens avec un musulman, 7th Controverse.* Paris: Cerf, 1966.

Kouvélakis, Stathis. *La France en révolte: Luttes sociales et cycles politiques.* Paris: Textuel, 2007.

Lagrange, Hugues, and Marco Oberti. *Émeutes urbaines et protestations: une singularité française.* Paris: Les Presses de Sciences-Po, 2006.

Mucchielli, Laurent, and Véronique Goaziou. *Quand les banlieues brûlent: retour sur les émeutes de novembre 2005.* Paris: Découverte, 2007.

Sifaoui, Mohamed. *L'Affaire des caricatures: Dessins et manipulations.* Paris: Éditions Privé, 2006.

Steyn, Mark. *America Alone: The End of the World as We Know It.* Washington, D.C.: Regnery, 2006.

6. The Challenge of Civilization

Wright, Lawrence. "The Rebellion Within: An Al Qaeda Mastermind Questions Terrorism." *New Yorker,* June 2, 2008, pp. 36–53.

Zacaria, Fareed. *The Post-American World.* New York: Norton, 2008.

ACKNOWLEDGMENTS

I was able to write this book thanks to the exceptional academic
and intellectual environment offered by the Chair in Middle Eastern and Mediterranean Studies at the Institut d'Etudes Politiques
in Paris. I wish to thank, first, all those who made it possible for
this resource center to exist: the associates from business and administration who contribute generously, as well as Mme Isabelle
de Vienne, who manages its daily work. Debating ideas with specialized master's and Ph.D. students linked to the chair provided
unparalleled terrain for experimentation on numerous hypothe-
ses, and allowed me to open up a great many paths. I benefited
greatly from the work of Lamiss Azab, Thomas Hegghamer,
Stéphane Lacroix, Hamid Nasser, Loulouwa al-Rashid, and Claire
Talon in particular; but I also owe a good deal to all their colleagues, with whom we regularly exchange discoveries and analyses
in the framework of a doctoral seminar.

I would also like to thank guests from all walks of life who participate in the conferences and seminars organized by the Chair.
Supervising and teaching at Menton campus, where B.A. students
from Europe and the Near East are educated together, in French,
English, and Arabic, also provided a unique opportunity to understand how the young, multilingual generation that will make up

tomorrow's elites perceives the challenges that face it, and the way in which it proposes to overcome those challenges.

I am also grateful to the Fondazione Giorgio Cini in Venice, and its director, Professor Pasquale Gagliardi, who drew my attention to the notion of martyrdom through the *Dialoghi di San Giorgio* and generously offered me hospitality to write part of this book. The Eurogolfe network and its coordinator, Frédéric Pouillot, spared no effort in organizing meetings and debates with figures, decision-makers, and intellectuals from both sides of the Gulf.

My colleagues Christophe de Voogd and Mehdi Mozaffari shared with me their intimate knowledge of the Netherlands and Denmark; Franck Debié and Albert Bressand were exacting "global" readers. My gratitude to them knows no limits.

Gwendoline Abou Jaoudé was an incomparable research assistant and guide through the labyrinth of Arabic-language websites. I would like to express my profound gratitude to Pascale Ghazaleh, once again, for her excellent work in translating my French text. In the preparation of this English-language edition, which was revised and updated from the French publication, I have benefited from the editorial advice of Joyce Seltzer and Susan Wallace Boehmer at Harvard University Press.

Finally, my family has patiently borne the many absences required by research and writing. With age, and as the young generation takes up the task with brio, I plan for this book to be one of my last. I hope to devote myself to returning, as I must, some of the love that my family has lavished on me, and without which there can be no inspiration.

INDEX

Islambuli, Khaled al-, 141
Islamic Army of Iraq, 146, 159, 180, 290n38
Islamic Jihad, 77, 87, 90, 101–102
Islamic law. *See Sharia*
Islamic Revolution (Iran), 49, 78, 80, 83, 87, 93, 152
Islamic Salvation Front, 41
Islamic State of Iraq, 59, 119, 127, 133, 139, 142, 145, 158–159, 258, 262
Islamic University of Medina, 155, 222
Islamist A. K. Party, 277
Islamists, 10, 47, 115, 122, 125, 134, 147, 154, 169, 174–175, 185, 207, 269; radical, 1, 9, 16, 18, 20, 43, 61, 98, 100, 110–114, 146, 160–161, 176, 180–182, 188, 191, 206, 209, 215, 239, 251, 254–255, 261; Hamas as, 3, 71, 77, 86–89, 101, 106–107, 109, 129, 145, 277; in Europe, 6, 167–168, 173, 180–182, 184, 188–189, 191, 193, 195, 198, 209, 214–215, 218, 221–224, 247, 251, 254–256; in Iraq, 37, 41, 43, 53, 61; in Iran, 48; Hezbollah as, 77, 180; moderate, 94, 152, 188, 211, 229, 233, 239, 242, 251; running in elections, 128–129, 140, 144; in Pakistan, 189; in Lebanon, 228; in Turkey, 270
Islam Online website, 229–230
Islam Today (Islam al-Yawm) website, 229, 239

Israel, 1–2, 9–11, 16, 23, 64, 76, 104, 125–127, 138–139, 141, 162, 168, 173–174, 184, 219, 222, 226, 232, 241, 257, 263, 277, 286n14; conflict with Palestinians, 3, 6, 8, 14–15, 39, 44, 58, 77, 85–102, 105–108, 158, 175, 220, 224, 271–272, 274; war with Hezbollah, 3, 52, 66, 69–72, 74–75, 121–122, 135–137, 232, 272; incursions in Lebanon, 66–68, 81–82, 87, 135, 141; and Oslo Accords, 86, 88, 90, 101–102, 108, 161, 274; Six-Day War, 145; Arab-Israeli War, 200
Israel Defense Forces (Tsahal), 39, 52, 66, 69–70, 85
Istanbul, Turkey, 233–234
Italy, 18, 174, 232, 243
Izzeddin al-Qassam Brigades, 85–87

Jaafari, Ibrahim, 53
Japan, 150
Jaysh-e-Mohammed, 189
Jenin, Palestine, 105
Jerusalem, 101, 135, 145, 272
Jerusalem Brigades, 87
Jesus, 106, 152, 237, 239
Jews/Judaism, 1, 98, 101, 104, 134, 163, 168, 174, 176, 207, 236, 254; and Holocaust, 64, 70, 149, 221, 225, 294n6; killing of, 91–92, 105, 141, 184, 239, 253, 286n14; Zawahiri on, 124, 132, 140–142; Bin Laden on, 149, 151; in Morocco, 149; Zarqawi on, 156; in